Many have heard the names o
gone before us and contribut(
church. But we know little abou
that contain short biographies
esting reading. Many do not hi
biographies. This delightful book meets this
read it through completely, or simply dip into it reading a
chapter or two when you want to be inspired by a "history
treat," or you may read a specific chapter on someone you
about whom are interested in knowing more.

AJITH FERNANDO
Teaching Director, Youth for Christ, Sri Lanka

That God's Word, written and incarnate, has the power
to transform lives is clearly evident in the narratives of
men and women throughout the history of the Christian
Church. Peter Barnes has provided a great service to the
Church in powerfully telling these stories of transformation,
demonstrating that God's Word is indeed a "lamp unto
our feet and a light to our paths." Readers will be moved
to faithful obedience to Christ as they read the accounts.

DENNIS P. HOLLINGER
President and Colman M. Mockler Distinguished Professor of Christian Ethics,
Gordon-Conwell Theological Seminary, South Hamilton, Massachusetts

These delightful sketches of Christian leaders remind us
that scripture shapes lives in many varied and rich ways.
From medieval monks to modern athletes — anybody who
peruses these biographical portraits will be encouraged
that God's word ministers to all in a relevant and apt way.

PETER SANLON
Lecturer in Doctrine and Church History, Oak Hill College, London

We owe Peter Barnes and Christian Focus our gratitude.
A *Lamp Unto My Feet* is just the kind of book we all need
at this time in our lives. We need to prayerfully meditate
upon the glorious stories that have surrounded the sacred

processional of men and women who have marched down the aisle of church history. As we do, we rediscover the centrality of God's inerrant and infallible Word in shaping those stories. Oh how we need Scripturally-centered stories today! Get Reverend Barnes' *A Lamp Unto My Feet* as soon as you can. Read the biographies and see how God's Holy Word writes a new story of faith in your own life. I commend this wonderful book to the Church with a prayer: read it slowly, carefully, and prayerfully before bed and let the faithfulness of God quiet your heart, calm your soul, and seal your sleep with a lamp of faithfulness that will cause you to dream dreams and have visions of how God's Word will change your life.

MICHAEL A. MILTON
Teaching Pastor, Truth That Transforms,
President, D. James Kennedy Institute for Christianity and Culture,
Charlotte, North Carolina

A
LAMP
UNTO MY
FEET

How God Has Used
His Word Through
The Ages

PETER BARNES

CHRISTIAN
FOCUS

Peter Barnes serves as the minister of Revesby Presbyterian Church, Revesby, New South Wales, Australia and also lectures in Church History at Presbyterian Theological Centre, Burwood, Sydney.

Unless otherwise indicated Scripture quotations are taken from the *New King James Version*. Copyright © 1982 by Thomas Nelson, Inc. Used by permission. All rights reserved.

Scripture quotations marked ESV are taken from *The Holy Bible, English Standard Version*, copyright © 2001 by Crossway Bibles, a division of Good News Publishers. Used by permission. All rights reserved.

Scripture quotations marked NLT are taken from the *Holy Bible, New Living Translation*, copyright © 1996. Used by permission of Tyndale House Publishers, Inc., Wheaton, Illinois 60189. All rights reserved.

Scripture quotations marked KJV are taken from the *King James Version*.

paperback ISBN 978-1-78191-121-1
epub ISBN 978-1-78191-176-1
mobi ISBN 978-1-78191-182-2

Published in 2013
Reprinted 2014
by
Christian Focus Publications
Geanies House, Fearn, Ross-shire,
IV20 1TW, Scotland

www.christianfocus.com

Cover design by DUFI-ART.com

Contents

Contents continued

Contents continued

Contents continued

Contents continued

Contents continued

Contents continued

Contents continued

PREFACE

The theme of this book might be illustrated from an episode in Mary Slessor's life. As a weaver who worked from six in the morning to six at night in Dundee, she was asked by a girl for something to read. Mary – who was destined to go to West Africa in 1876 as a missionary – gave her a Bible, and said: 'Take that; it has made me a changed lassie.' Down through the ages God has used His Word countless times to speak to His people. In the words of John Owen:

> Holiness consists in our actual obedience unto God, which is revealed to us in his Word. Indeed, the Word of God is the only adequate rule for all holy obedience. It is not to be found in our own imaginations or our inclinations. All that is commanded in the Word belongs to our obedience, and nothing else is binding.

Furthermore, there are some all-too-few accounts of people about whom we know little, to make the point that God's Word has come not just to the great heroes and heroines of the faith, but also to Christ's little ones. It is to be hoped that this work will give the reader some idea of the flow of Church history – or at least enough to make him or her want to investigate further. Finally, there has been a small attempt to include some accounts from many parts of the world, not just Europe and North America.

The New King James Version has been quoted, for the most part at least, partly to standardize the quotations and partly because so many of the Christians referred to in this book used the King James Version, and the NKJV is very close to it while being more readable and contemporary. The biblical texts cited are not necessarily those which had the most significant impact on the particular believer's life, but those which influenced him or her at one time or another. Occasionally, a text has been chosen because it summed up the life and witness of a particular Christian.

This is a modest project. It is not designed to push back the frontiers of historical knowledge. Quite simply, it is my prayer and hope that this volume will be an encouragement to Christians to see some examples of how God has used His Word down through the ages. This Book of books has laid the foundations for all that we can know truly about God, ourselves and the world in which we live. Here we have a lamp unto our feet, to lead us to the new heaven and the new earth; and without it, we dwell in darkness more terrible than Plato's cave where people live chained to the blank wall of a cave all their lives, and only ever get glimpses of the shadows of life.

1

JAMES THE LORD'S BROTHER

(c. 1 B.C.–c. A.D. 61)

Through the door to salvation

*I am the door. If anyone enters by Me, he will be saved,
and will go in and out and find pasture* (John 10:9).

During His life here on earth, Jesus made it clear that 'whoever does the will of My Father in heaven is My brother and sister and mother' (Matt. 12:50). Spiritual relationships count for more than physical ones. Matthew lists four brothers of Jesus, namely James, Joses, Simon and Judas, as well as sisters (Matt. 13:55-56). These are best understood not as cousins nor as children of Joseph from a previous marriage but as children of Joseph and Mary, born after the arrival of their firstborn, Jesus. As such, of course, they were Jesus' half-brothers and half-sisters since all were born to Mary, but Jesus, being conceived of the virgin, had no human father.

Presumably, James is listed first of the four brothers because he was the oldest. However, during the public ministry of their divine brother, the brothers seem to have regarded Him as out of His mind (Mark 3:21). The apostle John is quite specific that they did not believe in Him (John 7:5). The Holy Family is often idealized in an unrealistic way, but it was, it seems, something of a dysfunctional family.

The Bible nowhere records the conversion of James. It is highly probable that it was only when Jesus appeared to him alive, back from the dead, that James realized that Jesus was who He said He was – the incarnate Son of God (1 Cor. 15:7). Certainly, he appears as a prominent Christian leader from that time onwards. On Paul's first trip to Jerusalem, after his experience of conversion on the Damascus road, the great apostle met Cephas (Peter) and James, the Lord's brother (Gal. 1:18-19). On his second trip, Paul met with those who seemed to be the three pillars of the Church – James, Cephas and John (Gal. 2:9).

With Peter away (Acts 12:17), James led the church at Jerusalem. He presided over the Council of Jerusalem which decreed that circumcision was not necessary for salvation, with James himself pointing out Amos's prophecy that God would rebuild the fallen tent of David and call in the Gentiles (Acts 15:12-21; see Amos 9:11-12). Later he sought to diminish Jewish opposition to Paul's mission to the Gentiles and his refusal to maintain the Jewish 'boundary markers', particularly circumcision (Acts 21:18-25). It is almost certain that James is the author of the epistle of James that is canonized in the New Testament. After the death of the procurator, Festus, in A.D. 61, and before the arrival of his successor in A.D. 62, James was dragged before the scribes and Pharisees to explain what was meant by 'the door of Jesus' (John 10:9). James replied by referring to the words of Jesus about the Son of Man sitting in heaven at the right hand of the Great Power, and coming on the clouds of heaven (Matt. 26:64). This only antagonized the scribes and Pharisees who regarded it as blasphemy, and reacted by throwing him down from the sanctuary parapet. He survived the fall, but was then stoned and clubbed to death. The exclusive claims of Jesus, as the only door to salvation, were as offensive in the first century as they are today.

James had come to see what he had not seen during the public ministry of his brother (or half-brother, to be more exact). James's brother was also his Saviour and Lord! However, death was not the end for James, for Jesus is the door to heaven. Known as 'the Just One' because of his righteous lifestyle and as 'Camel-Knees' because of his fervent prayer life, James entered salvation by the only door that there is – the Lord Jesus Christ.

2

POLYCARP OF SMYRNA

(c. A.D. 69–c. 155)

Fearing God, not man

By this you know the Spirit of God: Every spirit that
confesses that Jesus Christ has come in the flesh is of
God, and every spirit that does not confess that Jesus
Christ has come in the flesh is not of God. And this is the
spirit of the Antichrist, which you have heard was coming,
and is now already in the world (1 John 4:2-3).

And do not fear those who kill the body but cannot kill
the soul. But rather fear Him who is able to destroy both
soul and body in hell (Matt. 10:28).

Polycarp (which means 'much fruit') is one of the Apostolic
Fathers – those who knew the apostles or who lived in the
apostolic era. In Polycarp's case, this was the apostle John at
whose feet he apparently sat. Polycarp became the Bishop of
Smyrna, one of the churches of Asia mentioned in Revelation
1–3, and seems to have pastored God's people there for over
fifty years.

Little is known of his life. He once met the dualistic heretic,
Marcion, probably in Rome about A.D. 154, after Marcion had
been excommunicated in A.D. 144. Marcion, who denied that
the creator God of the Old Testament was the God of the

New Testament, asked Polycarp to recognize him. Polycarp's firm reply was: 'I recognize you – as the firstborn of Satan!' It was Polycarp's biblical conviction that 'To deny that Jesus Christ has come in the flesh is to be Antichrist.'

Probably on this same visit to Rome, Polycarp had differed with the bishop, Anicetus, over the date of Easter. But as Irenaeus recorded: 'They parted from one another in peace, and the whole Church was at peace, both they who observed and they who did not observe.' To the church at Philippi, Polycarp wrote: 'Faith is the mother of us all; with hope following in her train, and love of God and Christ and neighbour leading the way.' A humble and loving pastor, Polycarp grieved at the lack of financial integrity shown by one of the Philippian presbyters, Valens, along with his unnamed wife.

As an old man, Polycarp was arrested, perhaps in 155 or 156, or even 166–7. A record of what happened was preserved in a letter written by a man called Marcion (not the heretic of the same name). Hearing that his arrest was likely, Polycarp had retired to a small farm not far from the city, before moving on to another farm. Here he was arrested, although he showed kindness to his captors by giving them food and drink. He was given permission to pray for an hour, although he managed to spend twice that in prayer.

Refusing to say 'Caesar is Lord', he was taken by carriage, then by foot, to the circus where the crowd was so noisy that nobody could be heard. Again he refused to swear by the Luck (or the Genius) of Caesar, and when asked to denounce the infidels, he did so while sweeping his hand towards the crowd. When pressed to curse Christ, he replied most memorably: 'Eighty-six years have I served Him, and He has done me no wrong. How then can I blaspheme my King and my Saviour?' Polycarp may have been baptized as an infant, or, less likely, he may have been almost a hundred years of age when he was martyred.

19

Polycarp was then threatened by the proconsul with being fed to the beasts and with being burnt to death, but he replied: 'The fire you threaten me with cannot go on burning for very long; after a while it goes out. But what you are unaware of are the flames of future judgment and everlasting torment which are in store for the ungodly ... Bring out whatever you have a mind to.'

For the last time, he prayed that he would be 'a sacrifice rich and acceptable' through 'the everlasting and heavenly High Priest Jesus Christ'. Glory was attributed only to the Father, His beloved Son and the Holy Spirit. The attempt to burn him at the stake proved difficult, so he was killed by the executioner's sword. Marcion was left to tell the story to Polycarp's congregation at Smyrna, and so the martyr was taken to heaven, unafraid of what man could do to him.

3

ATHANASIUS
(c. 298–373)

Against the world for the Word
The Word was God (John 1:1).
The Word became flesh and dwelt amongst us (John 1:14).
He who has seen Me has seen the Father (John 14:9).

Athanasius was the Bishop of Alexandria in Egypt from 328 until his death in 373. He became known, and widely admired eventually, for his strong commitment to the full deity of Christ, and for his preparedness to suffer for that belief. For his stance he was exiled five times – by the Christian emperor Constantine, twice by his Arian son Constantius II, then by the pagan Julian the Apostate, and finally by the Arian Valens. All in all, Athanasius spent something like seventeen out of his forty-five years as a bishop in exile.

To know something of Athanasius we need to know something of Arius, a tall and ageing Alexandrian presbyter, who, about the year 318, began to raise a furore by teaching that Christ is not God incarnate but the first of the created angels. In Arius's theology, 'God was not always Father. There was when God was alone and was not yet Father. He became Father subsequently.'

21

To Athanasius, 'The heresy which attacks Christ has no communion with the catholic church.' He considered those who referred to the Arians as Christians were 'in great and grievous error'. Yet when Christ's deity was truly acknowledged, and the dispute was only semantic, Athanasius was patient: 'We discuss the matter with them as brothers with brothers, who mean what we mean, and dispute only about the word.'

The emperor Constantine, the first Roman emperor to profess faith in Christ, had no appreciation of what was at stake, and thought that the dispute was a 'frivolous question'. Eventually he called together a council at Nicaea in Bithynia. In 325 this council declared that Christ the Son is 'God of God, light of light, true God of true God'. Furthermore, He is of the same essence (*homoousios* in Greek) as the Father.

Athanasius played some part in proceedings at Nicaea, despite his youth and the fact that he was as yet only a deacon. At this stage it seemed that the young but short Athanasius – described as 'almost childlike in size' – had triumphed over the 'Goliath', Arius. The next few years, however, made it clear just how fragile the Nicene victory was. Within a relatively short space of time, the Arian star was rising. Nicene bishops were deposed and exiled, and Arius's creed – with some conveniently ambiguous reworking – was accepted by Constantine as orthodox.

The two main factors in the change in the ecclesiastical climate were Constantine's desire for peace in the Church, and the Eastern suspicion of the term *homoousios*. Many Easterners thought that it might imply that the Son and the Father were the one Person, whereas the Bible teaches there are three divine Persons in the Godhead. In the midst of all these developments, on 8 June 328, Athanasius became the Bishop of Alexandria. His troubles began in earnest when Constantine wrote to him, saying: 'Now that you have been informed of my wishes, allow unhindered access into the church to all who wish to enter it.'

Not to do so would mean to suffer deposition and exile. Despite this threat, Athanasius refused to grant communion to Arius and his supporters. The scene was set for a clash, between the man of spiritual principle and the man of political concord.

Constantine lost his temper – his nickname was 'Bullneck' – and exiled Athanasius to Gaul. Athanasius spent the next two years there, before being allowed to return to Alexandria after the death of Constantine in May 337. It is likely that about this time Athanasius wrote his great treatise, *On the Incarnation of the Word*. Here he sought to maintain the truth that the Word who is God became flesh and dwelt among us. He says of the Word who made the universe: 'he took to himself a body, and that not foreign to our own.' In his classic statement of the purpose of the Incarnation, Athanasius wrote of Christ: 'For he became man that we might become divine; and he revealed himself through a body that we might receive an idea of the invisible Father; and he endured insults from men that we might inherit incorruption.'

Athanasius experienced more troubles under Constantine's son, Constantius, who was decidedly pro-Arian. Nicene churches in Alexandria were forcibly taken over. Athanasius says that the violence was 'dreadful beyond endurance'. Under threat of arrest, Athanasius sailed for Rome, perhaps in the Easter of 339. Constantius convened a number of Church councils, all of which supported some kind of Arianism or compromise with Arianism. After being allowed to return in 346, Athanasius was again forced to flee for his life on 8 February 356 when five thousand troops broke up Athanasius's vigil service.

Athanasius refused to pretend that all creeds are ultimately saying the same thing, and he was prepared to pay the price. He wrote:

> Our Churches have been taken away from us, and given to the Arians; they have our places, and we have been banished

23

from them. But we have the Faith: of that they cannot rob us. Which is the better of the two, the place or the Faith? Who, therefore, has lost most, or gained most? He who has the place and lost the Faith, or he who has lost the place and has the Faith? Every place is good where the Faith is. Wherever holy men dwell, the place is holy.

In all his troubles, Athanasius looked especially to the Psalms for comfort and wisdom. He saw in them history and prophecies but also 'the emotions of the soul'.

In 361 Julian the Apostate became emperor, and Athanasius was able to return to Alexandria. Julian hoped that Athanasius would be a disruptive influence on the church at Alexandria, and that it would self-destruct. When this tactic failed, Julian was wild and exiled Athanasius, not just from Alexandria but from Egypt. Athanasius does not seem to have been unduly worried and referred to the trauma as 'a small cloud which will soon pass'. That proved to be true, but when the emperor Valens ascended the throne, he favoured Arianism, and again Athanasius was exiled.

For a man whose life had been full of strife, Athanasius at least died in peace on 2 May 373. In 381, the Council of Constantinople finally reaffirmed the Nicene Creed.

4

HILARY OF POITIERS

(c. 315–367)

Seeing God in Christ

*Go therefore and make disciples of all the nations,
baptizing them in the name of the Father and of the Son
and of the Holy Spirit* (Matt. 28:19).
*He [Christ] is the image of the invisible God, the firstborn
over all creation* (Col. 1:15).

In 350 Constantius II became sole emperor of the Roman Empire – and he was a decided Arian. He placed increased pressure on the bishops of the West, and so the councils of Arles in 353 and Milan in 355 adhered to the Council of Tyre's condemnation of Athanasius passed back in 335. These were dark days for the cause of Trinitarian orthodoxy, but one of the Western bishops who stood firm in its defence was Hilary of Poitiers in Gaul (France).

Hilary's biography would be difficult to write, as we know relatively little about him. He was probably born between 310 and 320, and became Bishop of Poitiers around 350. He was married and had a daughter, Abra. Possessing a gift for poetic expression, he became one of the most prominent hymn-writers in the early Church. It is often assumed that he was converted

25

to Christ by reading the Bible. As a bishop, Hilary broke off communion with bishops who had condemned Athanasius. The result was that at the council of Béziers in 356 Hilary himself was deposed and exiled to Phrygia. Here he learned Greek and studied the works of the Greek fathers.

After some years, Constantius authorized Hilary to return home without subscribing to a profession of faith that was favourable to the Arian creed. Yet this was not regarded as a reinstatement – more like the removal of a troublemaker. Back in the West, Hilary was received in triumph, and was the moving spirit at a council in Paris in 361. Here he was a spokesman for moderation in doctrine and discipline. Like Athanasius, he only condemned decided Arian leaders, not those bishops who had wilted under coercion. At Milan in 364 he tried unsuccessfully to remove the Arian bishop Auxentius, who had been there since 355. Hilary had to return home, and Jerome records that he died in 367.

Hilary's chief doctrinal work, *On the Trinity*, appears in twelve books. In most ancient manuscripts it lacks a title. At the very outset, Hilary declares his position as equidistant from Arianism (the belief that Christ is the highest of the angels) and Sabellianism (the belief that the Father, the Son and the Holy Spirit are the one person acting in different roles). Furthermore, he interpreted *homoiousios* ('like essence') to be equivalent to *homoousios* ('same essence'). He considered that the baptismal formula in Matthew implied everything concerning God and His salvation. Indeed he asks, 'What is not contained in these words concerning the mystery of human salvation?'

Although he became known later as 'The Athanasius of the West', Hilary does not owe a lot to Athanasius. His Trinitarianism is anchored firmly in Scripture, and he was wary of analogies such as the root and the plant, the source and the stream, or fire and heat. He rightly emphasized that we can only know God as He has revealed Himself in Scripture.

As Hilary contemplated Christ as 'the visible image of God', he sought to describe the grace and mystery of the incarnation:

The one only-begotten God, ineffably born of God, entered the Virgin's womb and grew and took the frame of poor humanity. He who upholds the universe, within whom and through whom are all things, was brought forth by common childbirth; He at whose voice archangels and angels tremble, and heaven and earth and all the elements of this world are melted, was heard in childish wailing. The invisible and incomprehensible, whom sight and feeling and touch cannot gauge, was wrapped in a cradle. If any man deem all this unworthy of God, the greater must he own his debt ... He by whom man was made had nothing to gain by becoming man; it was our gain that God was incarnate and dwelt among us, making all flesh His home by taking upon Him the flesh of one. We were raised because He was lowered; shame to Him was glory to us. He, being God, made flesh His residence, and we in return are lifted anew from the flesh to God.

5
JOHN CHRYSOSTOM
(c. 349–407)

Applying the Scriptures

But someone will say, 'You have faith, and I have works.'
Show me your faith without your works, and I will show
you my faith by my works (James 2:18).
'Is not My word like a fire?' says the Lord (Jer. 23:29a).
For the word of God is living and powerful, and sharper
than any two-edged sword (Heb. 4:12a).

John Chrysostom once said that he looked like a spider – thin and short but with long limbs. He became the Bishop of Constantinople in 398, but he is best-known as the most eloquent preacher in the early Church. Hence he was given the nickname *'Chrysostomos'* which means 'golden-mouthed', an epithet which in later generations came to replace his given name. He was born about the year 349 in Antioch in Syria. John was raised as a Christian, but was also thoroughly educated in the rhetorical and literary traditions of Greek culture.

For some years, John lived in a semi-communal style. Each day began with the chanting of psalms, and was followed by meditating on the Scriptures, observing the rule of silence, carrying out various physical tasks (digging, planting, weaving, copying books – with the profits going to poor relief), and meeting together for the evening meal (which may have been only bread and salt). The lifestyle permanently injured John's health – he was to suffer from rushes of blood to the head, stomach troubles and insomnia for the rest of his life.

In 381 Chrysostom was ordained deacon, and five years later he was ordained presbyter. He belonged to the Antiochene school of literal, as opposed to allegorical, exegesis. A strict disciplinarian, who could nevertheless preach frankly on the joyous nature of the one-flesh union in marriage, he condemned the circus, slavery, abortion, prostitution, gluttony, swearing, horse racing, trusting in wealth, and the theatre. He had a golden mouth and an iron will, but some have considered that he was tactless.

Chrysostom was born for the pulpit: 'I cannot let a day pass without feeding you with the treasures of the Scriptures.' He constantly urged his hearers to meditate on the Scriptures and to obey them. Citing the words of the epistle of James, he said: 'If you are a Christian, believe in Christ; if you believe in Christ, show me your faith by your works.' He was especially adept at applying the text to his hearers. In one sermon against the theatre, he railed:

> If you see a shameless woman in the theatre, who treads the stage with uncovered head and bold attitudes, dressed in garments adorned with gold, flaunting her soft sensuality, singing immoral songs, throwing her limbs about in the dance, and making shameless speeches … do you still dare to say that nothing human happens to you then? Long after the theatre is closed and everyone is gone away, those images still float before your soul, their words, their conduct, their glances, their walk, their positions, their excitation, their unchaste limbs – and as for you, you go home covered with a thousand wounds! But not alone – the whore goes with you – although not openly and visibly … but in your heart, and in your conscience, and there within you she kindles the Babylonian furnace … in which the

peace of your home, the purity of your heart, the happiness of your marriage will be burnt up!

So vivid were his sermons that Chrysostom even had to tell his people not to applaud, and to beware of pickpockets while they were engrossed in the sermon!

It is obedience that proves the reality of faith. So Chrysostom told his people: 'The praise I seek is that you show forth all I have said in your works. Then am I an enviable and happy man, not when you approve, but when you perform with all readiness whatsoever you hear from me.' He made a point of hitting home in his sermons: 'Even if I do not have a knife, I have a word that is sharper than a knife. Even if I am not holding fire aloft, I have a teaching that is hotter than fire, which is able to burn more vigorously.' But it was his insistence on applying the Scriptures that landed Chrysostom in his final troubles.

Against his will, he was made Bishop of Constantinople in 398 and so became enmeshed in imperial and ecclesiastical politics – for which he was eminently unsuited. He fell out with the empress Eudoxia (the wife of Arcadius) mainly because of his disdain for the opulent lifestyle of the court. He apparently made an injudicious reference in a sermon to Eudoxia either as 'Jezebel' or 'Herodias'. When she threatened him, he gave the memorable reply: 'Go tell her I fear nothing but sin.'

In 403 at the Oak, in a suburb of Chalcedon, a synod packed with hostile Egyptian bishops condemned Chrysostom on a series of charges, some concocted and some more plausible (the latter would include uttering defamatory and treasonable words against the empress). Found guilty and deposed, John was almost immediately reinstated. Soon after, he was deposed again and exiled under military escort to a place near Antioch, then to an isolated village on the Black Sea. Here he lived out his final years in exile, until his death in 407. His last words were 'Glory be to God for everything! Amen.'

6
AUGUSTINE OF HIPPO
(354–430)

The quest for salvation and truth

Not in revelry and drunkenness, not in lewdness and lust,
not in strife and envy. But put on the Lord Jesus Christ,
and make no provision for the flesh, to fulfil its lusts
(Rom. 13:13b-14).
If you will not believe, surely you shall not be established
(Isa. 7:9).

Augustine stands like a colossus amongst the Fathers of the early Church. As the Bishop of Hippo in North Africa from 396 until his death in 430, he preached the gospel of God's electing grace to sinners, and stood against extremists and heretics. As the Roman Empire crumbled through its own corruption, he testified to God's sovereign and mysterious ways in history in his magisterial *The City of God*. Yet his path to heaven, like that of Bunyan's pilgrim, was fraught with struggles and tribulations.

Augustine was born in Thagaste in North Africa on 13 November 354, the son of a hot-tempered pagan father named Patricius and a doting, almost devouring, Christian mother named Monica. As a child, Augustine revealed more talent than wisdom. With some companions, he once stole some pears to throw to the pigs, and later recalled: 'Our real pleasure

31

consisted in doing something that was forbidden.' As he grew older, his sins take on a more modern hue. He lived for many years with a mistress and fathered a son named Adeodatus. At the time he consulted astrologers, and wept at the death of a friend, but his soul was in constant turmoil.

Reading a work by the pagan Cicero led Augustine to hunger after the wisdom of eternal truth, but dreaming of the fare and tasting it were two different things. He felt no attraction for paganism as such, and so joined a heretical cult, the Manicheans. The Manicheans taught that the physical world was evil, and so rejected the Old Testament. So far as sin was concerned, Augustine thought that his body was sinning while his spirit remained pure. Small wonder that Augustine felt divided against himself, unable to find himself, let alone God!

Finding the students at Carthage rather unruly, Augustine made his way to Rome in 382, and eventually became Professor of Rhetoric at Milan University. Here he heard the Bishop of Milan, Ambrose, preach on the Old Testament, and he came to see Manichaeism as a cul-de-sac. He left the cult, but still battled his ambitions and lusts; yet 'however great my indulgence in sensual pleasure, I could not find happiness.' After much struggle, he came to understand God as sovereign and good in His creation; the creation pointed to the Creator. This was a breakthrough, but it stopped short of conversion.

Augustine still experienced a frantic sense of desperation and fear that death might overtake him unprepared for eternity. He was tormented by his sins, yet unwilling and also unable to do anything about them. He dallied with prayer: 'Lord, give me chastity and continence: but not yet.' Weeping in a garden in Milan, he heard the voice of a child in a nearby house saying in a game, 'Take it and read, take it and read.' Grasping this as a message from God, Augustine picked up a copy of Paul's epistles, and his eyes fell on the passage in Romans 13:13b-14, 'Not in revelry and drunkenness, not in lewdness and lust, not in strife and envy. But put on the Lord Jesus Christ, and make no provision for the flesh, to fulfil its lusts.' It was enough; God had claimed him as His own.

Strangely enough, Augustine did not refer to the Romans text very often in his future life. Nor were revelry and drunkenness problems for him, even before he was a Christian. His mother was far more prone to drink too much than he ever was. Yet he had passed over from the death of sin to the life of righteousness in Christ. For the first time Augustine knew grace and peace: 'At last my mind was free from the gnawing anxieties of ambition and gain, from wallowing in filth and scratching the itching sore of lust. I began to talk to You freely, O Lord my God, my Light, my Wealth, and my Salvation.' His conversion illustrates what he said so masterfully in his prayer at the beginning of his *Confessions*: 'You have made us for Yourself, and our hearts are restless until they find their rest in You.'

In later life he would often cite Isaiah 7:9 in the form of – *If you do not believe, you will not understand*. In preparation for baptism, Ambrose had advised Augustine to read Isaiah, but at first Augustine struggled to understand it. He would explain to his congregation that 'faith means believing what you do not yet see, and the reward of this faith is to see what you believe.' He always sought both to believe and to understand whatever God had given him in His Scriptures.

7

AUGUSTINE OF HIPPO
(354–430)

Humbly receiving God's sovereign grace

*For who makes you differ from another? And what do
you have that you did not receive? Now if you did indeed
receive it, why do you boast as if you had not
received it?* (1 Cor. 4:7).

The letter kills, but the Spirit gives life (2 Cor. 3:6).

*Even so then, at this present time there is a remnant
according to the election of grace* (Rom. 11:5).

During his lifetime, Augustine was involved in three great controversies – with the Manicheans who denied the goodness of creation; with the Donatists who separated from the Church because of its unholiness; and with the Pelagians over whether salvation was by grace. B.B. Warfield considered that the Pelagian controversy was a struggle for the very foundations of Christianity.

Pelagius was a British monk, whom Jerome described as a huge dolt, raised on Scottish porridge, moving at the pace of a turtle. His spiritual understanding was less impressive than his physical dimensions. At Rome in 405 a bishop quoted a prayer from Augustine's *Confessions*: 'Give what You command and command what You will.' To Pelagius, this undermined human responsibility and took away any incentive to be holy.

When the Visigoths sacked Rome in 410, Pelagius and his friend Caelestius fled to North Africa. Pelagius never met Augustine, and moved on to Palestine while Caelestius was left in Carthage, where he was excommunicated. Caelestius then went to Ephesus, where he was ordained. Thus the controversy began to heat up.

At Diospolis (Lydda) in 415, fourteen bishops tried Pelagius, who renounced Caelestius and reassured the bishops of his own orthodoxy. Augustine declared that 'heresy was not acquitted, but the man who denied the heresy.' The African bishops (who were Western) appealed to the church of Rome in an attempt to overturn this Eastern synod, and, after some back flips, the Roman church supported the excommunications of both Pelagius and Caelestius. However, eighteen bishops led by Julian of Eclanum continued to support Pelagius.

The Pelagians taught that Adam set a pattern for disobedience and no more. Pelagius believed that we have 'a free will which is unimpaired for sinning and for not sinning', while Julian declared that 'our free will is just as full after sins as it was before sins.' Against this, Augustine spoke of 'a cruel necessity of sinning'. To Augustine, not even a one-day-old infant is free from sin. He wrote of original sin: 'Nothing is better known when the preacher declares it, nothing is more secret when we try to understand it.'

Predestination disturbed Augustine: 'I just cannot find what criterion to apply in deciding which men should be chosen to be saved by grace.' But he did not waver: 'What man, therefore, rages to such a degree of madness as not to offer ineffable thanks to the mercy of God, liberating whom He willed, when he could in no way rightly complain against God's justice, if He should condemn the whole of humanity?' In the end, Augustine was content to assert: 'I do not explain the inexplicable, but I commend what the apostle says.'

Augustine pictured the Christian man as a convalescent, not one who was entirely cured. In his *Confessions* he wrote: 'The mind commands the body, and the body obeys. The mind commands itself and is resisted.' The law is not our saviour: 'The use of the law is ... to convince man of his weakness, and force him to implore the medicine of grace that is in Christ.' But to Pelagius, God would never command the impossible – we are obliged to be holy (Lev. 19:2) and perfect (Matt. 5:48), and are able to be holy and perfect. Augustine, however, based his *Treatise on the Spirit and the Letter* on 2 Corinthians 3:6 ('The letter kills, but the Spirit gives life').

To Augustine grace was always free, and for that the sinner could only be deeply grateful. He often cited 1 Corinthians 4:7, and sought to plumb its depths. In his *Retractions*, issued in 426, four years before his death, Augustine wrote: 'I, indeed, laboured in defence of the free choice of the human will; but the grace of God conquered, and finally I was able to understand, with full clarity, the meaning of the Apostle: "For who singles you out? Or what have you that you have not received?"' A year before he died, Augustine lamented that in his earlier writings he had not sufficiently inquired of Romans 11:5, for grace 'is not grace, if any merits precede it; for what is given, not by grace, but according to what is due, is a reward for merits rather than a gift.'

What was at stake in the Pelagian controversy was the whole notion of the gospel of grace. For Augustine, grace means that 'The human will does not achieve grace through freedom, but rather freedom through grace.'

8

AUGUSTINE OF HIPPO
(354–430)

Dying with the Penitential Psalms

Behold, You desire truth in the inward parts ... Make me
hear joy and gladness ... Hide Your face from my sins,
and blot out all my iniquities ... The sacrifices of God are
a broken spirit, a broken and a contrite heart – these, O
God, You will not despise (Ps. 51:6a, 8a, 9, 17).

In pondering the meaning of life, Augustine also pondered the
meaning of death. His earnest and yearning soul struggled with
his ambition, his morals and his intellect – and the mortality
he saw around him and knew within. At nineteen, Augustine
was transformed by his reading of Cicero's *Hortensius*, which
is now lost. He recalled: 'All my empty dreams suddenly lost
their charm and my heart began to throb with a bewildering
passion for the wisdom of eternal truth.' This did not make
him a Christian, but God was dealing with his soul. At Thagaste
he was rocked by a friend's serious illness, his baptism while
comatose, his recovery, his subsequent attachment to his
baptism and to Christianity, and then his sudden death two
weeks later. Augustine wept, but then acknowledged that 'It is
time to confess, not to question.'

A year after his conversion in the garden in Milan in 386, Augustine was grieved by the death of his famous mother, Monica, and about two years after that by the death of his 16-year-old son, Adeodatus. By 391 Augustine had been chosen by the congregation of Hippo in North Africa to be its presbyter. By 396 he was the Bishop of Hippo, and in 397 he published his spiritual autobiography known as his *Confessions*. This is a work that is saturated with the Psalms. In fact, it contains something like 222 citations from the Psalms.

Augustine recorded his reasons for writing his *Confessions*: 'For love of Your love I shall retrace my wicked ways.' Here, as in no other work of ancient literature, we find the soul alone before God: 'You are the most hidden from us, the most beautiful and yet the most strong, ever enduring and yet we cannot comprehend You. You are unchangeable and yet You change all things.' Augustine pleaded: 'Do not hide Your face away from me, for I would gladly meet my death to see it, since not to see it would be death indeed.'

Sinners could but pray and beg for mercy: 'Let the strong and mighty laugh at men like me: let us, the weak and the poor, confess our sins to You.' Here there is hope. Let the wicked turn back, and 'they will find You in their hearts, in the hearts of all who confess to You and throw themselves upon Your mercy, in the hearts of all who have left the hard path and come to weep upon Your breast. Gently You wipe away their tears.' Indeed, 'What else can save us but Your hand, remaking what You have made?'

Death hangs over us all, so Augustine asked: 'If it steals upon me, shall I be in a fit state to leave this world?' He therefore kept asking: 'Where then does evil come from, if God made all things and, because he is good, made them good too?' Until he had grasped the significance of creation by God who is good, and the Fall by man who rebelled, there could be no peace: 'My anxiety was all the more galling for the fear that death might come before I had found the truth.'

Life was a struggle to know God and reality truly: 'How can I hope to understand the height and the depth of You, from the greatest to the most lowly of Your works? You never depart from us, yet it is hard for us to return to You.' Hence there was the need for humble prayer: 'Come, O Lord, and stir our hearts. Call us back to Yourself. Kindle Your fire in us and carry us away. Let us scent Your fragrance and taste Your sweetness. Let us love You and hasten to Your side.'

In all this Augustine took refuge in the Psalms: 'How I cried out to you, my God, when I read the Psalms of David, those hymns of faith, those songs of a pious heart in which the spirit of pride can find no place!' In his *Expositions on the Book of Psalms*, Augustine commented on them in an organized and orderly fashion; in the *Confessions*, he drew on the memory of them that had come from reciting and singing them daily. This love of the Psalms was lifelong. His friend Licentius had once offended Monica's sensibilities by singing a psalm rather too heartily in the toilet. Later, another friend, Evodius, would sing Psalm 100 on the occasion of Monica's death.

At the conclusion of the *Confessions*, Augustine prayed: 'O Lord God, grant us peace, for all that we have is Your gift. Grant us the peace of repose, the peace of the Sabbath, the peace which has no evening. For this worldly order in all its beauty will pass away.' Many years later, in 430, the Vandals were threatening North Africa. Augustine refused to leave his flock, declaring: 'I am a long-winded old man, and ill-health has made me anxious ... I will not desert you.' Before he died on 28 August, he had David's penitential Psalms hung on his walls (Psalms 6, 32, 38, 51, 102, 130, 143).

In teaching from Psalm 130, Augustine had emphasized the hope that the psalmist received: 'Though therefore he was weighed down with his sins, the mercy of God is present to him. For this reason, He went before without sin, that He may blot out the sins of those that follow Him.' Referring to Psalm 32, he had declared: 'For not by their own merits will they be holy, but by that acceptable time, that is, at His coming, who redeemed us from sin.' David's reception of grace, despite his great sin, is found in Psalm 51, on which Augustine commented: 'He who implores great mercy, confesses great misery.' Wonderfully, David's experience was also Augustine's: 'Of my own so deadly wound I should despair, unless I could find so great a Physician.' So the great sinner who had become one of the Church's greatest theologians died, weeping for his sins and rejoicing in the grace of Christ.

9

COLUMBA OF IONA
(c. 521–597)

Death is a good thing for the Christian

Gird Your sword upon Your thigh, O Mighty One, with Your glory and Your majesty. And in Your majesty ride prosperously because of truth, humility, and righteousness; and Your right hand shall teach You awesome things (Ps. 45:3-4).

One thing I have desired of the Lord, that will I seek: that I may dwell in the house of the Lord all the days of my life, to behold the beauty of the Lord, and to inquire in His temple (Ps. 27:4).

For a day in Your courts is better than a thousand [elsewhere]. I would rather be a doorkeeper in the house of my God than dwell in the tents of wickedness (Ps. 84:10).

Those who seek the Lord shall not lack any good thing (Ps. 34:10b).

Druidism was the religion that dominated pre-Christian Scotland and Ireland. This entailed a dread of innumerable spirits, as well as the worship of the rising sun and reverence for mistletoe. On one occasion Columba is supposed to have intimidated some Druids by singing Psalm 45 on the power and beauty of the divine king in his booming voice. Less reliably, he is also said to be behind the

Book of Kells, the introduction of whisky to Scotland and even the pacification of the Loch Ness monster through prayer and the sign of the cross.

It should be recognized that Columba was not the first Christian missionary to be concerned for the Celtic tribes, as Palladius, Ninian and Patrick had preceded him. Columba – whose nickname was Columcille ('Dove of the Church') – was born into a noble family, but became a monk. He joined Patrick's missionary establishment in Ireland, but, following temporary excommunication in 561 after being blamed for a quarrel leading to bloodshed, he sailed to the tiny island of Iona in 563. The story goes that Columba had to win as many souls from heathenism as were killed in battle – although this is not recounted in Columba's earliest biography, that written by Adomnan (or Adamnan), an abbot of Iona, who lived about a hundred years after Columba's time.

The Venerable Bede also refers to Columba in his *Ecclesiastical History,* written about 731. Whereas Adomnan portrays Columba as devout and gentle, Bede was wary of him, as the first English church historian disliked the Scottish way whereby the abbot possessed more prestige and power than the bishop. Columba was certainly a man of many parts – he engaged in prayer and in manual labour; he loved the sea and he loved reading; he slept on a bare rock with a stone for his pillow, yet he was warmly hospitable to guests. There is no reason to doubt the substantial truth of Adomnan's moving description of Columba: 'He was loving to all people, and his face always showed a holy gladness because his heart was full of the joy of the Holy Spirit.'

Iona became a training centre which maintained links with other missionaries – Cuthbert went to Lothian; Aidan to Northumbria; Moluag to the Picts; and Maolrubha to Ross, Sutherland, Caithness and Skye. Scotland was evangelized from Iona, as monks spread the gospel message wherever they went. When Aidan was consecrated as king of the Scots in Iona in 574 by Columba, he was probably the first ruler in Britain to be consecrated as a Christian ruler. All in all, Aidan was to reign for thirty-four years.

Columba loved the Psalms and knew them well. He prayed, as the least of saints, that 'I may keep even the smallest door, the farthest, darkest, coldest door, the door that is least used, the stiffest door, if only it be in Your house, O God, that I can see Your glory even afar, and hear Your voice, and know that I am with You, O God.' In 597 Columba, nearing death, was sitting in his hut and writing out a copy of the Psalms. When he reached Psalm 34:10b (*Those who seek the Lord shall not lack any good thing*), he knew that he had to stop, and that his time on earth was not long. Even his old white pony seemed to sense his master's imminent death, and whinnied in agitation. Columba went to the monastic church, prayed, and died that night. Engulfed in both hope and sorrow, the monks chanted some psalms that deal with death.

The best-known hymn attributed to Columba himself is 'Christ is the world's redeemer'. It includes the lines:

> *Christ the red cross ascended*
> *To save a world undone,*
> *And, suffering for the sinful,*
> *Our full redemption won.*

Herein is the secret of joy in the Holy Spirit. In death as in life, Columba remained cheerful, knowing that to the believer even death is turned into a good thing.

10

BONIFACE OF DEVON
(680–754)

Taking God's Word to the heathen

*Tear down the altar of Baal that your father has, and cut
down the wooden image that is beside it; and build an
altar to the Lord your God on top of this rock*
(Judg. 6:25b-26a).

*If the Lord is God, follow Him; but if Baal, follow him ...
and the God who answers by fire, He is God*
(1 Kings 18:21b, 24).

*[God] desires all men to be saved and to come to the
knowledge of the truth* (1 Tim. 2:4).

*Command those who are rich in this present age not to
be haughty, nor to trust in uncertain riches but in the
living God, who gives us richly all things
to enjoy* (1 Tim. 6:17).

Boniface's English name was Wynfrith (or Winfrid or Winfrith),
and he was born in 680 or thereabouts, in Wessex. He came
to love the Scriptures, and by the age of fourteen was a monk,
having overcome the objections of his father. He was such a
promising student that, at twenty-two, he moved about a
hundred miles to the east to Nutshell, now known as Nursling.
Here he undertook advanced study under Abbot Winbert. By
the age of twenty-five, he was a deacon, and at thirty he became

a presbyter. However, he felt a call to serve overseas and in 716 made an exploratory tour of Utrecht where the Duke at least did not seem to be hostile. Back in the fifth century Roman Britain had been overrun in the east and south by Germanic marauders, so it was not inappropriate that Boniface would want to return armed with a spiritual sword.

As a West Saxon, Boniface wanted to evangelize the Old Saxons. He hoped that Frisia would be the doorway to the Saxon tribes. In addition, the Frisian dialect was close to what an Englishman of the time could understand. However, his abbot, Winbert, died in 717, and Boniface was elected as his successor. He accepted this only as a temporary measure and was finally able to make his way to Rome to be commissioned on 15 May 719 by the bishop, Gregory II (who was known as the Vicar of Peter rather than the Vicar of Christ). In setting out from Rome to the Rhine, Boniface's pack animals carried chests containing the relics of saints – an indication that he was prone to the superstitions of the day. Gregory II had advised him to admit into the Church 'those who have some kind of belief in God'. Boniface learnt the Frankish language and at first refused episcopal ordination. By 722 or 723, however, he had relented, and Gregory II granted him a roving commission.

Boniface decided on a dramatic act about 724 or 725. The oak at Geismar – a place which cannot be located now with certainty – was sacred to the god Thor, so Boniface determined to fell it, much as the Lord had told Gideon to do in Judges 6. It is also said that he had Elijah's challenge to the prophets of Baal in mind. In front of a hostile crowd of heathens, and defying Thor to strike him dead, Boniface wielded his axe, although the task was made rather easier when a violent wind blew up and split the oak into four pieces. As was typical, the pieces were used to build a chapel on the spot.

The threat of Islam was also very real, until in 732 Charles Martel ('the Hammer') won a decisive victory against the Arabs between Tours and Poitiers. The Franks and the Germanic tribes were also frequently at war. After a period of some depression – something he experienced about every ten years in his life – Boniface sought to win the Old Saxons of eastern Frisia, and then move on to Hesse-Thuringia and Bavaria and Alamannia. Referring to I Timothy 2:4, Boniface tried to win the Germans from their worship of idols. He may have gained some 100,000 converts, and set up some 100 to 200 churches. He also sought to curb the clergy from indulging in immorality, hunting and bearing arms. In 745 he was consecrated as the archbishop of Mainz.

Boniface was fearless in his use of Scripture to admonish King Ethelbald of Mercia in 746–7 for his sexual immorality and his robbing of churches and monasteries. Wherever he went, Boniface carried his books with him. During a journey, he would read the Scriptures or sing psalms and hymns. He also distributed help to the poor. His copy of the epistle of James is heavily annotated with comments on morals, the sacraments and church order. In his letters he would comment on the shortness of life and the uncertainty of riches; and I Timothy 6:17 was a verse he urged upon his readers more than once. At the same time he was not averse to trying his hand at Latin acrostics and riddles. A monk's life was not all austerity. He wrote a letter to Egbert, Archbishop of York: 'We are sending you by the bearer of this letter two small casks of wine in token of mutual affection, beseeching you to use them for a merry day with the brothers.'

On his last missionary journey in 754, Boniface and his party of fifty men were attacked by some heathen Frisians. Boniface shouted to his men not to render evil for evil. To protect himself he held up a large book – which was possibly the Gospels – and finally had his skull hacked by a sword. Ironically enough, the murderers were apparently disappointed by the lack of expected treasure and so turned on each other. Boniface's body was recovered and buried at Fulda. He was a man who, despite his own longevity, knew that this life is short, and so he courageously sought to make the gospel known to all and sundry. His first biographer, Willibald, wrote of him: 'Zeal and vigour made him forceful, but gentleness and love made him mild.'

11

GOTTSCHALK

(c. 805–c. 868)

Witness to electing grace

Therefore He has mercy on whom He wills, and whom He wills He hardens (Rom. 9:18).

So then, those who are in the flesh cannot please God (Rom. 8:8).

But God demonstrates His own love toward us, in that while we were still sinners, Christ died for us. Much more then, having now been justified by His blood, we shall be saved from wrath through Him (Rom. 5:8-9).

Gottschalk was a ninth-century Saxon (i.e. German) monk, who at one stage sought relief from his monastic vows, but failed to win his case. He did, however, devote himself at the monastery of Orbais to the study of Augustine's works. On Christmas Day, 800, Pope Leo III crowned the French king, Charles (742–814), as the Emperor of the Romans. He has become known to history as Charlemagne, and the empire he ruled became known as the Holy Roman Empire. It was a deliberate attempt to revive the Roman Empire as a Christian realm. A period of some renewal of learning and culture resulted, known as the Carolingian Renaissance.

At this time Gottschalk studied the Bible and the Church Fathers, especially Augustine's writings, and sought to proclaim afresh the doctrines of grace. A fierce controversy resulted. In 848 at the Synod of Mainz, and then again in 849 at the Synod of Chiersy, Gottschalk was condemned, with the latter Synod deposing him from the priesthood. His major opponent in this dispute was Hincmar, the Archbishop of Reims. Gottschalk was publicly scourged, compelled to burn his books and imprisoned in the monastery of Hautvillers, near Epernay, for the remaining nineteen years of his life, despite appealing to Nicholas I of Rome (858–867). In all this, Gottschalk maintained the so-called double decree – that God's gracious election of a people to be in Christ necessarily means that the rest in Adam are reprobate.

Gottschalk refused to be intimidated by his persecutors, and, after a sad breakdown of some kind, he was denied Christian burial at his death. Yet his testimony remained: 'I believe and confess that God foreknew and foreordained the holy angels and elect men to eternal life, but that he almost equally foreordained the devil … with all reprobate men on account of their foreseen future evil deeds, by a just judgment to merited eternal death.' Hence salvation is all of unmerited grace, but damnation is all thoroughly deserved.

It has been customary to view Gottschalk as a lone August-inian voice testifying to the truth of divine predestination before an ecclesiastical world of Semi-Pelagians. It now appears that the Gottschalk controversy which erupted in 840 was an extension of earlier debate on matters related to predestination. For example, Smaragdus in the 820s was one who regarded Romans 8:32 as a text that revealed what he called 'the error of predestination'. Gottschalk was simply seeking to be faithful to Scripture as he understood it.

Against any teaching on free will, Gottschalk argued that 'After the first man fell by free will, none of us is able to use free will to do good, but only to do evil.' Being unable to do good in God's sight, we are naturally unable to please Him. Only Christ can save us, and He came to save only the elect, not all and sundry. Citing Romans 5:8-9, Gottschalk reasoned that 'If Christ died even for the reprobate, then the reprobate too, having been justified in His blood, will be saved from wrath through Him. But the reprobate will not be saved from wrath through Him. Therefore, Christ did not die for the reprobate.'

Not only did Gottschalk write theological works, he also wrote hymns, including one entitled 'A Hymn to God the Life-Giver'. Here he calls out to the Holy Spirit:

> *Together with the Father and the Son,*
> *You recreate Your elect souls,*
> *And when they are recreated,*
> *You also glorify them.*

In every era of the Church, God has maintained a witness to His free and undeserved mercy to sinners in Christ Jesus.

12

ANSELM OF CANTERBURY
(1033–1109)

The God-man pays the sinner's debt

And forgive us our debts, as we forgive our debtors
(Matt. 6:12).

*One was brought to him [the king] who owed him ten
thousand talents. But as he was not able to pay, his
master commanded that he be sold, with his wife and
children and all that he had, and that payment be made*
(Matt. 18:24b-25).

*For in Him [Christ] dwells all the fullness of the Godhead
bodily; and you are complete in Him* (Col. 2:9-10a).

*But you are those who have continued with Me in My
trials. And I bestow upon you a kingdom, just as My
Father bestowed one upon Me, that you may eat and
drink at My table in My kingdom, and sit on thrones
judging the twelve tribes of Israel* (Luke 22:28-30).

Although he became the Archbishop of Canterbury, Anselm was
actually born in north Italy, at Aosta, in 1033. At this time there
were no universities – only schools attached to cathedrals – so
prospective students would set off to find scholars to teach them.
After three years of wandering, Anselm came to Bec, where he
found Lanfranc lecturing both on classic works and the Bible.
As a student Anselm excelled, and in time Lanfranc left for the

monastery at Caen and then to be Archbishop of Canterbury, leaving Anselm in charge of the teaching at Bec.

After ten years of study in the monastery – mainly in the Bible and the works of Augustine – Anselm wrote his first book, the *Monologion*. His second work is the *Proslogion,* which sets out to prove the ontological argument for the existence of God, which is that God is something than which nothing greater can be thought. Anselm began to develop a theological method which placed great confidence in quiet reasoning.

Much against his inclination, Anselm was transferred to Canterbury as Lanfranc's successor in 1093. Here he clashed with the king, William Rufus, and twice went into exile. After writing *On the Incarnation of the Word*, he wrote *Cur Deus Homo (Why God Became Man)*. This was begun in England in 1094 and finished in exile in Italy in 1098. Anselm was never a rapid writer and agonized over everything he did, not wanting to imitate Augustine in his *Retractions* (or *Revisions*).

At the papal court in 1098, Urban II asked him to help with responses to the Eastern Orthodox Churches after the schism of 1054. So Anselm wrote *On the Procession of the Holy Spirit*, which was completed in 1102. His arguments do not make for short extracts and quotations.

Anselm's masterpiece is surely *Cur Deus Homo,* which is a dialogue between Anselm and an inquirer named Boso. It begins as follows: 'The question is this: For what reason or necessity did God become man and, as we believe and confess, by His death restore life to the world, when He could have done this through another person (angelic or human), or even by a sheer act of will?' Anselm answered by acknowledging the depths associated with such a question. He then begins his answer by saying that 'to sin is the same thing as not to render his due to God.' Therefore, 'everyone who sins must repay to God the honour that he has taken away, and this is the satisfaction that everyone ought to make to God.' If sin is not paid for or punished, it would be subject to no law, so sin is necessarily followed either by satisfaction or by punishment.

In Anselm's view, where Scripture is not clear there is liberty, but he saw the Scriptural teaching on the person and work of Christ as abundantly clear. Yet Anselm considered that he could set Christ aside for the sake of argument, and still prove the necessity of the God-man's sacrifice for sinners to be saved. In reply to Anselm's question about what he would give God to pay for sin, Boso replied in terms of repentance, a contrite and humble heart, fasting, giving and forgiving. Anselm's reply is that we owe these things to God even if we had not sinned. Boso is forced to the realization: 'I have nothing to repay Him for sin.'

Man has brought on himself his own inability to pay his debt to God. Even the Virgin Mary herself, said Anselm, was born with original sin. No one but God is able to pay this debt, and no one but man is obliged to pay it. Only one who is perfect God and perfect man can make satisfaction for sin. Boso thought that Anselm's explanation should even satisfy pagans, by reason alone. Anselm, however, moved from apologetics to adoration, and in his prayer to Christ addressed Him: 'Lord Jesus Christ, my Redeemer, my Mercy, and my Salvation.'

An old man in his seventies and in declining health, Anselm still pondered the origin of the soul. However, as he grew weaker, one of the monks present – perhaps his biographer Eadmer – read to him from Luke 22:28-30. His breathing grew slower, and he died soon after.

13

BERNARD OF CLAIRVAUX
(1090–1153)

For the love of the heavenly bridegroom

*Let him kiss me with the kisses of his mouth – for your
love is better than wine. Because of the fragrance of your
good ointments, your name is ointment poured forth;
therefore the virgins love you* (Song 1:2-3).

*Lord, make me to know my end, and what is the measure
of my days, that I may know how frail I am* (Ps. 39:4).

A contemplative monk, Bernard of Clairvaux was also much
involved in public affairs and controversies. These were not
always beneficial, as when he preached for the disastrous Second
Crusade which began in 1148. Other interventions could be
seen as more helpful and necessary, notably when he opposed
Peter Abelard for reducing the atonement to a demonstration of
God's love, and Bishop Gilbert of Poitiers for holding erroneous
views of the Trinity. In 1140 the Canons of Lyons proposed a
festival in honour of the Immaculate Conception, and Bernard
responded by declaring that it was contrary to Scripture and
to the Church Fathers. For all the high honour that Bernard
accorded to Mary, he also warned that 'the royal Virgin has no
need of a false honour'.

Bernard was born in 1090 – just five years before the calling of the First Crusade – at the château of Fontaines near Dijon in Burgundy, in what is now France. In 1112 Bernard entered the newly founded abbey of Cîteaux, belonging to the Cistercian order. Cîteaux was established as a response to perceived laxity in the Benedictine order, centred at Cluny. By 1115 Bernard had been appointed abbot of a new monastery, in the remote valley of Clairvaux.

For the last forty years of his life, Bernard spent more than half of each waking day in the reading and singing of, or the meditation on, Scripture – all done in Latin, as Bernard never mastered Hebrew or Greek. All 150 Psalms would have been recited aloud at least once a week.

Bernard knew the heart of the gospel of grace. In 1139 he wrote: 'I was made a sinner by deriving my being from Adam; I am made just by being washed in the blood of Christ.' He was strong on the forensic imputation of Christ's righteousness: 'Why should I not have someone else's righteousness since I have someone else's guilt? It was someone else who made me a sinner, it is someone else who justifies me from sin: the one through his seed, the other through his blood.'

On his deathbed, Bernard felt that the devil was accusing him of his sins; his reply was:

I admit that I am myself neither worthy nor able to obtain the kingdom of heaven by my own merits. But my Lord has obtained it by a double right: by inheritance from the Father and by the merit of His passion. Being content with the former, He gives the latter right to me. I claim it for myself on the basis of His gift and so will not be put to confusion.

He is supposed to have recited Psalm 39:4 in order to prepare for death.

Bernard is best known, however, as a preacher of Christ's love for the soul and the soul's love for Christ. This is seen in the allegorical approach taken in his *Sermons on the Song of Songs* (eighty-six in all, written between 1135 and 1153). Bernard only reached the beginning of chapter three of the Song of Songs – an average of about two sermons per verse! At the end of the twelfth sermon, Bernard prayed:

> Thank You, Lord Jesus, for Your kindness in uniting us to the Church You so dearly love, not merely that we may be endowed with the gift of faith, but that like brides we may be one with You in an embrace that is sweet, chaste, and eternal, beholding with unveiled faces that glory which is Yours in union with the Father and the Holy Spirit for ever and ever. Amen.

He interpreted 'kisses' to refer to the kiss of the feet initially, then the Bridegroom's hand by works of mercy, and finally the mouth whereby we experience His Spirit enter into the depths of our being. This would bring joy to the bride at the approach of the heavenly Bridegroom, which is 'a song that only the singer can hear'.

In Bernard's view, love leads to holiness. He wrote: 'Virtue is that by which man seeks continuously and eagerly for his Maker and when he finds Him, adheres to Him with all his might.' He could preach passionately, as in sermon 20 when he spoke of Christ: 'Learn to love Him tenderly, to love Him wisely, to love Him with a mighty love ... Let the Lord Jesus be to your heart sweet and pleasant, so as to destroy the false attractiveness of the carnal life.' Preaching on the Song of Songs 1:3-4, Bernard declared: 'I have need to be drawn for this reason, because the fire of Your love has grown somewhat cold in us; nor are we, on account of that coldness, able to run as we did yesterday and in former days.' Further on, he called on his hearers: 'Yes, let us run, but in the fragrance of Your perfumes, not in any confidence of our own merits.' Not all of Bernard's beliefs or activities measure up against Scripture, but he was a medieval Christian who knew grace and who yearned to grow in the love of Christ.

14

FRANCIS OF ASSISI

(1182–1226)

All creation celebrates the Lord

Praise the Lord! Praise the Lord from the heavens; praise Him in the heights! ... Praise Him, sun and moon; praise Him, all you stars of light! ... Beasts and all cattle ... kings of the earth and all peoples ... both young men and maidens; old men and children. Let them praise the name of the Lord (Ps. 148:1,3,10,11,12,13).

Provide neither gold nor silver nor copper in your money belts, nor bag for your journey, nor two tunics, nor sandals, nor staffs (Matt. 10:9-10a).

Casting all your care upon Him, for He cares for you (1 Pet. 5:7).

Francis was born in 1182, or perhaps 1181, in the Italian hill town of Assisi. He was actually baptized John, but his father called him Francis ('the little Frenchman') because he loved France; indeed, French was the language that Francis habitually used. Throughout his life he received little education and wrote only on rare occasions. Usually he signed his letters with a *T* to signify the cross.

As a youth, Francis indulged in much merrymaking. His first biographer, Thomas of Celano, declared that he was 'eager for foolishness of every kind'. Hoping to become a knight, he served as a soldier in 1202 but was captured while defending Assisi against the town of Perugia in what was more of a skirmish than a war. After spending a year in prison – during which time his father negotiated the price of his ransom – he was released.

But after resuming his former life, he soon fell gravely ill. He set out to participate in one of Pope Innocent III's Crusades in 1204, but a vision led him to return home to seek God's will for his life. He felt an increasing sense of alienation from the futility of worldly life and by 1205 had begun to adopt the life of a hermit. His project – also gained through a vision – was to rebuild the nearly abandoned church building at the edge of Assisi called San Damiano. This he did, singing all the while. Meanwhile, his father tried to have him imprisoned in the cellar of the family home because Francis was giving away too much money to the poor and leprous. He hauled his recalcitrant son before the local bishop, but Francis responded by stripping himself naked to signify his renunciation of all earthly possessions. Hence the Franciscan ideal of 'naked following the naked Christ'.

On 24 February 1208 in the little church of Saint Mary of the Angels, Francis heard the words of Christ to His twelve disciples recorded in Matthew 10: 'Take no gold or silver or copper in your wallet, no bag for your journey, nor two tunics nor sandals nor a staff.' This led him to change his hermit lifestyle for a more itinerant ministry. Gathering a band of followers, he began to preach the gospel of peace and penitence to the poor – very much as one of them. As Francis said: 'If we possessed property we should have need of arms for its defence.' He told his disciples: 'My brother, commit yourself to God with all your cares, and He will care for you.' Once, while riding on horse-back in Assisi, he met a leper. At first, Francis fled but he then reproached himself for his cowardly action and returned to kiss the leper's hand and give him all his money.

In 1209 Francis went to Rome, where he gained approval for his order from Innocent III. His *Later Rule* was approved in 1223. The beginning of the thirteenth century was the heyday of the dualist heresy of Catharism, which repudiated the beauty of the physical world, and hence of nature. It gained many converts in southern France but virtually disappeared in Italy – an indirect result of the Franciscan movement.

Great crowds gathered to hear Francis speak, and from 1210 to 1220 the Franciscan order grew at an impressive rate. Yet Francis was not ascetic in a gloomy way; he was joyful and genuinely loved poverty, referring to her as Lady Poverty. He was strict with himself and could be with others – to control temptation he would hurl himself into a ditch full of ice in the middle of winter; and on Cyprus he forced Brother Barbaro to eat a lump of ass dung because of his evil-speaking.

Everything in nature – such as the sun and birds – was referred to as a 'brother'. Rabbits, birds and even a wolf were supposed to have become tame before Francis. He once preached to some birds and then reproached himself for not having done so before this. If he saw a lamb being led off to the slaughter, he would try to rescue it by pleading or trading for it. Yet he was not a vegetarian.

Francis's *Canticle of the Sun* is a charming piece of work, composed in 1225, but it is sometimes criticized for being pantheistic because of its references to Sir Brother Sun, Sister Moon, Brother Wind, Sister Water, Brother Fire and Sister Earth. In fact, it is simply a celebration of the Creator through the creation and is based loosely on Psalm 148. It begins:

> *Most High, all-powerful, good Lord,*
> *Yours are the praises, the glory, the honour,*
>   *and all blessing.*
> *To You alone, Most High, do they belong,*
> *And no man is worthy to mention Your name.*

It concludes with further praise to the Lord, and a call to serve Him with great humility. Rejecting the world, Francis delighted in nature.

In 1194 Clare ('the clear one') was born into a noble family. After she grew up, she heard Francis preach and was converted to the Franciscan way of life. Although Francis was only a deacon, he received Clare's vows. Clare thus became the founder of the Poor Clares, although they originally called themselves the Poor Ladies. In one of the papacy's more bizarre efforts, Pope Pius XII in 1958 proclaimed Clare to be the patron saint of television.

Francis maintained that God chose him because 'he could find no one more worthless, and he wished here to confound the nobility and grandeur, the strength, the beauty, and the learning of this world.' In Egypt he predicted that the Crusaders would be beaten because of their weak moral condition. This prophecy was fulfilled in 1219. Actually, Christian victories disturbed him almost as much as Christian defeats. In 1219–20 he went to Syria, and probably to Bethlehem. Francis was able to meet the Egyptian sultan Malik-al-Kamil, and he was received with courtesy – one of the few high points during the Crusades. He even returned with a carved ivory horn, which was a present from the sultan.

On his deathbed Francis sang and cried, 'Welcome, Sister Death!' Francis was no theologian, and John Wesley had reason to portray him as 'a well-meaning man, though manifestly weak in intellect.' His abiding influence, however, is to be found in his uncompromising commitment to poverty, joy, a love of all creation, and peace.

15

RAMON LULL
(1235– c. 1316)

To die for Muslims

*Greater love has no one than this, than to lay down one's
life for his friends* (John 15:13).
*You shall love the Lord your God with all your heart, with
all your soul, and with all your strength* (Deut. 6:5).

In the thirteenth century, Islam was reaching into Europe, especially in Castile, Navarre and Aragon on the Spanish peninsula. This
was the time in which Ramon Lull was born, into a distinguished
family in the picturesque little port of Palma on the island of
Majorca in 1235. His father had served in the army of Aragon
when the island was reclaimed from the Saracens (Muslims). Little
is known of Lull's early life, but he did serve in the king's court
of Aragon. A highly intelligent man, gifted in many areas, he also
played, with considerable skill, the cithern (a stringed instrument,
not unlike a guitar), and was a court poet. He married Bianca
Picany, by whom he had two children, but his morals were low,
and he wrote licentious poetry to other women.

About the year 1266 he was converted through a vision of
Christ crucified, which came as Lull was contemplating another
sexual conquest. In response he took up an ascetic and ultimately

missionary life, having made provision for his wife and children. While he was meditating, John 15:13 came into his mind. He purchased a Saracen slave in order to learn Arabic, but the slave blasphemed Christ and Lull struck him. Sometime later, the slave brandished a knife and wounded Lull. This led to the slave's arrest, and, expecting the worst in prison, he hanged himself. Lull retired to pray, meditate and write for a time. By now his view was that the Holy Land would not be won by the methods of the Crusaders, but would only be conquered by 'love and prayers, and the pouring out of tears and of blood.' This should not be interpreted to mean that he opposed the Crusades, but that more was required than spears and swords.

Lull went on to set up a training school at Palma or Mont-pellier in order to reach Muslims. In the end, he was to under-take three missionary journeys to the Muslim world, the first one being to Tunis in 1291–2. This was by no means straight-forward, as he missed the first ship because of fear, and the second because he was ill with fever. Feeling something of the contrition of Jonah, he joined the third ship in good health.

Believing that faith, reason and passion needed to be com-bined, Lull challenged Muslim leaders to a debate, but this got him arrested and imprisoned. He was banished, and worked in univer-sities, including Paris. Almost certainly, he became a Franciscan. After more studies and missionary tours, he returned to Tunis about 1304 or possibly a little later. He here publicly criticized the character of Muhammad, whom Dante (c. 1265–1321) consigned to the deepest part of hell in his *Inferno*. A kindly mufti rescued Lull, and again he was deported.

About 1314 he returned to Bugia in North Africa, to minister to a little circle of converts. However, he was discovered, and was probably stoned to death in 1315 or early 1316 – or at least injured so badly that he later died. He and Francis of Assisi were the only two medieval Christians known to have reached out to Muslims in order to make Christ known to them.

Lull's intelligence was highly praised by some, leading to the refrain:

There have been three wise men in the world:
Adam, Solomon, and Ramon.

Today his numerous philosophical writings are treated as somewhat curious and picturesque. His life before conversion was disreputable, and even after conversion he considered it acceptable to God to neglect his wife and family. Yet there remains something to admire in his self-sacrificing courage and vision. The Great Commandment of Deuteronomy 6:5 became the foundation to his preaching and teaching. His motto later in life was: 'He who loves not lives not; he who lives by the Life cannot die.'

16

GERARD GROOTE
(1340–1384)

From magic to grace

*Also, many of those who had practised magic brought
their books together and burned them in the sight of all*
(Acts 19:19a).

*[Israel] has gone up on every high mountain and under
every green tree, and there played the harlot*
(Jer. 2:20b; 3:6b).

*For the kingdom of God is not eating and drinking, but
righteousness and peace and joy in the Holy Spirit*
(Rom. 14:17).

*Therefore whatever they tell you to observe, that observe
and do, but do not do according to their works; for they
say, and do not do* (Matt. 23:3).

Gerard Groote was born – an only child – in October 1340
in Deventer, a venerable old Dutch city in the eastern part of
the diocese of Utrecht, which was founded by an Anglo-Saxon
missionary in 768, not too long after Boniface's death. Both of
Groote's parents died of the plague in 1350, and he was looked
after by his uncle, and eventually sent to study at the University
of Paris. He seems to have studied virtually everything, including
astrology, alchemy and medicine, which were all viewed as
science.

It is certain that Groote owned books on the black arts and magic, and certainly he sought to show off his wealth and learning, but it is not at all certain that he was a kind of Doctor Faustus, who sold his soul to the devil. Whatever the case, in Deventer in 1372 Groote fell seriously ill, and was only able to receive Holy Communion if he first renounced his magic books and burned them. There had been a stand-off for a time between the Franciscan friar and Groote, but Groote finally came to the conclusion that only his soul mattered, and the books were burned, in imitation of what the new Christians at Ephesus did in New Testament times.

Groote lamented that he had 'committed every fornication under every shady tree and on every hill-top', and pleaded to heaven: 'God spare me.' He already held a number of ecclesiastical positions, including a canonry at St Martin's Cathedral at Utrecht, but now he denounced pluralism (the practice of holding more than one office at any one time). His views are something of a mixture; he favoured more frequent Communion (in the Middle Ages, most of the congregation would watch the priest celebrate Communion, and only participate themselves once a year, at Easter), and he recommended frequent short prayers during one's daily work; but he became a vegetarian, ate frugal meals and would only wash his dishes once a week. He tried to be practical in orientation. 'Labour is holy, but business is dangerous' is one of his sayings.

To prepare to preach, he went on a book-buying expedition to Paris. On his return, he was ordained as a deacon, probably in 1380. He was an itinerant preacher and sought to preach to the poor and the outcasts. His only surviving sermon in the vernacular is, typically, on Romans 14:17. He especially emphasized the importance of imitating Christ. Sometimes he would preach for three hours. He could overdo his denunciations of the body and of property. He warned: 'Do not love your body too much, that stinking sack, that rebellious jackass.' And he told of a monk who was buried in the dung pit for possessing three gold coins when he died.

Groote also set up monastic-like institutions at Deventer, albeit with no vows or distinctive dress. His followers became known as the Brethren and Sisters of the Common Life, and the movement was part of what became known as the *Devotio Moderna*, or Modern Devotion. When the Great Schism broke out in 1378, the pope in Avignon (Clement VII) confronted the pope in Rome (Urban VI), and all Europe lined up behind one or the other. Groote was grieved, and blamed simony (the practice of buying clerical office) and clerical immorality for the Schism, which was to last until 1417. Apparently his preaching became a little too fierce for some, as he claimed that the situation with regard to the priests was worse than in Matthew 23:3 where Jesus at least told His followers to observe what the Pharisees *taught* if not what they *practised*. In Groote's day neither the teaching nor the practice was safe. He wanted congregations to boycott a fornicating priest, although he still considered sacraments administered by immoral priests to be valid. In 1383 the bishop of Utrecht, in what Thomas à Kempis called 'a crafty edict', prohibited deacons from preaching, which effectively ended Groote's authority to preach.

Accepting for the moment the episcopal decision, Groote seems not to have preached, but he did appeal to Urban VI in Rome. He was not convinced that he was the true pope but inclined to think he was. However, in August 1384 he caught the plague and died. Thomas à Kempis, who was only four years of age in 1384, later recalled that Groote was remembered fondly: 'His features were pleasing, he had an agreeable voice and was affable to everybody.'

17

JOHN HUS
(c. 1372–1415)

Search the Scriptures

*When I say to the wicked, 'You shall surely die,' and you
give him no warning, nor speak to warn the wicked from
his wicked way, to save his life, that same wicked man
shall die in his iniquity; but his blood I will require at your
hand. Yet if you warn the wicked, and he does not turn
from his wickedness, nor from his wicked way, he
shall die in his iniquity; but you have delivered
your soul (Ezek. 3:18-19).*
Search the Scriptures (John 5:39).

The son of poor peasants, John Hus (or Huss) was born in 1372
or 1373 in Husinec in southern Bohemia. Hence he became John
of Husinec, which was abbreviated to Huss or Hus. Hus went
off to the University of Prague, destined for the priesthood.
As early as 1391 he read some of the writings of John Wyclif –
regarded by the Roman Catholic Church as heretical – but in
1393 he spent his last few coins to buy an indulgence (a piece
of paper whereby the buyer was promised some remittance
for sins committed). Although not an exceptional student, he
received his bachelor's degree in 1393 and his master's degree
in 1396. At this stage, he said: 'I had thought to become a priest

in order to secure a good livelihood and dress, and to be held in high esteem by men.'

By 1402 Hus was rector and preacher of the prestigious Bethlehem Chapel of the Holy Innocents (which still stands, albeit with some rebuilding), and Jerome of Prague was his most intimate companion and adherent. Jerome brought more of Wyclif's writings over from Oxford in 1402, and these emphasized the supreme authority of Scripture. Hus was converted to a more evangelical view of faith, and 'Search the Scriptures' became his constant admonition. He began to preach reform in the Church, denouncing simony, unworthy priests, and the alleged miracles such as the supposed appearance of Christ's blood on communion wafers. Zbynek, the Archbishop of Prague, became his bitter enemy, but Hus told him: 'I preach the sacred Scriptures.'

From 1378 to 1409 two rival popes had claimed authority over the Western Church. Then in 1409 a council at Pisa deposed both popes, installed another, but found that there were now three squabbling pontiffs! In all this, Hus was moving towards Scripture as God's final and sufficient Word. As late as 1409–10 he was chosen as rector of Prague University. On 16 July 1410, Zbynek had the works of Wyclif burned in his palace courtyard. Hus mocked: 'Such bonfires never yet removed a single sin from the hearts of men. Fire does not consume truth. It is always the mark of a little mind that it vents its anger on inanimate objects.'

Archbishop Zbynek excommunicated Hus in 1410, then placed him under 'aggravated excommunication'. In 1411 Hus was excommunicated (for the third time), but then Zbynek died, perhaps poisoned by his cook. Hus was excommunicated in 1411 for contumacy and non-appearance, not heresy. Cardinal Otto Colonna had cited Hus to appear before him, but Hus refused to go, and instead sent representatives. Hus warned against the priests of Antichrist, those 'who desire that human prescriptions be more strictly observed than the Word of God.'

After an indulgence was preached in 1412 – which Hus denounced – matters came to a head. An interdict was placed on Prague, and Hus felt torn between his responsibilities as a shepherd to die (John 10:11-14) or to flee (Matt. 10:23). Finally, to save the city, Hus left. For the next two years, Hus preached and wrote in the villages and fields of southern Bohemia. His views had crystallized: 'I humbly accord faith, i.e. trust, to the Holy Scriptures, desiring to hold, believe, and assert whatever is contained in them as long as I have breath in me.'

In the autumn of 1414, Pope John XXIII (not the pope who reigned from 1958–63, but one of the same name) convened an ecumenical council in Constance in Germany, and he called on Hus to attend. The emperor, Sigismund of Hungary, promised a safe conduct to Hus to go to the Council, but at Constance Hus was arrested on Pope John XXIII's orders. A promise given to a heretic was not regarded as binding and Hus was soon imprisoned for several months in a cell in the Dominican monastery on an island in Lake Constance (now a luxury hotel). The conditions were so terrible that he nearly died. He asked for a Bible, and thought much on the abuse of Christ at His trial.

Thirty charges were brought against Hus, including that he considered himself the fourth person in the Godhead! The presiding cardinal was Pierre d'Ailly, a conciliarist – one who believed that Church councils, not the pope, had the final authority. Hus was often shouted down during proceedings, and was condemned to die as a heretic. On 6 July 1415 at the cathedral in Constance, the Bishop of Lodi preached, with more intimidation than understanding, on Romans 6:6 ('that the body of sin be destroyed'). Hus, without his priestly garments, was asked to repudiate his own works.

Hus, however, refused to recant, his attitude being: 'He who fears death loses the joy of life. Truth conquers all things.'

From Ezekiel 3, he learned that silence is complicity: 'O faithful Christian, search the truth, hear truth, learn truth, love truth, speak the truth, hold the truth till death.' Only if he were shown by Scripture that he were wrong would he recant. He prophesied that though they might burn a goose (*Hus* means 'goose' in Bohemian), a swan would follow – a prophecy which was remembered in Luther's day.

Hus's views had become increasingly biblical but not radical. He only condemned unworthy popes (he listed fifteen of them) and he accepted the real presence in the Eucharist, complete with transubstantiation. He never denied the Assumption of Mary, the intercession of saints or the existence of purgatory. On the papacy he declared, without a great deal of logic: 'I acknowledge that the pope is the vicar of Christ in the Roman Church, but do not hold it as an article of faith.'

Finally, John Hus was burnt at the stake. His books were burnt first, then he was tied to the stake and was asked if he recanted. He refused, and the fire was lit. His final prayer was: 'Christ, thou Son of the living God, have mercy upon me.' He had prayed in preparation for this moment: 'Give us a valiant spirit, a fearless heart, the right faith, a firm hope, and perfect love, that we may offer our lives for Thy sake with the greatest patience and joy. Amen.'

18

MARTIN LUTHER
(1483–1546)

Justified by faith in Christ

For I am not ashamed of the gospel of Christ, for it is the power of God to salvation for everyone who believes, for the Jew first and also for the Greek. For in it the righteousness of God is revealed from faith to faith; as it is written, 'The just shall live by faith' (Rom. 1:16-17).

Knowing that a man is not justified by the works of the law but by faith in Jesus Christ, even we have believed in Christ Jesus, that we might be justified by faith in Christ and not by works of the law; for by the works of the law no flesh shall be justified (Gal. 2:16).

The blood of Jesus Christ His Son cleanses us from all sin (1 John 1:7b).

If You, Lord, should mark iniquities, O Lord, who could stand? But there is forgiveness with You, that You may be feared (Ps. 130:3-4).

Martin Luther is known to history as the one who, under God, initiated the Protestant Reformation of the sixteenth century. He was born on 10 November 1483 in the Saxon village of Eisleben, and died on 18 February 1546 at the same place. In July 1505 the young Luther, who had just earned his Master of Arts degree from Erfurt University, was walking towards

Stotternheim. A storm broke, and so terrified Luther that he cried out, 'St Anne help me! I will become a monk.' That is how he came to enter the strict Augustinian monastery at Erfurt, there to be given a cell nine feet by six feet. The first of the six daily worship services began at 2.00 a.m.

In May 1507 Luther was ordained to the priesthood, and in 1508 he began lecturing at the University of Wittenberg, a small town with a population of only 2,000 to 2,500. By 1512 Luther had obtained the degree of Doctor of Theology and began to lecture on the Bible. All this time he was a diligent monk, and claimed that 'if the monastic life could get a man to heaven, I should have entered.'

Luther's revolt against what the Roman Church was teaching came in 1517 when an indulgence was preached concerning the relics at Castle Church in Wittenberg. The Elector Frederick the Wise of Saxony had a huge collection of relics, including five particles of Mary's milk, four pieces of her hair, one piece of the swaddling clothes in which Jesus was wrapped, thirteen pieces of His manger, one piece of bread from the Last Supper, one piece of the burning bush, one hair of Christ's beard, one thorn, and various pieces of the cross. Viewing them on All Saints' Day (1 November) was supposed to reduce one's stay in purgatory by 1,902,202 years and 270 days. Luther felt compelled to speak out against such a travesty of the gospel, and posted his '95 Theses' on the Castle Church door.

By 3 January 1521 Luther was excommunicated by Pope Leo X, and in April 1521 he appeared at the Diet of Worms before the emperor Charles V. In all this he stood firm: 'Unless I am convinced by Scripture and plain reason – I do not accept the authority of popes and councils, for they have contradicted each other – my conscience is captive to the Word of God. I cannot and I will not recant anything, for to go against conscience is neither right nor safe. God help me. Amen.' He may have added: 'Here I stand, I cannot do otherwise.' So began the Protestant Reformation.

Finally, in 1546, Luther died, while trying to resolve a family dispute at Mansfield. He prayed Psalm 31:5 ('into Your hand I commit my spirit'), kept repeating John 3:16, and wrote on a slip of paper: 'This is true. We are all beggars.'

In an *Autobiographical Fragment* which was appended to the 1545 edition of his works, Luther placed his breakthrough to grace in the year 1519. Most historians would probably want to date this rather earlier – and Luther himself commented that 'I did not learn my theology all at once' – but the fragment does allow us to understand something of Luther's spiritual torment. Luther wrote: 'For I hated this word "righteousness of God", which by the customary use of all the doctors I had been taught to understand philosophically as what they call the *formal* or *active righteousness* whereby God is just and punishes sinners.' To continue in Luther's words:

> For my case was this: however irreproachable my life as a monk, I felt myself in the presence of God to be a sinner with a most unquiet conscience, nor could I believe him to be appeased by the satisfaction I could offer. I did not love – nay, I hated this just God who punishes sinners, and if not with silent blasphemy, at least with huge murmuring I was indignant against God, as if it were really not enough that miserable sinners, eternally ruined by original sin, should be crushed with every kind of calamity through the law of the Ten Commandments, but that God through the Gospel must add sorrow to sorrow, and even through the gospel bring his righteousness and wrath to bear on us.
>
> At last, as I meditated day and night, God showed mercy and I turned my attention to the connection of the words, namely – 'The righteousness of God is revealed, as it is written: the righteous shall live by faith' – and there I began to understand that the righteousness of God is the righteousness in which a just man lives by the gift of God, in other words by faith, and that what Paul means is this: the righteousness of

God, revealed in the Gospel, is *passive*, in other words that by which the merciful God justifies us through faith, as it is written, 'The righteous shall live by faith.' At this I felt myself straightway born afresh and to have entered through the open gates into paradise itself.

Galatians became his favourite epistle, and he spoke of it as 'my own epistle, to which I have plighted my troth. It is my Katie von Bora' (he had married Katherine von Bora in 1525). On Galatians 2:16, he commented: 'Most necessary it is that we should know this article well, teach it unto others, and beat it into their heads continually.' The article of justification is, said Luther, 'the principal article of all Christian doctrine, which makes true Christians indeed.' This gospel sustained him for the rest of his eventful life. He once dreamt that his Accuser came to him to set before him afresh all of his sins. Luther admitted them all, without denying any or seeking to justify himself in any way, but he also scrawled across the list: 'The blood of Jesus Christ cleanses us from all sin.' This was the message of the Reformation, summed up in Luther's hymn, based on Psalm 130:

> To wash away the crimson stain,
> Grace, grace alone availeth;
> Our works, alas! are all in vain;
> In much the best life faileth:
> No man can glory in Thy sight,
> All must alike confess Thy might,
> And live alone by mercy.

19

JOHN CALVIN
(1509–1564)

The testimony of Scripture

All Scripture is breathed out by God, and is profitable
for teaching, reproof, correction, and training in
righteousness (2 Tim. 3:16, ESV).

John Calvin – Jean Cauvin in French – was born at Noyon in France on 10 July 1509. His father originally intended his son for the priesthood, and at the age of twelve he received the tonsure. At Ourscamp Abbey, he kissed what was supposed to be the finger of St Anne. The young Calvin spent the next five years at the Collège de Montaigu in Paris, before switching to law at the University of Orleans in 1528–9. Calvin worked hard, to the detriment of his health.

On All Saints' Day in 1533 the rector of the Louvre University, Nicolas Cop, preached an evangelical sermon. Calvin clearly sensed danger. After the affair of the Placards (where placards appeared all over Paris denouncing the Mass), he fled to Basel in January 1535. The police seized Calvin's personal papers, and Etienne de la Forge (a friend of Calvin) was burned alive on 16 February 1535. By March 1536 the first edition of the magisterial *Institutes of the Christian Religion* had been published.

This leads us to ask: When was Calvin converted to the evangelical faith? Calvin rarely spoke of himself, but in the Preface to his *Commentary on the Psalms* (1557) he declared that 'God by a sudden conversion subdued and brought my mind to a teachable frame.' This probably took place between August 1533 when Calvin was at the general Chapter in Noyon and May 1534 when he was surrendering all ecclesiastical benefices.

Calvin's desires were simple: 'Being of a rather unsociable and shy disposition, I have always loved retirement and peace. So I began to look for some hideout where I could escape from people … My aim was always to live in private without being known.' However, Guillaume Farel persuaded – or bullied – him to stay in Geneva.

The Council at Geneva had abolished the Mass, and issued coins inscribed *post tenebras lux* ('after the shadows, light'). In January 1537 Farel and Calvin laid before the Council their *Articles on the Organization of the Church and its Worship at Geneva.* Calvin sought that the Lord's Supper be held monthly, and that the power of excommunication be the preserve of the Church, not the state. However, Calvin's reforms were resented by many, and the Council of Two Hundred expelled him, Farel and another minister. Calvin left Geneva, thinking that he would go to Basel to study, but Martin Bucer prevailed upon him to preach in Strasbourg.

At Strasbourg Calvin published the second edition of the *Institutes* in 1539, his first commentary on the Bible (Romans), his *Short Treatise on the Lord's Supper* and his noteworthy *Reply to Cardinal Sadoleto*. In 1540 he also married Idelette de Bure, the widow of an Anabaptist who had converted to the Reformed faith. Calvin knew tragedy, however – his wife died before the decade was out, and he had no surviving children. Calvin was left to care for her two children by her first marriage. His brother Antoine lived with Calvin and he had eight children, so for much of his life Calvin's house was full of little children.

Meanwhile, Geneva continued to experience troubles, so many in fact that in October 1540 Ami Perrin was sent to Strasbourg to retrieve Calvin, but not Farel. For a year Calvin agonized over the decision, but finally returned, not knowing that it would be for the rest of his life. Characteristically, he preached on his first Sunday in September 1541 from the text he had reached in his series when he had been banished three years previously.

For the rest of his life Calvin sought to teach and apply the Bible as the Word of God. He preached about 260 sermons a year, all delivered without notes. He had many opponents, although as Protestant refugees from Catholic persecution poured into Geneva, they tended to favour Calvin. The only man to be executed for heresy – on 27 October 1553 – was Michael Servetus, who denied the Trinity, and was fleeing from a death sentence passed by Roman Catholic authorities at Vienne.

Theodore Beza says that people called their dogs 'Calvin', and Calvin once complained to Heinrich Bullinger: 'If I simply said it was daytime at high noon, they would begin to doubt it.' Also, throughout his life Calvin seems to have suffered from migraine, gout, pulmonary tuberculosis, intestinal parasites, thrombosed haemorrhoids and irritable bowel syndrome. After 1555 the Consistory (the body of pastors) won the right to excommunicate – a contrast to the situation in Zurich under both Zwingli and Bullinger where the magistrates, not the clergy, handled excommunications, and in Berne where there were no excommunications.

In 1559 Theodore Beza was placed at the head of the newly founded College (the Genevan Academy) and Calvin finally took out Genevan citizenship. John Knox, one of Geneva's refugees, famously referred to the city as 'the most perfect school of Christ that ever was on earth since the days of the Apostles.' As he lay dying, Calvin wrote to Farel: 'It is enough that I live and die for Christ, who is to all his followers a gain both in life and in death.'

Calvin wanted a return to the Bible as the authoritative and sufficient Word of God. Duns Scotus (*c.* 1265–1308) – 'Doctor Subtilis' – spoke for medieval Catholicism when he declared that 'Nothing is to be held as of the substance of the faith except that which can be expressly derived from Scripture or which is expressly declared by the Church.' In his commentary on the classic text, 2 Timothy 3:16, Calvin set forth the Reformed, and biblical, view:

> This is the principle which distinguishes our religion from all others, that we know that God has spoken to us, and are fully convinced that the prophets did not speak at their own suggestion, but that, being organs of the Holy Spirit, they only uttered what they had been commissioned from heaven to declare. Whoever then wishes to profit in the Scriptures, let him, first of all, lay down this as a settled point, that the Law and the Prophets are not a doctrine delivered according to the will and pleasure of men, but dictated by the Holy Spirit.

He once said of 2 Timothy: 'As for me, I know that this epistle has profited me more than any other book in Scripture – and still profits me every day.' Calvin lived to preach, teach and apply the Word of God.

20

THOMAS BILNEY

(c. 1495–1531)

Grace to the chief of sinners

This is a faithful saying and worthy of all acceptance, that Christ Jesus came into the world to save sinners, of whom I am chief (1 Tim. 1:15).

But of Him you are in Christ Jesus, who became for us wisdom from God – and righteousness and sanctification and redemption (1 Cor. 1:30).

But now, thus says the Lord, who created you, O Jacob, and He who formed you, O Israel: 'Fear not, for I have redeemed you; I have called you by your name; you are Mine. When you pass through the waters, I will be with you; and through the rivers, they shall not overflow you. When you walk through the fire, you shall not be burned, nor shall the flame scorch you. For I am the Lord your God, the Holy One of Israel, your Saviour' (Isa. 43:1-3a).

Do not enter into judgment with Your servant, for in Your sight no one living is righteous (Ps. 143:2).

Little is known of Thomas Bilney's childhood, but in 1519 he was ordained by the Bishop of Ely in England. Throughout his life, Bilney remained a gentle and lovable little man, a bachelor, who was very studious and very generous (he would eat only one meal a day and would often give away his own meals to prisoners). As a Roman Catholic, he undertook fasts, vigils, Masses and pardons, but they brought him no relief. Later he was to criticize the Roman Catholic priests of his day: 'These men do not find pasture, for they never teach and draw others after them, that they should enter by Christ who alone is the door whereby we must come unto the Father; but set before the people another way, persuading them to come unto God through good works, oftentimes speaking nothing at all of Christ.'

When Erasmus's Greek and Latin New Testament was published in 1516, Bilney obtained a copy, as much for the Latin as for anything in the Word, but it had an immediate and abiding effect on him: 'And at the first reading, as I well remember, I chanced upon this sentence of St Paul (O most sweet and comfortable sentence to my soul), "It is a true saying and worthy of all men to be embraced, that Christ Jesus came into the world to save sinners; of whom I am the chief" (1 Tim. 1:15).' Bilney, who had been almost in despair, felt what he described as 'a marvellous comfort and quietness, insomuch as my bruised bones leaped for joy.' At this stage he had probably never heard of Luther. Yet he embraced a Luther-like grasp of saving faith: 'I see it all; my vigils, my fasts, my pilgrimages, my purchase of masses and indulgences, were destroying instead of saving me. All these efforts were, as St Augustine says, a hasty running out of the right way.'

Bilney was the first Cambridge scholar to embrace Reformation views. The White Horse Inn at Cambridge became known as 'Little Germany' because so many talked of Luther's theology there. About the year 1524, Bilney heard Hugh Latimer speak, and begged him to hear his confession. It was actually a form of evangelism, as Latimer learned more of the gospel from Bilney's confession than he had learned from books and priests. Latimer was to be burnt at the stake during Queen Mary's reign in 1555.

Bilney took Latimer with him to visit lepers and prisoners, but preaching Reformation doctrines was to land Bilney and

Latimer in trouble with the ecclesiastical authorities. Cuthbert Tunstall, the Bishop of London, asked Bilney to return to the Church, but Bilney replied that he had never left it. However, Tunstall was able to coerce a number of sad recantations from Bilney, but these gave Bilney no peace of heart. He continued to reject images, merits, the invocation of the saints and phoney miracles. Yet he did not reject the Mass as such.

In 1531, at the instigation of Richard Nix (the blind and embittered Bishop of Norwich), Bilney was arrested again and imprisoned. He knew what was in store for him. On the night before his execution, he put his finger into the flame of a candle, burning it down to the first joint, and cited Isaiah 43:1-3. The next day – either 10 March or, more probably, 19 August – he was burnt at the stake for believing in justification by faith in Christ alone. Having said that, Bilney had retained many Roman Catholic beliefs.

Bilney said that his only aim was to preach Christ: 'Whom with my whole power I do teach and set forth, being made for us by God His Father our wisdom, righteousness, sanctification, and redemption.' Sir Thomas More (the Lord Chancellor) and John Stokesley (the new Bishop of London) saw this persecution of Protestant 'heretics' as 'God's great cause'.

At the stake Bilney recited Psalm 143:2 three times, and then cried out 'Jesus!' and 'Credo!' ('I believe'). So 'Little Bilney' glorified his great and merciful God.

21

WILLIAM TYNDALE
(c. 1494–1536)

Hope through the Scriptures

*For whatever things were written before were written for
our learning, that we through the patience and comfort of
the Scriptures might have hope* (Rom. 15:4).

Tyndale seems to have been born about the borders of
Wales, perhaps around 1494 or a little earlier. He lived in times
when the Roman Catholic Church, while professing to believe in
the Scriptures, was very hostile to any attempts to translate them
into the vernacular. After graduating from Oxford University,
Tyndale went to Cambridge about 1516, in the aftermath of
Erasmus's stay there in 1511–14. He became convicted of what
was to become his life's work: 'I perceived by experience how
that it was impossible to establish the lay people in any truth,
except the Scriptures were plainly laid before their eyes in their
mother tongue.' He was well equipped to do this, as he was
proficient in seven languages – Hebrew, Greek, Latin, Italian,
Spanish, English and French.

Tyndale was hopeful that Bishop Cuthbert Tunstall of London
would possibly be supportive of his project to translate the Bible
into English, but he was soon disappointed. By May 1524 Tyndale

had left England for Hamburg, and never returned. Copies of Tyndale's translation of the New Testament, completed in 1525, were smuggled into England, but both civil and ecclesiastical authorities remained hostile. In late 1526 Tunstall ordered a bonfire at Paul's Cross of all the New Testaments. The Church which professed worship for God declared war on His Word. Among other 'crimes', Tyndale had used words like 'repentance' instead of 'penance', and 'senior' (in 1534, 'elder') instead of 'priest' in his translations.

John Foxe records that one day a Roman Catholic scholar at dinner with Tyndale declared: 'We were better be without God's law than the pope's.' Following the example of Erasmus (c. 1469–1536), Tyndale replied: 'I defy the Pope and all his laws … If God spare my life ere many years, I will cause a boy that driveth the plough, shall know more of the Scripture than thou dost.' He summarized the Bible's message to sinners: 'In the gospel, when we believe the promises, we receive the spirit of life; and are justified, in the blood of Christ, from all things whereof the law condemned us. And we receive love unto the law, and power to fulfil it, and grow therein daily.'

In October 1528 Tyndale published his *The Obedience of the Christian Man*, which sought to make it clear that the Reformers were not intending to be political revolutionaries. Tyndale wrote in a style that is densely biblical because his principle was that the Bible is self-sufficient in its authority and interpretation: 'One scripture will help to declare another.' Citing Romans 15:4 and referring to a multitude of other texts, Tyndale showed how the Old and New Testaments are connected and, rightly understood, are designed to give comfort and true hope to the sinner with faith in Christ.

By 1529 Sir Thomas More had become Lord Chancellor, and he became Tyndale's most virulent Roman Catholic opponent. More was to die bravely as a Roman Catholic, but as Chancellor he vehemently defended the existence of purgatory and was complicit in burning Protestants at the stake. King Henry VIII – or 'Squire Harry' as Luther called him – believed in a kind of Catholicism with himself taking the place of the papacy.

Henry Phillips, the third son of a parliamentarian and high sheriff, arrived in Antwerp in 1535, and wormed his way into Tyndale's favour by posing as an evangelical Christian, only to betray him. Tyndale was arrested in Antwerp in May 1535, and all his possessions were taken from him. His home for the next eighteen months was Vilvorde prison, from which he wrote a most affecting letter to the governor to ask for a warmer cap, a warmer coat, a piece of cloth, a lamp and a Hebrew Bible and dictionary. On 6 October 1536 he was first strangled, then burnt at the stake, crying aloud: 'Lord, open the King of England's eyes.' The following year saw Henry VIII allow the Bible to be printed in English. It came out under the pen name of Thomas Matthew, but most of it was Tyndale's work. Tyndale's final prayer had been answered to a surprising degree.

22

NICHOLAS RIDLEY

(c. 1500–1555)

The sufficiency of Christ's sacrifice

For such a High Priest was fitting for us, who is holy,
harmless, undefiled, separate from sinners, and has
become higher than the heavens; who does not need
daily, as those high priests, to offer up sacrifices, first for
His own sins and then for the people's, for this He did
once for all when He offered up Himself (Heb. 7:26-27).

Nicholas Ridley was born about the turn of the sixteenth century near the Scottish border. He became the vicar of Herne in Kent in 1538, and had learnt almost all of Paul's epistles by heart. He came to read a treatise by the monk Ratramm from the ninth century, which argued against understanding Christ's body and blood as being literally and physically present in the Lord's Supper. By 1546 Ridley was convinced of this and had convinced Thomas Cranmer, the Archbishop of Canterbury. In the following year, Cranmer convinced Hugh Latimer.

By 1547 Ridley was consecrated Bishop of Rochester, and in 1550 transferred to the see of London. A man who opposed breaking the law in things indifferent – and who could not understand John Hooper when he refused for a time to be consecrated as Bishop of Gloucester because he was required to wear vestments – he nevertheless broke down the high altar in St Paul's Cathedral in order to set an example for others in his diocese.

In Ridley's view, the Roman Catholic Mass, with its teaching on the real presence and its claim to sacrifice Christ again and again, was an offence to Christ's perfect work of atonement on the cross at Calvary. Ridley wrote: 'I fight in Christ's quarrel against the Mass, which doth utterly take away and overthrow the ordinance of Christ.'

The most influential contribution that Ridley made to the Reformation understanding of the Supper was his 46-page treatise *A Brief Declaration of the Lord's Supper*. With the death of the sickly young Protestant king, Edward VI, from tuberculosis at the age of sixteen in 1553, Mary Tudor came to the English throne. She was a determined and increasingly embittered Roman Catholic. By January 1555 Reginald Pole, a cardinal who at times seems to have had some kind of grasp of justification by faith, had absolved the House of Commons from the sin of schism, and the old legislation on heresy was restored. Nicholas Ridley, Thomas Cranmer, Hugh Latimer and the whole Protestant cause were now very vulnerable.

Ridley was arrested and brought to trial, where he made it clear that the Mass could not be a re-enactment of Calvary:

Christ made one perfect sacrifice for the sins of the whole world, neither can any man reiterate that sacrifice of His; and yet is the Communion an acceptable sacrifice to God of praise and thanksgiving. But to say that thereby sins are taken away (which wholly and perfectly was done by Christ's Passion, of the which the Communion is only a memory), that is a great derogation of the merits of Christ's Passion: for the Sacrament was instituted that we, receiving it, and thereby recognizing and remembering His Passion, should be partakers of the merits of the same.

Latimer too told his accusers that 'Christ made one perfect sacrifice for all the whole world, neither can any man offer Him again.' The Archbishop of Canterbury, Thomas Cranmer, who was to be burnt at the stake on 21 March 1556, explained: 'Figuratively He is in the bread and wine, and spiritually He is in them that worthily eat and drink the bread and wine; but really, carnally, and corporally, He is only in heaven, from whence He shall come to judge the quick [i.e. the living] and dead.'

For refusing to believe that the bread and wine became the literal body and blood of Christ in the Mass, Ridley and Latimer were condemned to die. On 16 October 1555 the two men prayed together for the last time, and were burnt together, back to back, at the stake. Latimer's last words to Ridley deserve to be long remembered: 'Be of good comfort, Master Ridley, and play the man; we shall this day, by God's grace, light such a candle in England as I trust shall never be put out.' The flames soon took Latimer, but Ridley suffered much before the flames reached the gunpowder around his neck, and he died. Trusting in the perfect sacrifice of Christ, he prayed that the Lord would receive his spirit.

HEINRICH BULLINGER
(1504–1575)

Hear Christ!

This is My beloved Son, in whom I am well pleased.
Hear Him! (Matt. 17:5b).

And I will put enmity between you and the woman, and
between your seed and her Seed; He shall bruise your
head, and you shall bruise His heel (Gen. 3:15).

All the paths of the Lord are mercy and truth, to such as
keep His covenant and His testimonies (Ps. 25:10).

Heinrich Bullinger is best known as the successor in Zurich to Ulrich Zwingli (who was killed in battle in 1531) and as the author of the *Decades,* much of the *First Helvetic Confession* (1536) and all of the very influential *Second Helvetic Confession* (1566). For 44 years – from 1531 to 1575 – he was the Antistes (the first pastor and doctor) of the Church of the Canton of Zurich, where Calvin was to visit him five times. Bullinger was born in 1504 in the little town of Bremgarten, the fifth and youngest son of a supposedly celibate Roman Catholic priest.

In his youth, Bullinger's intention was to become a Carthusian monk. Through the commentaries of Chrysostom and Jerome on Matthew's Gospel, he went back to the Bible itself, and about 1521 wrote: 'It was then that I finally abandoned the project of becoming a Carthusian monk and became utterly convinced of all the horror of papistic doctrine.' He came to delight in the *Loci Communes* of Luther's colleague, Philip Melanchthon, which was hot off the press in December 1521. He wrote in his *Journal*: 'I discovered that salvation came from God through Christ.'

In 1523 Bullinger was offered the post of director of the local monastic school at Kappel. He refused to attend Mass, and in six years at Kappel went through twenty-one of the twenty-seven New Testament books in a systematic way. When his commentaries on Paul's epistles were published, he wrote in the preface: 'The Bible is the only measuring stick for the truth. Where, then, you notice that I have not been quite correct in my interpretation, lay my commentary aside and follow the Bible.'

Bullinger became the preacher and pastor in Kappel, and later the pastor of Bremgarten, where he presided over his parents' marriage! In 1531 Zwingli fell in battle, and his corpse was subjected to a mock trial. He was cut to pieces and his remains burnt as those of a heretic. Zurich was left defenceless. As Bremgarten reverted to Roman Catholicism, Bullinger and his family had to flee, and in November 1531 they took refuge in Zurich. On 9 December 1531 Bullinger was elected Antistes or chief minister of the Zurich Church in very uncertain and turbulent times.

In 1564, the year of Calvin's own death, Bullinger lost his wife and several children to the plague and very nearly died himself. As a family man, Bullinger was loving, responsible and attentive. On 17 September 1575 he died quietly, murmuring the Lord's Prayer and verses from the Psalms. Calvin's successor, Theodore Beza, referred to Bullinger as 'the common shepherd of all Christian churches'.

The *Decades* – known in German as *Hausbuch* (a book to be read at home) – was a collection of fifty sermons covering Reformation doctrine, delivered originally in Latin to meetings of the Zurich pastors and teachers. It was published in 1549–51, and appeared in English in 1554. In 1549 he came to an agreement with Calvin on the Lord's Supper, the *Consensus Tigurinus*. One of Bullinger's most significant works is his *A Brief Exposition of the One and Eternal Testament and Covenant of God* (also known as *De Testamento*), which first appeared in 1534, with Matthew 17:5 on the title page. In fact, Bullinger used Matthew 17:5 or some variation of it either on the title page or the last page of all his books.

To Bullinger, 'There is therefore one covenant and one church of all the saints before and after Christ, one way to heaven, and one unchanging religion of all the saints.' With regard to the Old and New Testaments, he stated: 'The times are different, but not the faith.' In fact, 'Even the Spirit is the same in both Testaments.' In *The Decades* Bullinger pointed to Genesis 3:15 and wrote of God and His covenant:

> For He did first of all make it with Adam, the first father of us all, immediately upon his transgression, when He received him, silly wretch, into His favour again, and promised His only-begotten Son, in whom He would be reconciled to the world, and through whom He would wholly bestow Himself upon us, by making us partakers of all His good and heavenly blessings, and by binding us to Himself in faith and due obedience.

To Bullinger, there is but one covenant in history, first made with Adam, renewed with Abraham, and fulfilled by Christ. This Reformed faith is the only faith that ever was; it goes back to Adam. In Bullinger's view, 'There is only one church and one covenant, the same for the patriarchs and for us.' Bullinger acknowledged that there are two covenants mentioned or implied in Jeremiah 31:31-32, Ezekiel 36:26 and Galatians 4:24, but he pointed out that the patriarchs, living before Moses, did not have the law. Therefore, the ancient religion of the patriarchs can be seen as renewed and restored in the coming of Christ.

It is the papal religion, with its ceremonies and stipulations, that is new.

Bullinger's leadership helped Zurich to recover after the disaster of 1531. Bullinger's message was: 'This same God, therefore, even today will not fail those of His own who are bound to Him in the eternal covenant, no matter how the world might be seized with madness. To Him be the glory!' Fittingly, he concluded his *De Testamento* with Psalm 25:10: 'All the paths of the Lord are grace and faith to those who keep His testament and His covenant.'

24

JOHN KNOX
(c. 1514–1572)

Fearless faith in the sovereign God

Father, the hour has come. Glorify Your Son, that Your Son also may glorify You, as You have given Him authority over all flesh, that He should give eternal life to as many as You have given Him (John 17:1-2).

Then Jesus went into the temple of God and drove out all those who bought and sold in the temple, and overturned the tables of the moneychangers and the seats of those who sold doves. And He said to them, 'It is written, My house shall be called a house of prayer, but you have made it a den of thieves' (Matt. 21:12-13; see also John 2:13-17).

O Lord God of hosts, how long will You be angry against the prayer of Your people? ... Restore us, O God of hosts; cause Your face to shine, and we shall be saved! (Ps. 80:4, 7).

O Lord our God, masters besides You have had dominion over us; but by You only we make mention of Your name (Isa. 26:13).

John Knox was born in Haddington in East Lothian of humble folk about the year 1514, and studied at St Andrews University. He was ordained in April 1536, but did not take up a parish appointment because there was an excess of priests in Scotland. The details of his conversion remain unknown but John 17 was used to claim him. On his deathbed he described John 17 as the place 'where I first cast my anchor'.

The state of the Christian Church in Scotland before the Reformation was lamentable. John Knox recalled that Edinburgh in 1542 was 'for the most part, ... drowned in superstition'. Of the seventeen bishops at the Reformation, twelve had illegitimate children. From 1528 to 1560 about twenty reformers were burned at the stake. One of these was George Wishart, a field preacher who was burned at the stake in 1546. Knox had served as his bodyguard, and remembered him as 'a man of such graces as before him were never heard within this realm, yea, and are rare to be found yet in any man.'

In retaliation, Cardinal David Beaton was stabbed to death two months after the burning of Wishart. Knox only came to the Castle of St Andrews about ten months after Beaton's death. When called upon to preach, Knox was so overcome that he burst into tears, but he soon lost any diffidence when he stepped into the pulpit. However, he was soon taken prisoner by the French, and spent the best part of the next two years as a galley slave. It was as a galley slave that he was commanded to kiss a statue of Mary, but instead he threw it overboard. This was typical of Knox's fearlessness and his abhorrence of idolatry. In 1704 the novelist Jonathan Swift was to call him 'Knocking Jack of the North'.

After obtaining his release, Knox returned to England, but in 1554, after Mary Tudor had become Queen of England, Knox had to flee to France. At Frankfurt he opposed the use of the Prayer Book, and so disputed with Richard Cox. From 1555 to 1559 he was mostly in Geneva. In some circles, Knox's best-known treatise is *The First Blast of the Trumpet Against the Monstrous Regiment of Women*, published in 1558. It won him the undying animosity of Elizabeth I of England, and finished Knox's link with that realm.

On 2 May 1559 Knox arrived back in Scotland, and preached on 11 June 1559 at St Giles' Cathedral, Edinburgh, using texts from

Matthew and from John, on the ejection of the moneychangers from the temple. By the end of 1559 there were already two ecclesiastical structures in Scotland – one Roman Catholic and the other Reformed. The Lords of the Congregations began military operations and on 21 October 1559 suspended Mary of Guise, a Frenchwoman, from the regency. The Reformed Church was established in 1560 and endowed in 1567.

Knox's role was crucial in these testing times. Towards the end of 1559 the Protestant cause looked to be in trouble. Knox, who was in the habit of reading through the Psalms every month, preached on Psalm 80:1-3 at St Giles', then a few days later at Stirling on Psalm 80:4-8, where he chastised his hearers for their wavering in the face of the Roman Catholic and French threat. With confidence in the Word of God, he declared: 'For as it is the eternal truth of the eternal God, so shall it once prevail, howsoever for a time it be impugned.' The effect was electric, and morale revived. In 1561, Thomas Randolph, the envoy of Elizabeth I, commented regarding Knox: 'I assure you the voice of one man is able in one hour to put more life in us than 500 trumpets continually blustering [in] our ears.' Knox considered that his main task was to 'blow my master's trumpet'. Strangely enough, only one sermon was ever prepared for publication – it was on Isaiah 26:13-21. This was because he never wrote out his sermons, and he saw himself as a preacher rather than a theologian.

The Scots Confession (1560) and the First Book of Discipline (1561) were drawn up. Mass was forbidden, and the papal supremacy was overthrown, but there was no compulsion to subscribe to the new confession of faith. Unlike the situation in England, there was no act of supremacy, no act of uniformity, no deprivation of clergy, no dissolution of monasteries, and very little bloodshed. Mary Queen of Scots lost the Scottish throne, not because she was a devout Roman Catholic, but because she married the Earl of Bothwell who was suspected of murdering her previous husband, Lord Darnley. Mary was forced to abdicate in 1567 and to flee to England where she was later executed by order of Elizabeth I in 1587.

Due to the shortage of preachers – by 1567 there were 1,048 churches and only 257 ordained ministers – five superintendents were appointed, having been nominated by the lords, but these were not really bishops. Knox, as minister of the High Kirk of Edinburgh, was never a superintendent. On 24 November 1572 John Knox died, surprisingly quietly, having I Corinthians 15, then John 17 read to him by his wife. The new regent, the cynical Earl of Morton, is reported to have said over his grave: 'Here lieth a man who in his life never feared the face of man.' In 1920 Frank Boreham considered that Knox's memory was everywhere in Edinburgh: 'He is the most ubiquitous man you meet.' Sadly, that is no longer true, and Knox's grave has come to be covered by a car park.

25

ROBERT BRUCE
(c. 1555–1631)

'The lion roars'

The Lord roars from Zion, and utters His voice from Jerusalem (Amos 1:2).

A lion has roared! Who will not fear? The Lord God has spoken! Who can but prophesy? (Amos 3:8).

The Lord also will roar from Zion, and utter His voice from Jerusalem; the heavens and earth will shake; but the Lord will be a shelter for His people, and the strength of the children of Israel (Joel 3:16).

The king's wrath is like the roaring of a lion, but his favour is like dew on the grass (Prov. 19:12).

This being so, I myself always strive to have a conscience without offence towards God and men (Acts 24:16).

For I am persuaded that neither death nor life, nor angels nor principalities nor powers, nor things to come, nor height nor depth, nor any other created thing, shall be able to separate us from the love of God which is in Christ Jesus our Lord (Rom. 8:38-39).

Robert Bruce was raised in a family of Roman Catholic nobles, and seemed destined for a career that would be both prestigious and influential. As with Knox, the details of his conversion are uncertain. It apparently occurred in 1571 or even earlier, but in 1581 he went through much anguish of soul in deciding whether to enter the Reformed ministry. After studying divinity at New

College at St Andrews, he became minister of the Great Kirk of St Giles'. At first he could count as a close friend the king of Scotland, James VI (who in 1603 became James I of England).

During one church service James VI talked with his neighbours and paid little attention to the sermon. Bruce admonished him: 'It is said to have been an expression of the wisest of kings, "When the lion roars, all the beasts of the field are quiet": the Lion of the tribe of Judah is now roaring in the voice of His Gospel, and it becomes all the petty kings of the earth to be silent.' Bruce was probably a little nervous and seems to have combined two texts in his mind. He apparently thought the leonine reference came from Solomon (Prov. 19:12) rather than Amos or Joel, but his robust approach is an illustration of the Reformation's attempt to recapture the full authority of the Word of God. All had to submit to it, even kings and pontiffs. John Livingstone remembered the sermons of Bruce: 'Never man spake with greater power since the Apostles' days.'

By 1596 Bruce was offside with the king, and was compelled to leave Edinburgh for a year. This was a precursor of what was to come. In 1600 the Earl of Gowrie and his brother were killed, and James VI was present when they died. The king claimed that they were killed in making an attempt on his life, and ministers were ordered to give thanks from their pulpits for the king's deliverance. Bruce and four other ministers demanded evidence, were not given any, and so were exiled. Even when the king softened and sought to woo Bruce back, and Bruce himself accepted the decision of the Courts, Bruce made it clear that his conscience was captive to God.

Bruce's motives can be seen from his statement: 'Terrible it is to see the countenance of God in his justice ... When the Lord wakens thy conscience there is never a sin but it shall start to thy memory, and bring such a horror with it, that of all pains it is the greatest.' Hence he wrote: 'We claim no perfection, but a good conscience in all things.' Above everything else,

Bruce aimed at possessing a good conscience, and in preaching aimed at the conscience. To Bruce, 'There is no other lesson in Christianity than this; this is the first and the last lesson: to shake off your lust and affections more and more, and so more and more to renounce yourself that you may embrace Christ.'

From 1605 to 1613 Bruce spent most of his time banished to Inverness in the far north. Even when he returned, he was often under threat. In 1621 he was imprisoned without trial in Edinburgh Castle, and once survived an attempt on his life when he stopped to look at a bird's nest, and an assassin's bullet whistled past him. He preached whenever and wherever he could, and on one memorable occasion in June 1630 almost 500 hearers were greatly affected, with many coming to conversion.

In 1631 he was at breakfast, and, being nearly blind, had Romans 8 read to him by his daughter Martha, with particular emphasis on verses 38-39. Bruce stated: 'I have breakfasted with you, and shall sup with my Lord Jesus this night. I die believing in these words.' So it was that he died on 27 July 1631. No memorial sermon was preached, but the Latin inscription on his gravestone was (in English translation): *Christ in life and death gain.*

Postscript: In 1753–55 the American Presbyterian, Samuel Davies, was visiting Britain to raise funds for the College of New Jersey (later known as Princeton), and King George II was supposedly inattentive during a sermon. Davies was reported to have exclaimed: 'When the lion roars, the beasts of the forest all tremble; and when King Jesus speaks, the princes of the earth should keep silence.' It is an inspiring story, but it appears rather late, and is not found in Davies's own diary for his trip abroad.

26

RICHARD SIBBES
(1577–1635)

Ministering to the bruised reed

*Behold! My Servant whom I have chosen, My Beloved in
whom My soul is well pleased! I will put My Spirit upon
Him, and He will declare justice to the Gentiles. He will
not quarrel nor cry out, nor will anyone hear His voice
in the streets. A bruised reed He will not break, and
smoking flax He will not quench till He sends forth justice
to victory: And in His name Gentiles will trust*
(Matt. 12:18-21, citing Isa. 42:1-4).
Your heart was tender (2 Chron. 34:27a).

Richard Sibbes was born in Tostock in England, the son of a
wheelwright. He went off to study at Cambridge, and in 1608
was ordained in the Church of England as a clergyman of strong
Puritan convictions. Yet he was a moderate and conformed on
ecclesiastical matters, not making an issue of the wearing of the
surplice or the making of the sign of the cross. In all his pastoral
relationships, Sibbes would strive to be tender and Christ-like.
He served at Holy Trinity Church in Cambridge and also at Gray's
Inn in London. In 1626 he became master of St Catherine's
College, Cambridge. His ministry was known for its kindness
and charity to the poor, as well as its pastoral faithfulness.

Sibbes came to be known as the 'heavenly Doctor Sibbes' or 'the Sweet Dropper' because of his tender and encouraging sermons. 'Love is a boundless affection,' he declared. He was not one who was keen on seeing his own works published, but in 1630 he did see *The Bruised Reed and Smoking Flax* go into print. He noted that as a preacher, Jesus did not draw attention to Himself, and He was sensitive to the battered and fragile spiritual states of those who heard Him. As Sibbes said of Christ: 'He is a physician good at all diseases, especially at the binding up of a broken heart.' Noting the prophetess Huldah's description of King Josiah's tender heart, Sibbes commented that 'A soft heart is made soft by the blood of Christ.'

For all his suspicions that Puritan moralism ran the risk of sometimes being overdone, Sibbes still urged that God gave people the law in love in order to drive them from Sinai to Zion. In Sibbes's words, 'Christ's way is first to wound, then to heal. No sound, whole soul shall ever enter heaven.' The person who considered himself righteous has no reason to cast himself upon the righteousness of Christ as Saviour. Bruising was thus necessary, and beneficial: 'It is better to go bruised to heaven than sound to hell.' Nevertheless, he declared: 'Let us labour therefore to be always speaking somewhat about Christ, or tending that way. When we speak of the law, let it drive us to Christ; when of moral duties, let them teach us to walk worthy of Christ.'

Sibbes sought to avoid the twin dangers of weakness and severity, and to inculcate the virtues of strength and gentleness together. In his view, 'The best men are severe to themselves, tender over others.' It is true that 'Christ's sheep are weak sheep', but, to change the image somewhat, 'A weak hand may receive a rich jewel.' His dominant note was that of wooing grace: 'We are only poor for this reason, that we do not know our riches in Christ.' Hence there is strength in knowing our weakness: 'A Christian conquers, even when he is conquered.'

In the Christian scheme of things, it is the humble who will be exalted, and the exalted who will be humbled. As Sibbes wrote: 'Weakness, with acknowledgement of it, is the fittest seat and subject for God to perfect his strength in; for consciousness of our infirmities drives us out of ourselves to him in whom our strength lies.' The bruised reed is close to grace and victory, while the seemingly strong personality is close to his downfall. To cite Sibbes again: 'Nothing is stronger than humility, which goes out of itself, or weaker than pride, which rests on its own foundation.' It is perhaps significant that, as a preacher, Sibbes struggled with a lisp.

To Sibbes, union with Christ was everything: 'This is our comfort and our confidence, that God accepts us, because he accepts his Beloved; and when he shall cease to love Christ, he shall cease to love the members of Christ. They and Christ make one mystical Christ. This is our comfort in dejection for sin. We are so and so indeed, but Christ is the chosen Servant of God, in whom he delighteth, and delights in us in him. It is no matter what we are in ourselves, but what we are in Christ when we are once in him and continue in him. God loves us with that inseparable love wherewith he loves his own Son.'

Sibbes died in 1635, before the outbreak of the English Civil War, and well before the dramas of the Restoration in 1660 and the Great Ejection of 1662. Fittingly, Izaak Walton famously commented that 'Heaven was in him, before he was in heaven.'

27
ALEXANDER HENDERSON
(1583–1646)

Becoming a true shepherd of King Jesus

*Most assuredly, I say to you, he who does not enter the
sheepfold by the door, but climbs up some other way, the
same is a thief and a robber* (John 10:1).

*The LORD said to my Lord, 'Sit at My right hand, till I
make your enemies your footstool'* (Ps. 110:1).

*O Lord, I know the way of man is not in himself; it is not
in man who walks to direct his own steps* (Jer. 10:23).

Alexander Henderson was born about the year 1583, and
received his education at St Andrews University. After teaching
philosophy there, he became the minister at Leuchars. At this
stage Henderson was unconverted, and he had been intruded
into Leuchars against the will of the people. In fact, he was
ordained before an empty church after climbing in through
a window. All this took place against the background of King
James I's attempts to impose an episcopal system upon the
Church in Scotland. At this time Henderson was in favour as a
supporter of episcopacy.

Sometime around 1614 Henderson heard that Robert
Bruce was going to preach one day in his neighbourhood, and,
having disguised himself first, went to hear him, more out of

curiosity than anything else. In the providence of God, Bruce's text happened to be John 10:1, 'Most assuredly, I say to you, he who does not enter the sheepfold by the door, but climbs up some other way, the same is a thief and a robber.' Henderson was horrified at first, but became convicted of his sin – he described the words as 'drawn swords' – and he became a new man in Christ.

With conversion came an immediate concern to preserve the freedom of the Church from state interference, and opposition to episcopacy and an imposed Prayer Book. The situation became more serious after the death of James I in 1625. His successor, King Charles I, together with the Archbishop of Canterbury, William Laud, tried even more vigorously – indeed cruelly – to impose episcopacy, the Anglican liturgy and Arminian theology on Scotland. As the crisis unfolded, Samuel Rutherford looked to Alexander Henderson as the one to lead the Scottish Presbyterians. In 1637 Henderson refused to use the new liturgy, and by early 1638 it was obvious that the Scottish Presbyterians were left with two options: either submit to the king or go to war.

It was Henderson who, as Moderator, preached to the General Assembly on 13 December 1638 when six bishops were deposed and eight others were deposed and excommunicated. His text was Psalm 110:1, which emphasizes the crown rights of King Jesus, the one who is also priest forever (Ps. 110:4) and judge (Ps. 110:5-7). He made reference to Matthew 18:17-18; 1 Corinthians 5:1-6, and 1 Timothy 1:20, which all deal with discipline in the Church. On the abolition of the episcopal system, Henderson declared: 'We have now cast down the walls of Jericho, let him who rebuildeth them beware of the curse of Hiel the Bethelite.' (see Josh. 6:26; 1 Kings 16:34). Later he preached at the subscribing of the Solemn League and Covenant by the House of Lords, the House of Commons and the divines on 25 September 1643.

A fearless, albeit always courteous, man who never married, Henderson once rebuked King Charles I for playing golf on the Lord's Day. Charles seems to have responded with some urbanity. By 1638 Henderson was minister of Greyfriars Church, Edinburgh, and soon after was translated to the High Kirk, St Giles'. A most able man, Henderson was one of the five Scottish commissioners to the Westminster Assembly that drew up the Westminster Confession, the Shorter and Larger Catechisms, and other related documents. Strangely enough, he himself published little apart from a tract, *The Government and Order of the Church of Scotland.*

Henderson was to die in Edinburgh in 1646. In looking over his life, he thought of the words of Jeremiah: 'O Lord, I know that the way of man is not in himself; it is not in man that walketh, to direct his steps (Jer. 10:23, KJV).' He had every reason to contemplate the providence of God, who had led him remarkably from being a minister who curried the favour of the world to being a capable and judicious leader of the Presbyterian cause in Scotland during difficult days.

28

JOHN OWEN
(1616–1683)

Glorifying Christ for His grace

But He said to them, 'Why are you fearful, O you of little
faith?' Then He arose and rebuked the winds and the sea,
and there was a great calm (Matt. 8:26).

For if you live according to the flesh you will die; but if by
the Spirit you put to death the deeds of the body,
you will live (Rom. 8:13).

But there is forgiveness with You, that You may be feared
(Ps. 130:4).

John Owen was born in 1616, the son of a vicar with Puritan convictions. At the age of twelve he went to Oxford University, where he studied hard, competed in athletics and learnt to play the flute. He tried to get by on only four hours' sleep each night. In 1635 he graduated with a Masters of Arts degree, and was ordained into the Anglican ministry by Bishop John Bancroft. In 1642 he went to hear the renowned Presbyterian preacher, Edmund Calamy, at St Mary's Church, Aldermanbury. For one reason or another, Calamy was not present and, to Owen's disappointment, an unknown country preacher took his place. His text was Matthew 8:26, and it had a profound and unexpected effect on Owen. Here he was either converted or, more likely, experienced a deep sense of assurance.

Later, Owen was to tell Richard Davis, the minister at Rothwell, Northamptonshire: 'I myself preached Christ some years, when I had but very little, if any, experimental acquaintance with access to God through Christ; until the Lord was pleased to visit me with sore affliction, whereby I was brought to the mouth of the grave, and under which my soul was oppressed with horror and darkness; but God graciously relieved my spirit by a powerful application of Psalm 130.' So affected was John Owen by the fourth verse, that when he came to write his exposition on Psalm 130, which ran to 322 pages, he devoted some 226 pages to this one verse!

Owen's first book also appeared in 1642, entitled *A Display of Arminianism*. This was a rather vigorous, even violent, assault on the notion of free will ('an opinion fitter for a hog of the Epicurus herd than for a scholar in the school of Christ') and universal atonement (he argued that a Christ who died for everyone in effect died for no one). A year later he was pastor of a small parish in Fordham, Essex. As an Independent (a Congregationalist), Owen was to serve as a chaplain to Oliver Cromwell, and in 1652–7 he was the Vice-Chancellor of Oxford University.

Owen preached the full Christ, one who both saves and sanctifies. In 1647 he published *The Death of Death in the Death of Christ*, which set out the sufficiency of Christ's death for the elect. In 1656 he wrote *On the Mortification of Sin in Believers*, based on Romans 8:13. He summed this up as, 'Be killing sin or it will be killing you' – one of the few succinct statements found in Owen's wordy writings. He declared that 'my heart's desire unto God, and the chief design of my life ... are, that mortification and universal holiness may be promoted in my own and in the hearts and ways of others, to the glory of God.'

Owen knew suffering – he outlived all eleven of his children. After the Restoration of the monarchy in 1660, Owen was virtually a fugitive – a pastor on the run – until his death in

1683. However, he was not imprisoned, and he found time to write, including a massive seven-volume commentary on the book of Hebrews. On the day of his death, 24 August 1683, William Payne called to tell him that his final work, *Meditations on the Glory of Christ*, was being printed that day. Owen responded: 'I am glad to hear of it; but, O brother Payne! the long-wished-for day is come at last, in which I shall see that glory in another manner than I have ever done, or was capable of doing in this world.'

To Owen, a right apprehension of Christ is everything: 'One view of Christ's glory by faith will scatter all the fears, answer all the objections and disperse all the depressions of poor, tempted, doubting souls.' That which believers behold by faith on earth is beheld by sight in eternity (2 Cor. 5:7-8; 1 Cor. 13:12). Owen's view of the faith is thoroughly Trinitarian – it is the Father who chooses His people, the Son who dies for them alone, and the Spirit who works in the lives of these chosen ones to bring them to a greater measure of Christ. Indeed, as Owen's last letter, dictated from his deathbed, affirmed: 'I am going to him whom my soul hath loved, or rather hath loved me with an everlasting love; which is the whole ground of all my consolation.'

29

JOHN BUNYAN
(1628–1688)

A struggling pilgrim

Still there is room (Luke 14:22).

Jesus Christ is the same yesterday, today, and forever
(Heb. 13:8).

*But of Him you are in Christ Jesus, who became for us
wisdom from God – and righteousness and sanctification
and redemption* (1 Cor. 1:30).

*But you have come to Mount Zion and to the city of the
living God, the heavenly Jerusalem, to an innumerable
company of angels, to the general assembly and church
of the firstborn who are registered in heaven, to God the
Judge of all, to the spirits of just men made perfect, to
Jesus the Mediator of the new covenant, and to the blood
of sprinkling that speaks better things than that of Abel*
(Heb. 12:22-24).

*Leave your fatherless children, I will preserve them alive;
and let your widows trust in Me* (Jer. 49:11).

*And he carried me away in the Spirit to a great and
high mountain, and showed me the great city, the holy
Jerusalem, descending out of heaven from God, having the
glory of God. Her light was like a most precious stone,
like a jasper stone, clear as crystal* (Rev. 21:10-11).

John Bunyan was born in Elstow, near Bedford, in 1628, and
grew up to suffer during the restoration of the monarchy under
Charles II in 1660. A somewhat uneducated man – whose father
was illiterate – he became a tinker who repaired tools and pots

and pans for a living. Yet he came to write one of the enduring classics of English literature, *The Pilgrim's Progress*.

As a youth, he lied, blasphemed and carried on with religion as the least of his thoughts. He served in the Civil War, presumably on the Parliamentary side, but his only reference to it in his writings concerned a man who took his place and was shot dead while he stood sentinel. About two years after leaving the army in 1647, Bunyan married a woman who seems to have curbed his wild lifestyle to some degree. However, he swung between loose living and legalistic rules for some considerable time without finding any evangelical peace.

In the agonized process of becoming a Christian, Bunyan became so depressed that he envied the toads in the grass. He would be convicted of sin for a time, then return to that sin and become utterly downcast. Dreams tormented him. Once he was much moved by the godly conversation of some Christian women at Bedford who were discussing the new birth. He remembered them as 'far above, out of my reach', but loitered nearby in order to learn from them. In this time of turmoil he was comforted by words from the parable of the great supper: 'yet there is room'. Later he was to write: 'Conversion is not the smooth, easy-going process some men seem to think ... It is wounding work, of course, this breaking of the hearts, but without wounding there is no saving.'

Bunyan's autobiographical work, *Grace Abounding to the Chief of Sinners,* tells in its own rather chaotic way of his struggles to come to faith. One day, while passing in the field, he was thinking that his righteousness was in heaven, and he thought of Hebrews 13:8, that Jesus Christ is the same yesterday, today and forever. He felt his chains fall off, and he went home rejoicing for the grace and love of God. However, at home he found no verse in Scripture that declared 'Thy righteousness is in heaven.' His heart sank until he remembered that Christ is our righteousness (1 Cor. 1:30). Bunyan rejoiced: 'Now Christ was all; all my wisdom, all my righteousness, all my sanctification, and all my redemption.'

Bunyan agonized about whether he could be assured that he was in Christ. One night he contemplated Hebrews 12:22-24, and could scarcely lie on his bed for joy and peace and triumph through Christ. He later recalled the effect of these words: 'Through this blessed sentence the Lord led me over and over, first to this word, and then to that, and showed me wonderful glory in every one of them. These words also have oft since this time been great refreshment to my spirit. Blessed be God for having mercy on me.'

Finally, in 1653 he joined the Baptist church at Bedford. By 1655 Bunyan was a deacon in the church and had begun to preach. In 1656 he became the pastor. However, he was arrested on 12 November 1660, and was to spend almost twelve years in prison. To be released, all he needed to do was sign a paper to say he would not preach again. He refused to do this. In prison he made himself a flute, wrote books, made shoelaces to sell, and sought to shepherd others as best he could. His first child, Mary, had been born blind and was aged ten by 1660, and Bunyan especially felt the trial of being separated from her. He drew comfort from Jeremiah 49:11, and his resolution remained as he put it in his most characteristic hymn:

> There's no discouragement
> Shall make him once relent,
> His first avowed intent
> To be a pilgrim.

One of his most powerful sermons was preached to his fellow prisoners on the subject of the New Jerusalem (Rev. 21:10-11).

The Pilgrim's Progress first appeared in 1678, with part two following in 1684. Bunyan was initially concerned about using fiction as a vehicle for truth, but his sanctified imaginative powers, his own spiritual struggles, and his wonderful grasp of

Scripture – Spurgeon said that his blood was 'bibline' – meant that he could convey Scriptural truth in a very vivid way. To Bunyan, struggle is part of the Christian life:

> A Christian man is never long at ease,
> When one fright's gone, another doth him seize.

He said: 'I preached what I felt, what I smartingly did feel.' Reversing the usual order, he would write his sermons out *after* he had preached them. In 1688 he was caught in the rain while returning from London, and died of fever on 31 August. The pilgrim had reached home.

30

JAMES DURHAM
(1622–1658)

The freeness of grace

*Therefore, to you who believe, He is precious; but to
those who are disobedient, 'The stone which the builders
rejected has become the chief cornerstone' (1 Pet. 2:7).*

*All that the Father gives Me will come to Me, and the one
who comes to Me I will by no means cast out (John 6:37).*

*But He was wounded for our transgressions, He was
bruised for our iniquities; the chastisement for our peace
was upon Him, and by His stripes we
are healed (Isa. 53:5).*

James Durham was born just four years after King James
I had imposed the Five Articles of 1618 on the Church in
Scotland, in favour of kneeling at communion, observing holy
days, confirmation by a bishop, private baptism and private
communion. Raised into a wealthy family, Durham studied at
St Andrews University, and served as a captain in the Scottish
army. He was converted not long after he was married, when
his wife's family pressed him to come to church during a
communion season. On the Sunday morning, Ephraim Melville
preached with power and effect on 1 Peter 2:7.

While in the Army, Durham prayed with his soldiers, and
David Dickson was so impressed that he told Durham to

go home and study for the ministry. Durham studied under Dickson at Glasgow University, and in 1647 was ordained into the Glasgow Blackfriars' parish. Three years later he was appointed to teach divinity at Glasgow University, and soon afterwards he became minister of the High Church in Glasgow.

At this time the Scottish Church was racked by division between the milder Resolutioners (such as David Dickson) and the uncompromising Protesters (such as Samuel Rutherford). They differed over how far churchmen could make concessions in dealing with the Stuart king, Charles I's son, who later became Charles II. By 1653 there were two General Assemblies of the Church meeting in Edinburgh. Durham tried to mediate between the two parties in a work which has been republished with the title *Concerning Scandal*.

If any man ever preached the freeness of God's grace, James Durham did. He declared that 'if it were possible that a soul would come without a sense of sin, grace would embrace it.' The love of Christ is everything to the believer: 'It is only the love of Christ that secures believers in their battles and march against their spiritual adversaries; and indeed they may fight, who have love for their colours and banners.' Durham preached Christ as a sweet Saviour and a sweet Lord.

After only ten years in ministry his health broke, and after some months confined to his home, he died in 1658. However, his widow, Margaret, and her sister's husband, John Carstairs, published his works, including seventy-two sermons on Isaiah 53. On verse five, Durham commented: 'It is hard to tell whether the subject of this verse, and almost of this whole chapter, is more sad or more sweet.' He added that these sad but most sweet words hold out what he called 'a short sum of the substance and marrow of the gospel'.

Durham and Dickson collaborated to produce *The Sum of Saving Knowledge*, which aimed to present federal covenant theology in a simple way to readers. Some historians have made much of James Durham's supposed lack of assurance on his deathbed, but they fail to tell the whole story. John Howie admits that Durham, who was only thirty-five when he died, was 'under considerable darkness about his state', and wondered whether he could rest upon the offer of John 6:37, 'Whosoever cometh unto Me, I will in no wise cast out.' John Carstairs's brother replied comfortingly: 'You may depend upon it, though you had a thousand salvations at hazard.' According to Howie, Durham died full of assurance, crying out: 'Is not the Lord good? Is he not infinitely good? See how he smiles! I do say it, and I do proclaim it.' So he died in the same comfort that he had preached to others.

31

THOMAS WATSON
(c. 1620–1686)

All things for good

*And we know that all things work together for good
to those who love God, to those who are the called
according to His purpose* (Rom. 8:28).

*But his delight is in the law of the Lord, and in His law he
meditates day and night* (Ps. 1:2).

*Who may ascend into the hill of the Lord? Or who may
stand in His holy place? He who has clean hands and a
pure heart, who has not lifted up his soul to an idol, nor
sworn deceitfully* (Ps. 24:3-4).

*Then those who feared the Lord spoke to one another,
and the Lord listened and heard them; so a book of
remembrance was written before Him for those who fear
the Lord and who meditate on His name. 'They shall be
Mine,' says the Lord of hosts, 'on the day that I make
them My jewels. And I will spare them as a man spares
his own son who serves him.' Then you shall again discern
between the righteous and the wicked, between one who
serves God and one who does not serve Him*
(Mal. 3:16-18).

Virtually nothing is known of the early life of Thomas Watson.
After studying at Cambridge University, he became the lecturer,
then the rector, of St Stephen's, Walbrook, in London, in 1646.
By this time the English Civil War had been going for some four
years, between the Royalist forces and those of the Parliament.

A Puritan by conviction, Watson was also a Presbyterian, and he opposed the execution of Charles I in 1649. He was under suspicion for favouring the future Charles II and spent several months in the Tower of London, but by 30 June 1652 was back with his flock at Walbrook. The restoration of the monarchy in 1660 led to the passing in 1662 of the Act of Uniformity, which obliged all ministers to use the Book of Common Prayer and to be ordained by a bishop. This led to the Great Ejection, where some 2,000 ministers were ejected from the national Church and forced to become nonconformists. Watson defied the law by setting up conventicles of believers.

As a preacher, he hid his learning behind a popular style that was both simple and memorable. Illustrations were his strong point as he painted 'word pictures' in his sermons. For example, he wrote: 'A covetous man is like a bee that gets into a barrel of honey, and there drowns itself.' Comparing Adam and Christ, he declared: 'We die through the tree of knowledge; we rise through the tree of the cross.' The sinner must know that he cannot save himself, but in this there is hope for 'God pours the golden oil of mercy into empty vessels.' All godliness flows from Christ whom we own by faith: 'By faith a man possesses God and by patience he possesses himself.' This has most helpful consequences, for 'Patience is a star which shines in a dark night.' And, most wonderfully, 'The blood of Christ has quenched the flame of divine fury.'

In 1663, a year after Watson was expelled from his living in the Great Ejection, he published *A Divine Cordial* which has recently been reprinted as *All Things for Good*. It deals with Romans 8:28. Its conclusion is this: 'Our graces are imperfect, our comforts ebb and flow, but God's foundation standeth sure.' Watson specialized in epigrammatic, picturesque and balanced sentences. He considered that 'There are two things which I have always looked upon as difficult. The one is, to make the wicked sad; the other is, to make the godly joyful.'

All things work for good for God's people: 'The worst that God does to His children is to whip them to heaven.' So, 'You shall be a gainer by your losses. Your crosses shall be turned into blessings.'

For all his belief in providence, Watson nevertheless warned that 'Providence should be the Christian's diary but never his Bible.' He struggled to answer the question: 'What was God doing in 1662?' He wanted Christians to go back to the Bible: 'Think in every line you read that God is speaking to you.' On Psalm 1:2, he pointed out how godliness is linked to God's Word: 'Grace breeds delight in God, and delight breeds meditation.' Like every Puritan, he emphasized the need for godliness. Pointing to Psalm 24:4, he urged that 'This is the grand business that should swallow up your time and thoughts.' Law and gospel work together to save and sanctify the sinner, and 'They who will not have the law to rule them, shall never have the gospel to save them.'

Watson set great store by fellowship with God's people and godly conversation, and wrote with reference to Malachi 3:16-18: 'I believe that one main reason for the decay of the power of godliness is a lack of Christian conference.' What we say is vital before God, for 'The tongue is the index of the heart.' In his celebrated *Body of Divinity* he said: 'Be among the spices and you will smell of them ... Nothing has a greater power and energy to effect holiness than the communion of saints.'

Like David Livingstone two hundred years later, Watson died in the act of prayer – which he called 'the soul's traffic with heaven' – and was buried on 28 July 1686.

32

SAMUEL RUTHERFORD
(1600–1661)

Seeing the King in Immanuel's land

Then He said to her: 'For this saying go your way; the demon has gone out of your daughter' (Mark 7:29).

Your eyes will see the King in His beauty; they will see the land that is very far off (Isa. 33:17).

They shall call His name Immanuel which is translated 'God with us' (Matt. 1:23b).

Born in the little village of Nisbet in the rural part of the Scottish Borders, Samuel Rutherford grew up in contentious times. During his reign (1603–25), King James I of England sought – admittedly with some restraint – to impose bishops on the Church in Scotland. As James's reign moved towards its end, Rutherford took up tutoring in Latin at the University of Edinburgh, but had to demit in 1625 over some irregularity to do with his marriage. This did not stop his becoming the pastor of Anwoth in south-west Scotland. Here he preached the loveliness of Christ: 'O what a happiness for a soul to lose its excellency in His transcendent glory.' The 'fair little man' was also diligent in pastoral visitation and catechizing.

Rather famously, Alexander Whyte was to comment that Rutherford's work, *Lex Rex* ('The Law is King', published anonymously in 1644), has as much emotion in it as the multiplication table, while his *Letters* are 'overcharged with emotion'. Rutherford revelled in the Song of Songs, the Psalms, and the books of Revelation and of Isaiah, and was almost mystical, indeed sensuous, at times in his yearning for fellowship with Christ, whom he called his 'lovely Jesus, fair Jesus, King Jesus'. As Rutherford once acknowledged to David Dickson: 'I am made of extremes.' He experienced blessing in suffering, and declared that 'Grace groweth best in winter', although he also acknowledged that 'it is hard to keep sight of God in a storm.'

Because of his outspoken opposition to rule by bishops, Rutherford was taken from Anwoth in 1636 and confined in Aberdeen. He wrote: 'I had but one joy out of heaven next to Christ my Lord, and that was to preach Him.' The Second Reformation was almost under way, and Scotland was in rebellion against the more decidedly episcopalian and Arminian policies of Charles I (1625–49) and the Archbishop of Canterbury, William Laud. By July 1638 Rutherford was back in Anwoth, but in 1639 he became the Professor of Theology at St Andrews.

When the Westminster Assembly was called to meet in London from 1643 to 1647, Rutherford was one of the four Scottish ministerial commissioners, along with Alexander Henderson, Robert Baillie and George Gillespie. Rutherford was both a decided Calvinist and a tender pastor. As George Gillespie lay dying in 1648, at the age of thirty-five, Rutherford wrote to him and cited Galatians 2:20. Rutherford taught that 'a little hand with small fingers may receive a great heaven and lay hold on the great Saviour of the world.'

Noting Christ's initial rebuff of the Gentile woman from Tyre and Sidon (Mark 7:24-30), Rutherford comments that 'It is but Christ's outside that is unkind.' Indeed, 'Christ may give rough answers, when he hath a good mind.' When this woman was lying in the dust, Christ would have her lying below the dust. But grace is sweet indeed, so 'Bring hell, and sins red as scarlet and crimson; come and be washen: come at the eleventh hour, and welcome; fall, and rise again in Christ; run away, and come home again, and repent.'

In the events leading up to the final days of Oliver Cromwell as Lord Protector, and finally the Restoration of the monarchy in 1660, Rutherford did not trust Charles II, and so, as a Protester, opposed the Resolutioners. By October of that year copies of *Lex Rex* were publicly burned in Edinburgh and in London by the hangman. To Rutherford, Christ is the true king of all the earth, and he argued that 'Tyranny being a work of Satan, is not from God ... and, therefore, a power ethical, politic, or moral, to oppress, is not from God, and is not a power, but a licentious deviation of a power; and is no more from God, but from sinful nature and the old serpent, than a license to sin.' Charles II sought Rutherford's life, but on 27 March 1661 Rutherford was a dying man and wrote: 'Tell them ... I behove to answer my first summons, and ere your day come, I will be where few kings and great folk come.' He died three days later. Among his last words were 'Glory, glory dwelleth in Immanuel's land!'

The hymn 'The sands of time are sinking' was not written by Rutherford but put together by Mrs A.R. Cousins, using the words of Rutherford. One stanza goes like this:

> The King there in His beauty,
> Without a veil, is seen;
> It were a well-spent journey,
> Though seven deaths lay between.
> The Lamb, with His fair army,
> Doth on Mount Zion stand,
> And glory – glory dwelleth
> In Immanuel's land.

That sums up the recurring message of Rutherford's *Letters*. Hence he once declared: 'I am so in love with His love that if He were not in Heaven, I would not want to go there.'

33

DONALD CARGILL
(1627?–1681)

Victory in death

*Moreover He said to me, 'Son of man, eat what you find;
eat this scroll, and go, speak to the house
of Israel' (Ezek. 3:1).*

*For I will pour water on him who is thirsty, and floods on
the dry ground; I will pour My Spirit on your descendants,
and My blessing on your offspring (Isa. 44:3).*

*Stand fast therefore in the liberty by which Christ has
made us free, and do not be entangled again with a yoke
of bondage (Gal. 5:1).*

*Now to you, O profane, wicked prince of Israel, whose
day has come, whose iniquity shall end, thus says the
Lord God: 'Remove the turban, and take off the crown;
nothing shall remain the same. Exalt the humble, and
humble the exalted. Overthrown, overthrown, I will make
it overthrown! It shall be no longer, until He comes whose
right it is, and I will give it to Him (Ezek. 21:25-27).*

*The right hand of the Lord is exalted; the right hand
of the Lord does valiantly. I shall not die, but live, and
declare the works of the Lord. The Lord has chastened me
severely, but He has not given me over to death. Open to
me the gates of righteousness; I will go through them, and
I will praise the Lord. This is the gate of the Lord, through
which the righteous shall enter. I will praise You, for You*

*have answered me, and have become my salvation. The
stone which the builders rejected has become the chief
cornerstone. This was the Lord's doing; it is marvellous
in our eyes. This is the day the Lord has made; we will
rejoice and be glad in it. Save now, I pray, O Lord; O Lord,
I pray, send now prosperity. Blessed is he who comes in
the name of the Lord! We have blessed you from the
house of the Lord. God is the Lord, and He has given us
light; bind the sacrifice with cords to the horns of the
altar. You are my God, and I will praise You; You are my
God, I will exalt You. Oh, give thanks to the Lord, for He
is good! For His mercy endures forever* (Ps. 118:16-29).

We know more about Donald Cargill's death than his birth, or indeed his early life. He appears to have graduated in philosophy from St Andrews University in 1647, but became so convicted of his sin that he sought to commit suicide. As he was about to throw himself down a mineshaft, he heard a voice: 'Son, be of good cheer, thy sins are forgiven.' Being gripped by Ezekiel 3:1, he soon went off to St Andrews to study for the ministry under Samuel Rutherford, and probably finished his divinity course in 1652. He eventually received a call to Barony in Glasgow in 1655 after a woman rebuked him for his initial reluctance to come among such a rebellious people.

In 1656 he married a widow with six children and many debts, but she died four months later, leaving Cargill in financial straits. Not surprisingly, he never remarried. After solemnly promising to uphold the government of the Church of Scotland, King Charles II proceeded to restore bishops, dismantle the presbyteries and synods, and forbid the conventicles (unlawful religious meetings). Some 400 ministers were ejected from their parishes. Even before then, Cargill had been exiled, and his movements are not known, but from 1670 he seems to have resided around Glasgow. He joined a kind of 'field presbytery' at a time when preachers at field conventicles were threatened with death.

Sometimes thousands would gather in the field to hear the preachers. After preaching on Isaiah 44:3, with his voice almost broken down, he himself recovered and the revival intensified. He became convinced that no compromise was possible with the Privy Council, and argued that Galatians 5:1 is 'not a liberty from ceremonies only, but from all subjection to men in things that concern God.' When James Sharp, the Primate of Scotland, was murdered on 3 May 1679, Cargill rather recklessly viewed the deed in terms of the righteous killings by Phinehas (Num. 25:6-9) and Jael (Judg. 4:17-21; 5:24). He did, however, say that 'it is no zeal that has no tenderness, and it is no tenderness that has no zeal.' On 12 September 1680, citing Ezekiel 21:25-27, he excommunicated Charles II, along with six others.

With a price of 5,000 merks on his head, Cargill was captured, and on 27 July 1681 in Edinburgh, he was hanged. At the scaffold he took out his weather-beaten Bible, turned to Psalm 118 and sang verses 16-29 in the metrical version. As he was ordered to climb the ladder, he declared: 'The Lord knows, I go up this ladder with less fear and perturbation of mind than ever I entered the pulpit to preach.' On the morning of his execution, he had written: 'I have followed holiness, I have taught the truth, and I have been most in the main things.' There is a monument in a graveyard in Edinburgh which honours the Covenanters who lost their lives in the persecutions of 1660–1688. It cites the words of Revelation 7:13-17 which tell of those who have washed their robes and made them white in the blood of the Lamb, and who now serve the Lord day and night, without hunger or thirst or pain.

34

MARGARET WILSON

(1667–1685)

'Nothing shall separate us from the love of Christ'

I now rejoice in my sufferings for you, and fill up in my flesh what is lacking in the afflictions of Christ, for the sake of His body, which is the church (Col. 1:24).

Who shall separate us from the love of Christ? Shall tribulation, or distress, or persecution, or famine, or nakedness, or peril, or sword? As it is written: 'For Your sake we are killed all day long; we are accounted as sheep for the slaughter.' Yet in all these things we are more than conquerors through Him who loved us. For I am persuaded that neither death nor life, nor angels nor principalities nor powers, nor things present nor things to come, nor height nor depth, nor any other created thing, shall be able to separate us from the love of God which is in Christ Jesus our Lord (Rom. 8:35-39).

Do not remember the sins of my youth, nor my transgressions; according to Your mercy remember me, for Your goodness' sake (Ps. 25:7).

In the view of King Charles II, 'Presbyterianism was no religion for a gentleman.' Like the other Stuart kings (James I, Charles I, and later James II), Charles II persecuted Presbyterians and Puritans. In 1670, three years after Margaret Wilson was born, the conventicles in Scotland were made treasonable. Ten years after that, in 1680, Charles II's brother – the Duke of York, the man who became James II in 1685 – was appointed High Commissioner to Scotland. So began 'the killing time' in Scotland. The novelist Daniel Defoe claimed that 18,000 were killed, exiled, imprisoned or tortured, although this is now regarded as exaggerated. Nevertheless, the government of Charles II indulged in barbaric measures against the Covenanters. After Donald Cargill excommunicated Charles and James at a large conventicle at Torwood, he was hunted down, captured and hanged. His head was fastened over one of the main gates leading into Edinburgh.

These were the times in which Margaret Wilson lived and died. She was a daughter of Gilbert Wilson, a farmer from Wigtownshire in Scotland. Troops would scour the countryside in search of those who refused to conform to the king's demands that the Church be governed by accommodating bishops. In order to worship as they believed God had commanded, Scottish Presbyterians were forced to defy the king. Three of the Wilson children would wander in the woods, mountains and caves of Carrick, Nithsdale and Galloway in order to hear the field preachers and then to evade the authorities.

In such circumstances, capture was almost inevitable. Margaret Wilson eighteen, and her sister, Agnes thirteen, were discovered at Wigtown, and arrested. The two sisters and a sixty-three-year-old widow, Mrs M'Lachlan, were condemned by the head judge, Sir Robert Grierson of Lagg, to be drowned. The father of the Wilson girls was able to obtain, with a bond of one hundred pounds, the release of his younger daughter, but a reprieve for Margaret and for widow M'Lachlan was not acted upon.

On 11 May 1685 the widow M'Lachlan was tied to a stake at the bottom of the channel so that the rising waters of the Solway Firth would drown her first. The intention was to break the spirit of Margaret Wilson. A nearby soldier, or perhaps even Grierson himself, asked her: 'What do you see now?' Margaret's reply was: 'I see Christ in one of his members wrestling here.' She may have had Colossians 1:24 in mind. In any case, she recited the words of Romans 8:35-39, and sang from the Psalter:

> *My sins and faults of youth,*
> *Do thou, O Lord, forget;*
> *After thy mercy, think of me,*
> *And for thy goodness great.*

Her mother pleaded with Margaret to take the abjuration oath to recognize the king's authority but, even on the stake, Margaret refused. After the drownings, the bodies of the two Margarets were buried in the churchyard at Wigtown.

35

JOHN FLAVEL
(c. 1628–1691)

The mystery of providence

If anyone does not love the Lord Jesus Christ, let him be accursed. O Lord, come! (1 Cor. 16:22).

I will cry out to God Most High, to God who performs all things for me (Ps. 57:2).

Behold, I stand at the door and knock. If anyone hears My voice and opens the door, I will come in to him and dine with him and he with Me (Rev. 3:20).

When the Lord saw her, He had compassion on her and said to her, 'Do not weep' (Luke 7:13).

John Flavel was born in Bromsgrove, Worcestershire, the son of a Puritan minister who, along with his wife (John's mother), was to die of the plague in 1665 while in Newgate Prison for resisting the decrees of Charles II. Flavel knew bereavement, having married four times and outliving three of his wives. In 1656 he became the minister of the port town of Dartmouth, but he was ejected in 1662 for the same reasons that his father suffered the same fate.

Flavel met his congregation in the woods for secret services of public worship. In 1665 the Five Mile Act meant that services could only be held more than five miles from a place of public worship. Flavel obliged by moving to Slapton and continuing to preach. In 1672 Charles II issued the Declaration of Indulgence which gave nonconformists some freedom of worship, but this was rescinded in the following year. Flavel would preach as the Congregational minister of Dartmouth in private homes and out in the forests. He also took up a ministry of writing.

In 1687 King James II issued another indulgence for Non-conformists, but this was widely, and rightly, perceived to be an attempt to favour the Roman Catholics, of which James was one. The so-called Glorious Revolution of 1688 gave freedom to nonconformists, and Flavel was able to preach at Dartmouth for the last four years of his life, until he died suddenly of a stroke in 1691. Because of his ministry in a seaport, Flavel would often preach with seamen especially in mind, and so he wrote treatises which spiritualized life at sea.

When he was about the age of fifteen, Luke Short heard Flavel preach on 1 Corinthians 16:22. Later, he emigrated to America, where, at the age of over 100 and not before time, he pondered the issues of death and eternity, and remembered Flavel's sermon from some eighty-five years previously and was converted. In 1678 Flavel published his oft-reprinted *Mystery of Providence*, based on Psalm 57:2, written when David was on the run from Saul. Flavel explained that 'Saul is high, but God is the most high, and without His permission he is assured Saul cannot touch him.' He told of how a man cut his throat in a suicide attempt, but after Flavel brought the gospel to him, he recovered. All things come from God, even the most minute and ordinary affairs of our lives. This sets boundaries to our sufferings. In Flavel's words: 'All your losses are but as the loss of a farthing to a prince.'

Whereas Oliver Cromwell was overly fond of reading the providences, Flavel was far more cautious: 'a man may easily get a strain by over-reaching.' For all that, he still advised Christians to meditate on their providences: 'Set the grace and goodness of God before you in all afflictive providences' and 'Set the faithfulness of the Lord before you under the saddest providences.' Finally, 'How Providence will dispose of my life, liberty and labours for time to come, I know not; but I cheerfully commit all to Him who has hitherto performed all things for me.'

In his last years he preached eleven sermons on Revelation 3:20. In his preaching, Flavel portrayed a very different Christ to the somewhat helpless figure painted by Holman Hunt in his 'The Light of the World'. Flavel pointed out that the Spirit makes the sinner willing to hear Christ's knock. Nor is it a case of the sinner simply inviting Jesus into his or her heart. Flavel declared of Christ: 'He knocks by the particular convictions of the word upon the conscience; this knock by conviction rings and sounds through all the rooms and chambers of the soul; particular and effectual conviction wounds to the very centre of the soul.' He pressed the issue of conversion to hesitant sinners: 'Thousands have missed of Christ by their unwillingness, but Christ never put off one soul upon account of its unworthiness.'

Flavel's death was sudden, but earlier he had sought to comfort his congregation with the words of Christ to the widow at Nain at the funeral of her only son: 'Do not weep.' Flavel, as a faithful Puritan, wrote in words that applied to himself as well as all believers: 'The resurrection of her son from the dead is the ground upon which Christ builds her consolation and relief.'

36

THOMAS GOODWIN
(1600–1680)

Alive through the Word

Now as He drew near, He saw the city and wept over it, saying, 'If you had known, even you, especially in this your day, the things that make for your peace! But now they are hidden from your eyes' (Luke 19:41-42).

And when I passed by you and saw you struggling in your own blood, I said to you in your blood, 'Live!' Yes, I said to you in your blood, 'Live!' (Ezek. 16:6).

I have been crucified with Christ; it is no longer I who live, but Christ lives in me; and the life which I now live in the flesh I live by faith in the Son of God, who loved me and gave Himself for me (Gal. 2:20).

And the Lord passed before him and proclaimed, 'The Lord, the Lord God, merciful and gracious, longsuffering, and abounding in goodness and truth, keeping mercy for thousands, forgiving iniquity and transgression and sin, by no means clearing the guilty, visiting the iniquity of the fathers upon the children and the children's children to the third and the fourth generation' (Exod. 34:6-7).

But let patience have its perfect work, that you may be mature and complete, lacking nothing (James 1:4).

Thomas Goodwin was raised in a Puritan household in Norfolk, and as a child seems to have possessed a tender conscience. At thirteen he was sent off to Christ's College, Cambridge, but was offended when his tutor restrained him for taking the Lord's Supper.

At the age of twenty, Goodwin went to a funeral on 2 October 1620, and was awakened by the sermon by Thomas Bainbridge on Luke 19:41-42. This threw him into turmoil of heart over his sins, and he struggled to know where he stood before God. A few hours later he was greatly comforted by reading 'Live!' from Ezekiel 16:6. He wrote:

> So God was pleased on the sudden, and as it were in an instant, to alter the whole Course of His former Dispensation towards me, and so of and to my Soul, Yea live, yea live I say, said God: and as He created the World and the Matter of all things by a Word, so He created and put a new Life and Spirit into my Soul, and so great an Alteration was strange to me.

Creation, conversion, and the resurrection of the dead all come about by the power of the Word of God. God speaks and it is done. Goodwin did not immediately come to an assurance of faith, but continued to learn, especially from Richard Sibbes, and in 1625 was licensed as a preacher. With William Laud as the Archbishop of Canterbury, there were increasing restrictions on Puritan preachers, and Goodwin moved to embrace Independent (Congregationalist) views and fled to the Netherlands. With rise to power of the parliamentary party, and of Oliver Cromwell, Goodwin returned to England, and was appointed to the Westminster Assembly, which went from 1643 to 1647. He was very vocal during its meetings, and spoke 357 times!

In 1650 Goodwin became the president of Magdalen College, Oxford, where he worked with John Owen. He was also close to the Lord Protector, Cromwell, and ministered to him on his deathbed in 1658, especially encouraging him concerning the perseverance of the saints. About the same time he helped to draw up the Savoy Declaration of Faith. Since Goodwin was an Independent and so already outside the national Church, the Great Ejection of 1662 did not affect him directly, although he spent the rest of his life trying to evade persecuting authorities. Yet he was never imprisoned.

When the plague broke out in London in 1665, to be followed by the Great Fire of 1666, Goodwin remained to minister to those who were suffering. Finally, at the age of eighty, Goodwin died full of assurance, saying: 'Christ cannot love me better than he doth; I think I cannot love Christ better than I do; I am swallowed up in God.'

As a preacher, he was simple and clear, but he would seek to cover every possible point, 'to study them down', as he put it. This was his very great strength, but it also means the reader needs a considerable amount of time to read him. In his work on *The Object and Acts of Justifying Faith,* he refers to Exodus 34:6-7 as 'the sweetest sermon that ever was preached, and preached by God himself, upon the highest subject, and therefore the richest text the whole Bible affords.'

Goodwin's greatest sermons were those which concentrated on Christ as our glorious mediator, and what it means to trust in Him. He seems to have especially delighted in the epistle to the Ephesians, but he has a particularly pertinent comment on Galatians 2:20, where he declared that 'Faith is not a sleeping thing, nor merely not doubting that Christ is mine, but a continually active whetting of my thoughts on Christ as mine, or casting myself upon Him to be mine. It is living on Him and in Him.' Doctrine and application were joined together in his ministry. Indeed, after much of his personal, and massive, library was destroyed in a fire, he published four sermons on James 1:1-5 to encourage a spirit of patience and submission. Fittingly, he speaks of adoring God in His sovereignty – something Goodwin sought to do all his Christian life.

37

RICHARD BAXTER
(1615–1691)

A shepherd in action

Therefore take heed to yourselves and to all the flock,
among which the Holy Spirit has made you overseers, to
shepherd the church of God which He purchased with His
own blood (Acts 20:28).

Richard Baxter was born on 12 or 13 November 1615 at Rowton in Shropshire, and lived a long time for a sickly man. He lived through the reigns of the Stuart kings who ruled seventeenth-century England – James I, Charles I, Charles II and James II. He thus witnessed the days of Cromwell's Commonwealth, the civil wars (where the Parliamentary Roundheads fought the king's Cavaliers), the overthrow of the monarchy and the Church of England, and the restoration of the monarchy and the Church of England. He also lived through the plague (1665), the Great Fire of London (1666), the Westminster Assembly (1643–7), the Great Ejection (1662) and the Glorious Revolution (1688).

In his youth Baxter read widely but he never went to university. In 1638 he became headmaster of a newly established school at Dudley, and was ordained by the Bishop of Worcester. He could never state exactly when he was converted, and this at first made him introspective. Later he determined to 'look oftener on God, and Christ, and heaven, than upon my own heart.'

In 1641 Baxter became Lecturer of St Mary's in Kidderminster, Worcestershire, a township of about 3,000 people where the vicar preached only once a quarter, and haunted the taverns rather more frequently. Here Baxter's work has made him well-known in the annals of Puritanism. Suffering from ill health, and expecting to die soon, he wrote the first of his 168 books, *The Saints' Everlasting Rest*. Baxter served as pastor of Kidderminster from 1647 to 1660, and he and an assistant catechized 800 families annually by having fourteen or fifteen come to his home on Mondays and Tuesdays. On Thursdays he settled cases of conscience, and all the time he wrote. He loved books, and they filled his shelves and covered his floor at Kidderminster. Caring little for style, he never bothered to revise or correct his works, but raced quickly on to the next one.

In 1662 he suffered removal in the Great Ejection, whereby 2,000 Puritan ministers were thrown out of the national Church by the Act of Uniformity. Despite being ordained by a bishop, Baxter refused to say that it was necessary for pastoral ministry. He quoted the proverb from Rupert Meldenius: 'Unity in things necessary, liberty in things unnecessary, and charity in both.' Baxter begged to be allowed to minister without a stipend, but Bishop Morley of Worcester told him: 'Better none than you.'

In the same year Baxter married Margaret Charlton, and it proved a very happy union. From 1662 to 1691 he suffered persecutions, fines and imprisonment, and only preached when he was able. On the accession of James II to the throne, he was brought to trial under Judge Jeffreys, who called Baxter 'an old blockhead, an unthankful villain, a conceited, stubborn, fanatical dog', and wanted to hang him. 'Richard, I see the rogue in your face,' shouted the judge. 'I was not aware my face was so true a *mirror*,' retorted Baxter, for which he was fined and imprisoned for about eighteen months. In 1691, on his deathbed, when asked how he was, he replied either 'Almost well!' or 'Better than I deserve to be, but not so well as I hope to be.'

Baxter is best known for his pastoral ministry. He declared: 'It is the converting and saving of souls that is our business.' *The Reformed Pastor* was published in 1656, and is his most enduring work. It came about through a meeting of Worcestershire's voluntary association of ministers, and was originally a sermon based on Acts 20:28. By 'Reformed', Baxter meant 'Revived' – pastors with spiritual life in them. His well-known lines are:

> *I'll preach as though I ne'er should preach again,*
> *And as a dying man to dying men.*

He lived out these lines. He tried to preach from full notes, but this was not always possible.

Baxter's two principles were, first, that 'All churches either rise or fall as the ministry doth rise or fall (not in riches or worldly grandeur) but in knowledge, zeal and ability for their work'; and secondly, that 'it is usually far more effectual to preach it privately to a particular sinner.' Initially, Baxter hesitated to carry out his programme of individual catechizing because he thought the people would scorn it, and he did not have the strength to carry it out. But he came to urge it, telling ministers to 'not slightly slubber over this work, but do it vigorously.'

In the first part of the address, Baxter dwells on the oversight of ourselves. His preaching was vigorous and searching: 'Many a preacher is now in hell, who hath a hundred times called upon his hearers to use the utmost care and diligence to escape it.' 'O brethren!' he cried, 'it is easier to chide at sin, than to overcome it.' He warns preachers to 'preach to yourselves the sermons which you study, before you preach them to others.'

The second part of the address covers the oversight of the flock. Family religion was the key: 'You are not like to see any general reformation, till you procure family reformation.' In summary: 'The whole of our ministry must be carried on in tender love to our people. We must let them see that nothing pleaseth us but what profiteth them; and that what doeth them good doth us good; and that nothing troubleth us more than their hurt.'

The third part of Baxter's address deals with the application. 'You cannot break men's hearts by jesting with them, or telling them a smooth tale, or pronouncing a gaudy oration.' It is quite possible for a sermon to be nothing more than 'a well-dressed carcase'. Only a true Christian can be a true shepherd.

38

RICHARD BAXTER
(1615–1691)

A mere Christian

What then? Only that in every way, whether in pretence or in truth, Christ is preached; and in this I rejoice, yes, and will rejoice (Phil. 1:18).

Now I plead with you, brethren, by the name of our Lord Jesus Christ, that you all speak the same thing, and that there be no divisions among you, but that you be perfectly joined together in the same mind and in the same judgment (1 Cor. 1:10).

Say to them: 'As I live,' says the Lord God, 'I have no pleasure in the death of the wicked, but that the wicked turn from his way and live. Turn, turn from your evil ways! For why should you die, O house of Israel?' (Ezek. 33:11).

Therefore, since all these things will be dissolved, what manner of persons ought you to be in holy conduct and godliness, looking for and hastening the coming of the day of God? (2 Pet. 3:11-12a).

For I am hard-pressed between the two, having a desire to depart and be with Christ, which is far better (Phil. 1:23).

C.S. Lewis was to appeal to Baxter's 'mere Christianity', since Baxter did not fully identify with the Anglicans, Presbyterians or Independents. Baxter had said: 'My religion is merely Christian.' He was more Anglican than anything else, but he said: 'Be it by Conformists or Non-Conformists, I rejoice that Christ is preached.' He favoured the toleration of all professing Christians except Roman Catholics and Socinians; and declared that if all the Episcopalians had been like Archbishop Ussher, all the Presbyterians like Stephen Marshall, and all the Independents like Jeremiah Burroughs, then 'the breaches of the church would soon have been healed.' He lamented that some of the godly wanted to 'shut up the church of God in a nutshell'.

Baxter was no admirer of Oliver Cromwell, but he seized the opportunity once to preach before the Lord Protector on 1 Corinthians 1:10 on divisions in the Church. Baxter wanted a creed no larger than God's own; he wanted Christians to 'unite in necessary truths, and bear with one another in things that may be borne with.' Later he recalled of this sermon: 'The plainness and nearness, I heard, was displeasing to him and his courtiers: but they put it up' (i.e. they put up with it). In 1654 he drew up a statement entitled *Fundamentals of Religion* in the hope of promoting unity.

For all that, Baxter was a man born for contention. Later in life he confessed: 'I have perceived that nothing so much hinders the reception of the truth as urging it on men with too harsh importunity and falling too heavily on their errors.' But he showed courage in speaking both to Cromwell and to Charles II. The Civil War began in 1642, and most of Worcestershire was Royalist. Baxter sided with the Parliament, but tried to remain loyal to the monarchy.

Suffering from ill-health and expecting to die soon, Baxter wrote books, and wrote them quickly. *The Saints' Everlasting Rest* declared: 'It is too soon to go to hell at a hundred years old, and not too soon to go to heaven at twenty.' His *Christian Directory* was published in 1673, and ran to 1,133 folio pages. His other great work was *The Call to the Unconverted*, written in 1657 and based on Ezekiel 33:11. Here he does not hold back:

> Miserable souls ... who has bewitched your minds into such madness, and your hearts into such deadness, that you should

... go on so obstinately towards damnation, that neither the word of God nor the persuasions of men can change your minds, or hold your hands, or stop you, till you are past remedy! Well sinners, this life will not last always; this patience will not wait upon you still.

Baxter's preaching was personal and powerful in its appeal.

In 1660 he was summoned to London to aid, as a moderate Puritan, in the recall of the king. He was appointed one of ten or twelve chaplains to Charles II, to whom he preached. His text was Hebrews 11:1, and the title was *The Life of Faith*. He presented heaven and hell before Charles and his courtiers:

Dare you now be drunk, or gluttonous or worldly? Dare you be voluptuous, proud or fornicators any more? Dare you go home and make a jest at piety and neglect your souls as you have done? ... Princes and Nobles live not alwaies: you are not the Rulers of the unmoveable Kingdom, but of a boat that is in a hasting stream, or a ship under sail, that will speed both Pilot and Passengers to the shore ... The inexorable Leveller is ready at your backs, to convince you by unresistible argument that dust you are and to dust you shall return ... No man will fear you after death: much less will Christ be afraid to judge you ... Live as if you saw the glorious things which you say you do believe. That when worldly titles are insignificant words and fleshly pleasures have an end, and Faith and Holiness will be the marks of honour, and unbelief and ungodliness the badges of perpetual shame, and when you must give an account of your stewardship and shall be no longer stewards, you may then be brought by Faith unto Fruition and see with joy the glorious things which you now believe. Write upon your Palaces and Goods that sentence: 'Seeing all these things shall be dissolved, what manner of persons ought you to be in all holy conversation and godliness looking for and hasting to the coming of the Day of God.'

The Puritans were not lacking in courage!

It must be said that Baxter excelled more in pastoral theology than in doctrinal matters. In his *Aphorisms of Justification* he argued that Christ died conditionally for all, to reconcile man to God, not God to man. He emphasized the subjective righteousness of a person's repentance and faith: 'To affirm therefore that our Evangelical or new Covenant righteousness is in Christ and not in ourselves, or performed by Christ and not by ourselves, is such a piece of Antinomian doctrine that no man who knows the nature and difference of the Covenant can possibly entertain and which every Christian should abhor as insufferable.' As J.I. Packer writes: 'Baxter was a big man, big enough to have large faults and make large errors.'

As he contemplated death, he meditated on Philippians 1:23. His testimony is most moving:

> In this world I have had many of God's mercies and comforts; but their sweetness was their taste of divine love, and their tendency to heavenly perfection ... Every place I have lived in has its monuments of divine love. Every year and hour of my life has been a time of love. Every friend, neighbour, and even enemy, has been the messenger and instrument of love. Every state and change of my life, notwithstanding my sin, has opened to me the treasures and mysteries of love.

In this world, God's love is good; but in the world to come it is far better.

39

WILLIAM BRIDGE
(1600–1671)

Student of the Word and counsellor
of the downcast

*Because you have made the Lord, who is my refuge, even
the Most High, your dwelling place, no evil shall befall
you, nor shall any plague come near your dwelling*
(Ps. 91:9-10).

*Why are you cast down, O my soul? And why are you
disquieted within me? Hope in God; for I shall yet praise
Him, the help of my countenance and my God*
(Ps. 42:11).

*O God, You have taught me from my youth; and to this
day I declare Your wondrous works. Now also when I am
old and greyheaded, O God, do not forsake me, until I
declare Your strength to this generation, Your power to
everyone who is to come* (Ps. 71:17-18).

*They shall still bear fruit in old age; they shall be fresh
and flourishing* (Ps. 92:14).

Like many of the Puritans, William Bridge came through Cambridge University. In 1627 he was ordained into the priesthood of the Church of England, but by 1634 he was suspended by the consistory court for a time for attacking Arminianism. Two years later, Bridge was deprived, and then excommunicated and exiled. When he fled to Holland, as did so many Puritans, Charles I said: 'Let him go: We are well rid of him.'

In Rotterdam in Holland, Bridge was ordained as an Independent, and later became co-pastor with Jeremiah Burroughs. In 1641 he returned to England and became a member of the Westminster Assembly. From 1643 until he was ejected in 1662 by the Act of Uniformity, he was the Independent pastor of Yarmouth. As a pastor, Bridge took his work very seriously. He used to study the Bible and pray each day from 4.00 a.m. to 11.00 a.m., yet he was also a warm-hearted pastor of souls. The last decade or so of his life was spent at Yarmouth and Clapham in Surrey. Here he ministered to an Independent church with considerable success, and here he died, in 1670 or 1671.

As plague ravaged London in 1665, Bridge published *The Righteous Man's Habitation in the Time of Plague and Pestilence*. This was an exposition of Psalm 91 – a Psalm that was to mean much to Corrie ten Boom in the dark days of the Nazi occupation of Holland in World War II when she and her family set up a hiding place to help persecuted Jews to escape. Bridge pressed his hearers and readers: 'It is not enough to trust in the Lord, but you must go to God and tell him, that you do trust in him, that you make him your habitation; say, "Lord, I make thee my habitation, I trust in thee, thou art my refuge, and my fortress, in thee do I trust."'

Earlier, in 1649, Bridge had published *A Lifting Up for the Downcast* which is a series of thirteen sermons on Psalm 42:11. Depression and discouragement are not a monopoly of modern Western society. Bridge sought to take the depressed person out of himself: 'All your discouragements are from self-love,' he wrote. He cited the advice of Martin Luther: 'When God seems to be mine enemy and to stand with a drawn sword against me, then do I cast and throw myself into His arms.' Bridge never underestimated how difficult it is to exercise faith, but he pointed out that 'Affliction is God's soap.' To change the image: 'Affliction is a bag of gold given unto the people of God; though it seem a leathern bag without, yet there is gold within.'

Bridge also wrote to minister to the aged, where he noted that older people are susceptible to becoming remiss in the things of God, too covetous for the things of the world, fearful, apt to be touchy and peevish, unteachable, hard to please, full of complaints, of all men likely to be the most impenitent. Like Psalms 71 and 92, which he cited in his *Word to the Aged,* Bridge urged the older saint to continue to look to Christ, and to bear fruit in old age. In his pastoral ministry, Bridge used his hours of laborious study particularly to help those who were struggling in the Christian life.

40

PAUL GERHARDT

(1607–1676)

Joy through believing

When they had twisted a crown of thorns, they put it on His head ... And they bowed the knee before Him and mocked Him, saying, 'Hail, King of the Jews!'
(Matt. 27:29).

If God is for us, who can be against us? (Rom. 8:31b).

Commit your way to the Lord, trust also in Him, and He shall bring it to pass (Ps. 37:5).

Rest in the Lord, and wait patiently for Him; do not fret because of him who prospers in his way, because of the man who brings wicked schemes to pass (Ps. 37:7).

Paul Gerhardt lived in troubled times, during the disastrous period of the Thirty Years War of 1618–48, where the Hapsburg (Spanish) and Bourbon (French) dynasties fought one another, mainly on German soil. The Protestant nations favoured the French. Gerhardt's father was the mayor of the village of Gräfenhainichen, but he died when Paul was only twelve. Gerhardt seems to have done everything quite late in life. From 1628 to 1642 Gerhardt studied theology at Luther's old university at Wittenberg. He worked as a family tutor in Berlin for a time, but in 1651 obtained his first pastorate, in the war-torn and devastated village of Mittenwalde. Gerhardt only married at the age of 48, to Anna Maria Berthold, who was nearly sixteen years younger.

In 1657 Gerhardt became the first deacon (i.e. the third pastor in seniority) of the Lutheran Church of St Nicholas in Berlin. He became a popular preacher, and continued the hymn-writing which he had begun in the 1640s.

The Christian testimony has suffered many detractions down through the ages, but two lamentable features are how Christians have understood Church-state relations, and how they have differed from one another. Both issues were combined in the troubles which engulfed Gerhardt from 1662. The Elector of Brandenburg, Freidrich Wilhelm, who was Reformed, issued an Edict of Toleration, which forbade attacks on each other's confessions by Lutheran and Reformed ministers. Such legislation invariably makes matters worse, and Gerhardt considered that he could not in conscience sign away his commitment to the Lutheran Formula of Concord. For this, he was dismissed.

In 1668 Anna died, leaving Gerhardt with his only surviving child (out of five) – a six-year-old boy. On her deathbed, Anna asked her husband to read his passion hymns to her, including:

> O sacred Head, now wounded,
> With grief and shame weighed down,
> Now scornfully surrounded
> With thorns, Thine only crown.

The comfort for the believer lies in the truth of substitution:

> My burden is Thy passion,
> Lord, Thou hast borne for me,
> For it was my transgression
> Which brought this woe on Thee.

In 1669 Gerhardt was called as archdeacon to the comparative backwater of Lübben where he worked until his death in 1676.

He never wrote the thousands of hymns that Charles Wesley was later to write, and restricted himself to something like 133 to 139. They reveal the depth of his biblical knowledge, his grasp of the sinful human condition and his joy in Christ.

After the funeral of a fellow pastor who had suddenly dropped dead after himself conducting a funeral, Gerhardt wrote the hymn which is essentially a meditation on Romans 8:31-39. It begins with his thoughts on verse 31:

> *If God Himself be for me,*
> *I may a host defy;*
> *For when I pray, before me*
> *My foes confounded fly.*

Gerhardt wrote long hymns that were saturated in Scripture.

In the aftermath of the appalling Thirty Years War, Gerhardt turned to Psalm 37:5 and wrote the hymn, which was translated by John Wesley:

> *Commit thou all thy griefs*
> *And ways into His hands*
> *To His sure truth and tender care,*
> *Who heaven and earth commands.*

Psalm 37 evidently gripped him because he also wrote a hymn based on the seventh verse. This hymn begins:

> *Be thou content; be still before*
> *His face, at whose right hand doth reign*
> *Fullness of joy forevermore,*
> *Without whom all thy toil is vain.*

It is entirely appropriate that in the 1940s, in the dark days of Nazi brutality, as Dietrich Bonhoeffer languished in prison, he sought to learn by heart all of Gerhardt's hymns.

41

BLAISE PASCAL
(1623–1662)

A sinner yet righteous

Moreover He said, 'I am the God of your father – the God of Abraham, the God of Isaac, and the God of Jacob.' And Moses hid his face, for he was afraid to look upon God (Exod. 3:6).

For there is one God and one Mediator between God and men, the Man Christ Jesus (1 Tim. 2:5).

Also He spoke this parable to some who trusted in themselves that they were righteous, and despised others ... for everyone who exalts himself will be humbled, and he who humbles himself will be exalted (Luke 18:9, 14).

Blaise Pascal lived at a time when Roman Catholicism in France saw a prolonged theological dispute between the Jesuits and Jansenists. In 1638 the Belgian Roman Catholic bishop, Cornelius Jansen, died, but two years later his huge work *Augustinus* was published. Here he tried to reproduce the teaching of Augustine of Hippo and the doctrines of grace. In summary, he detested the notion that grace is given according to merits. Saint-Cyran (who took the name of his own abbey) formed a party of followers of Jansen which included the convent of Port Royal and the Arnauld family. Meanwhile, in 1588, Luis de Molina (a

Spanish Jesuit) published his *On the harmony of free will with the gifts of divine grace*. This taught that sufficient grace becomes efficacious by the free cooperation of the human being – equivalent to what became known as Protestant Arminianism.

Blaise Pascal was born on 19 June 1623. The three Pascal children – Jacqueline, Blaise and Gilberte – were all educated at home, and never went to school. After the death of their father in 1651, Jacqueline joined the convent at Port Royal. Pascal himself seemed destined for a distinguished career in science. He mastered sound and vibrations, and established the existence of atmospheric pressure, which led to hydraulics. In the study of the vacuum, he has left us with what has become known as Pascal's principle. He also invented the mechanical calculator, and a year before his death he was involved in setting up the first public transport system in Paris.

Pascal's conversion to a radical version of Jansenism came after a worldly period on 23 November 1654 – the night of fire – when he surrendered to 'the God of Abraham, the God of Isaac, the God of Jacob' and not the God of the philosophers and scholars. He wrote, 'Certainty, Certainty, emotion, joy, peace, God of Jesus Christ ... Oblivion of the world and of everything except God ... Renunciation sweet and total.' He kept a record of this experience on his person for the rest of his life. From this time on, he led an austere and charitable life. Despite his own poor health, he visited those in need and gave away money.

The pope at this time, Innocent X (1644–55), issued a papal bull in 1653, reaffirmed in 1654, which condemned five propositions contained in *Augustinus*. The Five Propositions of Jansen were that some of God's commandments are not possible for righteous persons to fulfil; grace is irresistible; reward or forfeiture does not demand free will; semi-Pelagians are heretical; and to say that Christ died and shed His blood for all mankind is semi-Pelagian.

Innocent X's successor, Alexander VII (1655–67), held similar views. Hence Pascal wrote that the 'Disciples of St Augustine' were 'between God and the Pope'. The controversy raged within both church and state. Pascal refused to support the signing of the formulary but professed submission to the Church. The faculty at the Sorbonne condemned Antoine Arnauld in January 1656, depriving him of his degrees and expelling him from the university. Fearful of the police, and in disguise, Arnauld turned to Pascal for help. To help the Jansenist (Augustinian) cause, he published anonymously the *Provincial Letters* of 1656–7. These consisted of eighteen letters plus the fragment of a nineteenth. They were a devastating attack on the Jesuits for their worldliness, and a defence of the tenets of Jansenism. Referring to the Jesuits, Pascal asserted: 'You let your opinions grow bit by bit. If they appeared all at once in their extreme and final form, they would arouse horror; but such slow imperceptible progress accustoms people to them gently and obviates scandal.' Not surprisingly, the *Provincial Letters* ended up being condemned by the Roman Inquisition.

In 1660 King Louis XIV denounced Jansenism. In 1661 an anti-Jansenist text was read out in all churches, and clergy were given fifteen days to subscribe to it (not being a cleric, Pascal did not have to sign). Pascal's sister Jacqueline (a nun at Port Royal) signed the formulary and then died of a broken heart. Pascal's better-known work is the *Pensées*, which consisted of draft notes of an intended work of apologetics and which was published in 1670 by Gilberte. The book portrays the inconstancy, boredom and anxiety of the human condition, and sets great store by prophecies as the essential proofs of the Christian revelation. Pride cuts man off from God, and sensuality binds him to the earth. Christianity does not offend reason nor does it submit to it. Yet 'We only know God through Christ Jesus. All contact with God is severed without this Mediator.'

A few of Pascal's thoughts are:

Man is great in so far he realises that he is wretched. A tree does not know its own wretchedness.

Self will can never be satisfied, even if it were to secure everything it wanted; but we are satisfied the moment we give it up.

I discovered that all the unhappiness of man stems from one thing, that he cannot remain alone in a room.

There are only two kinds of men: the righteous who think they are sinners and the sinners who think they are righteous.

One who suffered much ill-health during his life, Pascal died of a brain haemorrhage at the age of thirty-nine. When he died, he was found to possess virtually nothing except his Bible and Augustine's *Confessions*. His last spoken words were 'May God never abandon me.' Earlier he had written: 'I stretch out my arms to my Saviour.'

42

MATTHEW HENRY
(1662–1714)

Treasure in heaven

The sacrifices of God are a broken spirit, a broken and a contrite heart – these, O God, You will not despise (Ps. 51:17).

Do not lay up for yourselves treasures on earth, where moth and rust destroy and where thieves break in and steal; but lay up for yourselves treasures in heaven, where neither moth nor rust destroys and where thieves do not break in and steal. For where your treasure is, there your heart will be also (Matt. 6:19-21).

Her ways are ways of pleasantness, and all her paths are peace (Prov. 3:17).

The churches of Asia greet you. Aquila and Priscilla greet you heartily in the Lord, with the church that is in their house (1 Cor. 16:19).

For His mercy endures forever (refrain in Ps. 136).

Born in the year of the Great Ejection, Matthew Henry might be regarded, along with John Howe (1630–1705), as the last of the Puritans. He was raised in a Puritan household, his father being Philip Henry, who was known as 'Heavenly Henry'. At ten, Matthew recovered from a life-threatening fever, and this played a significant part in leading him to consider the things of eternity and to come to saving faith in Christ. He had especially been gripped for a number of years by Psalm 51:17. Initially he studied law, but after some preaching in private houses, he was secretly ordained in 1687 in London by six ministers in the home of Richard Steele. He only ever served in two Presbyterian pastorates – at Chester (1687–1712) and at Hackney in London (1712–14).

Although he wrote quite a number of other works, Matthew Henry is best known as the great biblical commentator, whose commentary on the whole Bible is still in print. He began it in November 1704, and left it incomplete at his death ten years later. Henry was an extremely industrious worker who sought to make maximum use of his time, and wrote prayerfully in his diary: 'God, by his grace, help me to fill up time – to be busy while working time lasts.' He died at a relatively young age. In May 1714 he fell from his horse while riding back to London, and died the next day. But friends finished off his commentary – the section from Romans to Revelation – by using his notes.

On Sunday 8 March 1713 Matthew Henry was travelling in London in order to preach. On the way home he was robbed of all his money, which was about ten or eleven shillings. Later he recorded his response to the experience:

(a) his gratitude that he had never been robbed before;
(b) an acknowledgment of the evil of the love of money;
(c) an acknowledgment of the power of Satan;
(d) the vanity of worldly wealth.

He concluded: 'How loose, therefore, we should sit to it.' Earlier, in his own commentary on Matthew 6:19-21, he had written that 'It is folly to make that our treasure which we may so easily be robbed of.' Not every pastor is so prophetic, or so readily adheres to his own teaching!

Elsewhere Henry commented on Proverbs 3:17, that 'We are not yet home, but we should long to be there.' Henry's grasp of the spiritual life can be seen in his pithy, proverb-like sayings: 'A godly man's way may be melancholy, but his end shall be peace and everlasting light. A wicked man's way may be pleasant, but his end and endless abode will be utter darkness.' As in the book of Proverbs, Henry saw that wisdom, godliness and joy were all joined together.

Henry was always very family-centred, and in 1704 he published *A Church in the House: Family Religion,* based on 1 Corinthians 16:19. He maintained to his friends and family that 'A life spent in the service of God and communion with him, is the most comfortable life anyone can live in this world.' He took family worship seriously, with prayer, reading and praise both morning and evening. Invariably after supper, he would sing Psalm 136 before catechizing and testing what had been learnt from sermons. He sought to live out what he wrote: 'Sincere love is that which looks at God, and not self in what it doth. It is "love unfeigned" (2 Cor. 6:6; 1 Pet. 1:22).'

43

THOMAS HALYBURTON
(1674–1712)

Finding rest in grace

Take My yoke upon you and learn from Me, for I am
gentle and lowly in heart, and you will find rest
for your souls (Matt. 11:29).

Then they brought little children to Him, that He might
touch them; but the disciples rebuked those who brought
them. But when Jesus saw it, He was greatly displeased
and said to them, 'Let the little children come to Me,
and do not forbid them; for of such is the kingdom of
God. Assuredly, I say to you, whoever does not receive the
kingdom of God as a little child will by no means enter
it.' And He took them up in His arms, laid His hands on
them, and blessed them (Mark 10:13-16).

Thomas Halyburton was born in 1674 in Dupplin, Perthshire, in Scotland, the son of a minister who was ejected in 1676. Despite his father's troubles with the laws against dissenters, Halyburton received a good classical education in Greek, Latin and Dutch. Raised on a steady, indeed overdone, diet of sermons, lectures and prayer meetings, Halyburton grew weary of the weekly grind of religious exercises.

Nevertheless, he went off to Edinburgh University and then St Andrews to study philosophy and to try to settle his religious convictions. At university he struggled with ill health and religious doubts, and only after he left did he come, in 1698, to some kind of assurance of faith. By 1700 he was ordained as the minister of Ceres, Fife, not far from St Andrews. The following year saw his marriage, but he and his wife, Janet, lost three children, who all died in infancy.

Although he did well as a parish minister, despite possessing no musical abilities whatsoever, his health declined, so in 1710 he was installed as Professor of Divinity at St Andrews, but he died in 1712 at the age of thirty-seven and was buried next to Samuel Rutherford. No doubt drawing on his own struggles with philosophy and Deism, Halyburton repudiated the notion of John Locke that reason was to be the Christian's guide in all matters.

Like Augustine and Bunyan before him, and 'Rabbi' Duncan after him, Halyburton struggled for faith. He took the doctrine of original sin seriously, but says that he mistook amendment for atonement: 'I engaged to live a new life with an old heart.' In fact, he says, 'I never parted with any sin till God beat and drove me from it.' After binding himself to serve the Lord in 1697, he failed again, but soon after came to find rest in Christ (Matt. 11:29) and His commandments (1 John 5:3; Ps. 119:128). He still struggled, and considered that true Christians may walk in darkness (Isa. 50:10), but he struggled in a different spirit: 'Sorrow formerly flowed from discoveries of sin as it brings on wrath; now it flowed from a sense of sin as containing wretched unkindness to one who was astonishingly kind to an unworthy wretch.'

Halyburton came to see Christ as the answer to atheism. He loved God's law, but said: 'I dared not trust in anything but sovereign grace.' When his baby daughter was dying, he was comforted by the simple account of Christ's love for children recorded in Mark 10:13-16. When he himself came to die, he wrote: 'I loved to live preaching Christ, and love to die preaching Christ.' In fact, 'All is of grace. He has chosen me, called me, justified me, and sanctified me by His grace.' He lamented: 'I repent I did not more; but I have peace in it, that what I did I did in sincerity.'

Halyburton's restless soul and weak body found their rest in Christ alone. He was assured on his deathbed, and looked forward to glory – 'There are no coughs in heaven.' Christ in His free grace achieved what legal preaching could never achieve – rest and assurance for a troubled soul.

44

THOMAS BOSTON
(1676–1732)

Plain, useful, searching and safe preaching

*For we are the circumcision, who worship God in the
Spirit, rejoice in Christ Jesus, and have no
confidence in the flesh* (Phil. 3:3).

*Cry aloud, spare not; lift up thy voice like a trumpet; tell
my people their transgression, and the house
of Jacob their sins* (Isa. 58:1).

*He is like a man building a house, who dug deep and laid
the foundation on the rock* (Luke 6:48a).

*Truly, this only I have found: that God made man upright,
but they have sought out many schemes* (Eccles. 7:29).

*Then the master of the house, being angry, said to his
servant, 'Go out quickly into the streets and lanes of
the city, and bring in here the poor and the maimed
and the lame and the blind' ... Then the master said to
the servant, 'Go out into the highways and hedges, and
compel them to come in, that my house may
be filled'* (Luke 14:21b, 23).

Thomas Boston was born in Duns in Berwickshire, the home-
town of the medieval theologian Duns Scotus, on 17 March
1676, and he died at Ettrick on 20 May 1732. In 1700 Boston
married Katherine Brown, but she was to suffer from a
distressing disorder of the mind, particularly in Boston's later
years when she was barred from the public ordinances of the

Church. They had ten children, but only four of them outlived their father. Boston only ever served in two parishes, both of them small, in his lifetime. In 1699 he was ordained to Simprin, and then he moved to Ettrick, near the English border, in 1707, and remained there until his death 25 years later.

As a youngster, Boston was impressed by a number of events:

(a) a visit to his father who was in prison for his anti-prelatic views;
(b) his own conviction of sin for having played pins on the Lord's Day, and for having stolen David Dickson's commentary on *Matthew* from a notary;
(c) the sight of a corpse in an open coffin;
(d) the awakening sermons of Henry Erskine, father of Ebenezer and Ralph.

Boston's finest work was his *Human Nature in its Fourfold State*. His premise was 'You cannot be in the way to heaven, who never saw yourselves by nature in the high road to hell.' He dealt with human nature in innocence, nature, grace and eternity. He always aimed to preach simply and faithfully to his people. Indeed, his declared aim can be found at the conclusion of a series of sermons on Philippians 3:3, entitled *The Distinguishing Characters of Real Christians*. Boston himself regarded these sermons as his best. As he drew his sermons to a close, he trusted that his teaching had been 'plain, useful, searching, and safe'.

So committed was Boston to plainness of speech that in speaking of what it means to 'worship God in the Spirit' (Phil.3:3), he made potent use of repetition:

> Ye need Christ, ye cannot be without him. O how does the profane world need Christ! But, O sirs, ye need him as really when ye are going to your prayers, as the man that is going to the devil's fetters to his cups and his drunken companions need

him; ye need him as really when ye are going to the sermon on the Lord's day, as he who profanely casts contempt on God's ordinance, by loitering at home on the Lord's day ... Ye need himself. Sinners, ye need himself, to be united to him, to be one spirit with him.

Succinct summaries are Boston's speciality. For example, the act of justification is set out in a most memorable way: 'God the Father takes the pen, dips it in the blood of his Son, crosses the sinner's accounts, and blots them out of his debt-book.' Union with Christ is described in no less vivid terms: 'Christ takes the soul, as one marries a widow under a burden of debt: and so when the creditors come to Christ's spouse, she carries them to her Husband, confesses the debt, declares she is not able to pay, and lays all upon him.' He also aimed to hit his target in preaching, and so noting Isaiah 58:1, he warned against the temptation of bringing people on little by little by being smooth. He remained convinced that 'There is need of a digging deep for a thorough humiliation in the work of conversion' (Luke 6:48).

This was because, citing Ecclesiastes 7:29, he saw the doctrine of man's natural state as 'the foundation of all real religion'. He told the natural man: 'You were wont to divide your works into two sorts; some good, some evil: but you must count again, and put them all under one head; for God writes on them all "only evil".'

Yet we should not be left with the impression that Boston worked on his congregations in the same way that a hammer works on an anvil. Pointing to 1 John 2:13-14, Boston affirmed: 'There are saints of several sizes in Christ's family.' There was thus a powerful wooing note in the preaching of Boston. In a sermon preached in 1719 on *A Rich Feast Prepared for Hungry Souls*, Boston cried out that 'the invitation is given to all who come in its way, without distinction, or exception of any sort of persons ... The invitation is to the Gentiles, as well as to the

Jews, to those in the highways and hedges as well as those in the city. All who will come are welcome.'

Pointing to numerous passages (Matt. 22:3; Isa. 55:1; Rev. 3:20; Luke 14:23; Ezek. 33:11; Matt. 23:37; Luke 19:41-42), Boston emphasized the freeness of the offer of Christ: 'He commands sinners to come to him. The invitations are all commands; they are most peremptory.' Indeed: 'Where all are invited, none are excluded.'

As a safe preacher, Boston sought to be reliable and orthodox, worthy of our trust. He sought to live out the truth of Philippians 3:3, for 'It is good for all, especially ministers, to be emptied of themselves, and to have Christ and the good of souls before their eyes.'

JOHANN SEBASTIAN BACH
(1685–1750)

Music to God's glory

*Not unto us, O Lord, not unto us, but to Your
name give glory* (Ps. 115:1a).

*In the multitude of my anxieties within me, Your comforts
delight my soul* (Ps. 94:19).

*Return to your rest, O my soul, for the Lord has dealt
bountifully with you* (Ps. 116:7).

*Moreover David and the captains of the army separated
for the service some of the sons of Asaph, of Heman, and
of Jeduthun, who should prophesy with harps, stringed
instruments, and cymbals* (1 Chron. 25:1).

I will not leave you nor forsake you (Josh. 1:5c).

*For in much wisdom is much grief, and he who increases
knowledge increases sorrow* (Eccles. 1:18).

*So he who was dead sat up and began to
speak* (Luke 7:15a).

The life of Johann Sebastian Bach cannot be said to have been extraordinary, but he was one of the finest composers who ever lived, and he was a strong Christian of the Lutheran faith. None of his personal letters to family members seem to have survived. He possessed two sets of Martin Luther's complete works, and he was in the habit of marking his three-volume Bible with his comments.

Bach's family had music in their genes. His great-grandfather was a baker who used to play the guitar to the rhythmic accompaniment of the flour mill wheels. Bach himself was born in Eisenach in 1685, the last of eight children. After the death of his mother in 1694 and his father in 1695, he went to live with Christoph Bach, his married brother. At Arnstadt in 1703–7, with a salary from the church treasury and the beer tax, he became the church organist, and began to compose his own works. In 1707 he married Maria Barbara Bach, a distant cousin, by whom he had seven children. After her death in 1720, he married Anna Magdalena Wilcke, a professional singer, by whom he was to have thirteen children. It is small wonder that of the eleven children who survived him, Bach could write that 'they are all born musicians'.

Psalm 115 provided Bach with the motto *Soli Deo Gloria* which he attached to the end of many of his scores. He worked at Weimar (1708–17), Cöthen (1717–22), and then at Leipzig from 1723 until his death in 1750. He also frequently performed in Zimmermann's Coffee House! It was his view that 'the goal of all music should be nothing but the glory of God and the recreation of the mind.' His abilities to improvise, sight-read and perform were remarkable, and his son, Carl, considered that he could hear the slightest wrong note even in the largest ensemble. His use of counterpoint is masterful, perhaps unrivalled.

For years during the 1720s Bach would write a cantata a week, with cantata 21 being his favourite. It was based on Psalm 94:19 and Psalm 116:7. His two greatest works were *St Matthew Passion* and *St John Passion*. Perhaps his best-known piece is the haunting and enchanting *Jesu, Joy of Man's Desiring*. On 1 Chronicles 25 he underlined the names of Asaph, Heman and Jeduthun, and commented that 'This chapter is the true foundation of all God-pleasing music.' He also marked Joshua 1:5c in his Bible, and many passages from Ecclesiastes, including Ecclesiastes 1:18.

Bach never met his great contemporary, George Handel, who worked in England as well as Germany. On 22 July 1750 he received the Lord's Supper at home, and five days later he died. Back in 1716 he had written *Come, Sweet Hour of Death* to go with the reading from Luke 7:11-17, which tells of Christ's power over death.

46

NICHOLAS LUDWIG VON ZINZENDORF
(1700–1760)

Taking the gospel to all

These are the ones who were not defiled with women, for they are virgins. These are the ones who follow the Lamb wherever He goes. These were redeemed from among men, being firstfruits to God and to the Lamb (Rev. 14:4).

I have set watchmen on your walls, O Jerusalem; they shall never hold their peace day or night. You who make mention of the Lord, do not keep silent, and give Him no rest till He establishes and till He makes Jerusalem a praise in the earth (Isa. 62:6-7).

I am a debtor both to Greeks and to barbarians, both to wise and to unwise (Rom. 1:14).

For none of us lives to himself (Rom. 14:7a).

The earth is the Lord's (Ps. 24:1a).

Behold, all souls are Mine (Ezek. 18:4a).

You did not choose Me, but I chose you and appointed you that you should go and bear fruit, and that your fruit should remain (John 15:16a).

Nicholas Ludwig von Zinzendorf was born into an aristocratic household on 26 May 1700. Zinzendorf never forgot his experience as a four-year-old when 'the father of Pietism', Philipp Spener, who had only a year to live, laid his hands on him. By the age of six, Zinzendorf was holding prayer meetings, and was writing: 'I firmly resolved to live for him alone, who had laid down his life for me.' At ten, he entered the Paedagogium at Halle, where he fared badly with tutors and students. At the age of fifteen, he was involved in a public oration which proved to be a near disaster, and afterwards he wrote: 'Since that time I have lost my passion to excel and have begun to satisfy myself with doing my duty.' In 1716 he went reluctantly to Wittenberg to study law. He disliked mathematics, wrote in German and French, and read the Greek New Testament.

In 1722 he married Erdmuth Dorothea, Countess of Reuss, although it was never a deep love relationship. That same year saw the arrival of Protestant (Hussite) refugees from Moravia on his Berthelsdorf estate in Upper Lusatia. This led to the founding of Herrnhut ('the watch of the Lord'), with the Lord's Watch of Prayer whereby for over a hundred years twenty-four men and twenty-four women – not always the same persons, of course – prayed constantly.

By 1727 Zinzendorf had quit his government post in order to devote himself to the Herrnhut community. He had founded a Christian fraternity which finally took the name of the 'Order of the Mustard Seed'. This group held to three pledges:

(a) be kind to all men;
(b) be true to Christ;
(c) send the gospel to the heathen.

Each member wore a ring with Romans 14:7a on it. Zinzendorf was strong on the communal aspects of Christianity: 'I acknowledge no Christianity without fellowship.' The Order of the Mustard Seed was actually a corresponding fellowship, and included John Potter (Archbishop of Canterbury), Thomas Wilson (Anglican bishop of Sodor and Man), Cardinal Noailles of Paris (a Jansenist) and General Oglethorpe of Georgia. Zinzendorf wrote to Noailles: 'When God enters into judgment with a sinner, then nothing avails but the righteousness of Jesus, through faith in his blood; and our salvation does not depend upon the pope or any other man, but merely and alone on the merits of Christ.' Pope Clement XI had issued the bull *Unigenitus* in 1713, to combat Jansenism, and Noailles finally capitulated, to Zinzendorf's sadness.

Zinzendorf sought to combine the Lutheran Pietists and the Moravian Brethren in a single body of prayerful, missionary-minded people, devoted to good works. Missionaries were sent out to Greenland, the West Indies and America. He also sought the conversion of the Jews. His manifesto was: 'The earth is the Lord's; all souls are His; I am debtor to all.' At Herrnhut he would contemplate a picture of twenty-five Moravian converts in their native costumes, and underneath was his favourite text, Revelation 14:4.

Zinzendorf had a particular love for the Gospel of John and the epistle to the Hebrews. The Count did much to revive hymn singing, and contributed personally to evangelical hymnody. His best-known hymn was composed on a ship to the West Indies:

> Jesus, Thy blood and righteousness,
> My beauty are, my glorious dress.

Not all of the Pietistic practices are to be commended. For some inexplicable reason, he rejected biblical inerrancy. The 'lot' was used to choose elders, missionary enterprises and marriage partners. A child of four drew the lot that decided that the Brethren would not unite with the Lutherans. Yet Zinzendorf was ordained in the Lutheran Church in 1734, and three years later was ordained as a bishop.

As a missionary church, the Moravians were without parallel in history. Missionaries were sent to the West Indies in 1732 (with Leonard Dober prepared to sell himself into slavery in order to reach the slaves with the gospel), to Greenland in 1733 (where, almost starving, the missionaries were forced to eat raw seaweed), and to Georgia in America in 1734 (where

Wesley and Whitefield were to go). These missionaries were to live humbly among the heathen; preach Christ crucified, rather than start with the creation and the fall; and would aim at individuals, not tribes. They were also to earn their own living.

In 1736, after being exiled by the king from Saxony, Zinzendorf went to an old castle at Ronneberg where he set up free schools for children, and distributed food and clothing for the poor. John Wesley was so impressed by Herrnhut that he declared: 'I would gladly have spent my life here.' After spending some eleven years in exile (1736–47), and suffering financial difficulties, Zinzendorf died in 1760. He was buried at Herrnhut, with the inscription being: 'He was appointed to bring forth fruit, and his fruit remains.'

47

SUSANNA WESLEY
(1669–1742)

Raising godly children

Foolishness is bound up in the heart of a child; the rod of correction will drive it far from him (Prov. 22:15).

My little children, for whom I labour in birth again until Christ is formed in you (Gal. 4:19).

Then I saw a great white throne and Him who sat on it, from whose face the earth and the heaven fled away. And there was found no place for them. And I saw the dead, small and great, standing before God, and books were opened. And another book was opened, which is the Book of Life. And the dead were judged according to their works, by the things which were written in the books (Rev. 20:11-12).

Susanna Wesley is best known in evangelical circles today as the mother of John and Charles Wesley, and the woman who bore nineteen children in all. But she herself was one of twenty-five! A strong-minded girl who became a strong-minded woman, at age thirteen she left the church where her Puritan father was the pastor in order to join the Church of England. In 1688 she married Samuel Wesley, who from 1697 until his death in 1735 ministered in the Anglican parish of Epworth in Lincolnshire.

The marriage between Samuel and Susanna proved to be quite stormy, and Samuel actually left his wife for a year when she did not say 'Amen' to the prayer for the king. This probably led her to devote her love and care to her children. Her child-rearing methods would raise the ire of many who claim to be experts today, but she took the doctrine of original sin seriously, and considered self-will to be 'the root of all sin and misery'. She taught her children six days a week, and, in her own testimony, recorded in 1732, she declared that by the age of one, 'they were taught to fear the rod and to cry softly, by which means they escaped abundance of correction ... and that most odious noise of the crying of children was rarely heard in the house.' Regarding childish follies, she wrote: 'Some should be overlooked and taken no notice of, and others mildly reproved; but no wilful transgression ought ever be forgiven children without chastisement, less or more, as the nature, and circumstances of the offence may require.'

Once a week, Susanna would have a private conference with each of her children (nine of the nineteen born to her died early). Her motives can be seen from a letter she wrote to one of her sons in 1705:

> I have such a vast inexpressible desire of your salvation, and such dreadful apprehensions of your failing in a work of so great importance, and do moreover know by experience how hard a thing it is to be a Christian, that I cannot forbear, I cannot but most earnestly press and conjure you, over and over again, to give the most earnest heed to what you have already learned, lest at any time you let slip the remembrance of your final happiness, or forget what you have to do in order to attain it.

She did in fact write a treatise for her eldest daughter, Emilia, based on Galatians 4:19.

Susanna once expressed the sentiment that it is easier to mourn ten children who had died than one who was living but dead spiritually. There was much affection in the household as well as discipline and order. She used to call John 'Jacky', and she prayed constantly for his salvation, as well as that of his siblings. After John and Charles were converted, she wrote to Charles that 'Jesus is the only Physician of souls; his blood the only salve that can heal a wounded conscience.'

Yet for all that, Charles thought that his mother lived in 'a legal night' for almost seventy years, and only really came to understand grace as God's free mercy in the last two years of her life. At the Lord's Supper in 1739 she had felt assured by the words 'The blood of our Lord Jesus Christ, which was given for thee.' Indeed, she had scolded Charles in 1740 when he expressed doubts as to the reality of his own Christian standing. She told him that this was in effect 'to tell Christ to his face that you have nothing to thank him for.' She went on: 'I think myself far from being so good a Christian as you are, or as I ought to be; but God forbid that I should renounce the little Christianity I have: nay, rather let me grow in grace and in the knowledge of our Lord and Saviour Jesus Christ.'

Whatever the case – and it is probably best to understand her experience of 1739 as one of assurance rather than conversion – as she lay dying, death held no terrors for her, and she said: 'Children, as soon as I am released, sing a psalm of praise to God.' At her funeral, John Wesley read from Revelation 20:11-12. It was a fitting reading for a woman whose life was – despite being marred by sin – essentially one of self-sacrificing goodness. She was buried in the Bunhill Fields cemetery, along with John Bunyan, John Owen and Isaac Watts. But her earnestness, her methodical methods of child-rearing and her biblical common sense were to leave a lasting impact on all her children, particularly John and Charles. She was truly a mother in Israel!

48

JOHN WESLEY
(1703–1791)

Saved from fire to proclaim the
riches of Christ

Is this not a brand plucked from the fire? (Zech. 3:2).

*And I will be even more vile [or undignified] than this, and
will be humble in my own sight* (2 Sam. 6:22a).

*For you know the grace of our Lord Jesus Christ, that
though He was rich, yet for your sakes He became poor,
that you through His poverty might become
rich* (2 Cor. 8:9).

John Wesley was born in 1703, the fifteenth child of Samuel
and Susanna Wesley, in Epworth, Lincolnshire where Samuel
was the Anglican rector. On 9 February 1709 a fire broke out
in the rectory. Young John Wesley was only six years old, and
he ran to the window to peer out, just as the roof was about
to collapse. Thankfully, a man in the village was resourceful
enough to know what to do. He bade another man climb on his
shoulders and reached young John only seconds before the roof
crashed in. The relieved father, Samuel Wesley, invited all to
join him in prayer: 'Come, neighbours, let us kneel down. Let
us give thanks to God. He has given me all my eight children.
Let the house go. I am rich enough.'

John never forgot this experience, and each year he would observe the anniversary of that dramatic night. He referred to himself in terms of Zechariah 3:2, and when he came to sit for his portrait by George Vertue, the background was a house in flames, with the words underneath: 'Is this not a brand plucked out of the fire?' In 1753 Wesley became so ill that he expected to die, and he wrote his own epitaph, calling himself 'A brand, not once only, plucked out of the fire.'

By 1724 Wesley had graduated from Christ Church College, Oxford He was ordained in 1728, and continued to seek after holiness through the Holy Club at Oxford which his brother Charles had founded. This was devoted to spiritual improvement and to good works. They were assailed as 'Methodists', and John was derided as 'His Holiness'. The two Wesleys went over to Georgia in the American colonies in 1735 to work as missionaries. This was not a great success, and they returned after a few years.

The courage of the Moravian Brethren on board the *Simmonds* during a storm while on the way to Georgia deeply impressed Wesley, and caused him to ponder more deeply about his own spiritual state. He lamented: 'I have a fair summer religion. I can talk well; nay, and believe myself, while no danger is near. But let death look me in the face, and my spirit is troubled.' He met the Moravian Peter Böhler who emphasized justification by faith, and urged Wesley: 'Preach faith until you have it; and then, because you have it, you will preach faith.'

On 24 May 1738 Wesley went to Aldersgate in London to hear a reading of Luther's *Preface to the Epistle to the Romans*. His words have deservedly become famous: 'I felt my heart strangely warmed. I felt I did trust in Christ, Christ alone for salvation; and an assurance was given me that He had taken away my sins, even mine, and saved me from the law of sin and death.' This is usually regarded as Wesley's conversion, although some contend that it should be understood in terms of assurance, not conversion.

Wesley's friend, George Whitefield, took to preaching in the open air in Bristol. His first congregation numbered over 200, and the hardened colliers melted before the sound of the gospel. Whitefield recorded: 'Having no righteousness of their own to renounce, they were glad to hear of a Jesus who was a friend of publicans.' Wesley was convinced: 'Having been all my life (till very lately) so tenacious of every point relating to decency and order, I should have thought the saving of souls almost a sin if it had not been done in a church.' But in April 1739 he, like David dancing before the ark of the covenant, 'submitted to be more vile'.

From 1739 until his death in 1791, Wesley travelled some 250,000 miles, usually on a horse, and preached some 40,000 sermons, never taking a holiday. He could sleep anywhere, and travelled in any kind of weather. He calmly looked mobs in the face, even when he was pelted with stones.

Wesley's aims were transparent: 'To reform the nation, particularly the Church, and to spread Scriptural holiness over the land.' He also set up dispensaries for the sick, a mutual benefit society, a school for colliers' children at Kingswood, and an orphan house at Newcastle. So great was the impact of the revival that Eli Halévy claimed that Methodism and Evangelicalism saved England from something like the violence and brutality that engulfed France after 1789.

Wesley had kept good health all his life. The day before he died, he was often asleep. During one of his waking moments, he asked what he had preached on a little while before at Hampstead. He was informed that his text was 2 Corinthians 8:9: 'For you know the grace of our Lord Jesus Christ, that though He was rich, yet for your sakes He became poor, that you through His poverty might become rich.' His response – indicating his physical weakness but his lucid spirituality – was: 'That is the foundation, the only foundation; there is no other.'

49

CHARLES WESLEY
(1707–1788)

Singing praise to the Lamb

*I have been crucified with Christ; it is no longer I who live,
but Christ lives in me; and the life which I now live in the
flesh I live by faith in the Son of God, who loved me and
gave Himself for me (Gal. 2:20).*

*Blessed is he whose transgression is forgiven,
whose sin is covered (Ps. 32:1).*

*He has put a new song in my mouth – praise to our God
(Ps. 40:3a).*

*'Comfort, comfort My people!' says your God
(Isa. 40:1).*

Behold the Lamb of God! (John 1:36b).

It is somewhat strange that the Wesley whose name has become so entwined with Methodism should be John Wesley, although most Christians have not read a word of what John wrote, while Charles's hymns are sung all over the globe. Charles was born on 18 December 1707, the eighteenth of the nineteen children born to Rev. Samuel and Susanna Wesley, and died in London in 1788. He was a gifted child who apparently learnt the alphabet in one day. At the age of eight, he left Epworth to study at Westminster School in London, where elder brother Samuel taught.

Charles went to Oxford in 1726 where he struggled spiritually for a time before founding the Holy Club. By 1735 he was ordained by the Bishop of London, and John virtually dragged him to Georgia in the American colonies to work as a missionary. However, sickness and a sense of failure soon saw him back in England within six months (John lasted twenty-two months).

Charles's experience of grace took place before John's heart was famously 'strangely warmed' on 24 May 1738. Charles's conversion is usually dated three days before John's, but it was associated with much spiritual struggle. He met with George Whitefield and Peter Böhler (a Moravian), and lived with John Bray, whom he described as 'a poor ignorant mechanic, who knows nothing but Christ; yet by knowing him, knows and discerns all things.'

On 14 May 1738 Charles wrote: 'I longed to find Christ, that I might show him to all mankind; that I might praise, that I might love him.' Within a few days, on 17 May, he recorded: 'I spent some hours this evening with Martin Luther [i.e. with Luther's commentary on Galatians], who was greatly blessed to me, especially his conclusion of the second chapter. I laboured, waited, and prayed to feel "who loved *me* and gave himself for *me*."'

On 21 May 1738 (the Day of Pentecost) Charles was prayerful but physically unwell. A number of influences struck him that day. John Bray read Psalm 32:1 to him, and Charles responded: 'I found myself convinced, I knew not how nor when.' He heard the voice of the wife of a 'poor ignorant mechanic' say: 'In the name of Jesus of Nazareth, arise, and believe, and thou shalt be healed of all thy infirmities.' Charles turned to his Bible and read from the Psalms: 'He hath put a new song in my mouth, even praise unto our God' (Ps. 40:3) and from Isaiah 40: 'Comfort ye, comfort ye my people, saith your God.' He recorded: 'I now found myself at peace with God, and rejoiced in the hope of loving Christ.' This was his conversion. He exclaimed: 'I was in a new heaven and a new earth!' Yet he also wrote: 'I never knew the energy of sin till now that I experience the superior strength of Christ.'

Charles took to preaching, although for the first five months after his conversion, he read his sermons. At Newgate prison he preached with success to condemned prisoners. He recorded: 'I found myself overwhelmed with the love of Christ to sinners.'

Itinerant evangelism had its dangers. The evangelists all faced riots, and on one occasion, Charles's horse rolled on him, and left him so dazed that he could not think properly for a day. Clergymen closed church doors to the Wesleys and to Whitefield, and they were heckled as madmen. Yet the impact was irresistible, and Charles wrote: 'All opposition falls before us, or rather is fallen ... This also the Lord wrought.'

Charles is best known as the poet of the revival. All in all he composed around 6,500 hymns – perhaps even as many as 9,000 – including 'Hark, the Herald Angels Sing'; 'Jesus, Lover of My Soul'; 'O for a Thousand Tongues to Sing'; 'And Can it Be?'; and 'Love Divine, All Loves Excelling' (Isaac Watts wrote about 600 hymns). They are literally saturated in Scripture. Charles was in the habit of jotting down thoughts, even as he rode his grey horse.

In 1749 Charles married Sarah (often known as Sally) Gwynne. Yet he even preached on his honeymoon! Sarah proved to be a capable and musical woman who died in 1822 at the age of 96. This was a happy union – unlike John's marriage to Molly Vazeille in 1751. Even in her eighties Sarah possessed a beautiful singing voice, and sang from Handel's *Messiah*. In her widowhood she was kindly provided for by William Wilberforce.

Worn out by his labours, Charles died in London in 1788. His life may be best illustrated from a hymn usually known today as 'Jesus! the Name high over all' (the original has 22 verses!):

O that the world might taste and see
The riches of His grace;
The arms of love that compass me
Would all mankind embrace.

His only righteousness I show,
His saving truth proclaim;
'Tis all my business here below
To cry 'Behold the Lamb!'

Happy, if with my latest breath
I may but gasp His Name;
Preach Him to all, and cry in death,
'Behold, behold the Lamb!'

50
GEORGE WHITEFIELD
(1714–1770)

Searching Spirit-filled preaching

You must be born again (John 3:7b).

*Who then is Paul, and who is Apollos, but ministers
through whom you believed, as the Lord gave to
each one?* (1 Cor. 3:5).

*Examine yourselves as to whether you are in the faith.
Test yourselves. Do you not know yourselves, that Jesus
Christ is in you? – unless indeed you are
disqualified* (2 Cor. 13:5).

George Whitefield's father died early, leaving his mother to
run 'The Bell' inn at Gloucester. Whitefield was to claim later
that, as a youth, he was addicted to lying, filthy talking, the
theatre, cards and reading romances. Yet he went to Oxford
University where he joined the Holy Club, fasted twice a week,
wore a patched gown and dirty shoes, and did not have his hair
powdered. He read William Law, Richard Baxter, Joseph Alleine
and Matthew Henry, but on reading Henry Scougal's *The Life
of God in the Soul of Man,* Whitefield realized his need to be
reborn.

Finally, in 1735 Whitefield was converted: 'O! with what joy
– joy unspeakable – even joy that was full of and big with glory,

was my soul filled, when the weight of sin went off, and an abiding sense of the pardoning love of God, and a full assurance of faith, broke in upon my disconsolate soul!' Ordination into the Church of England followed – as deacon in 1736 and as priest in 1739. After his first sermon, Whitefield heard that a complaint was made to the bishop that he had driven fifteen people mad. Charles Wesley commented: 'The whole nation is in an uproar.' After a quick trip to Georgia, Whitefield took to preaching in the open air in Bristol.

As a preacher, Whitefield was unrivalled. The actor David Garrick said he would give 100 guineas to be able to say 'Oh!' like Whitefield. He claimed that Whitefield could move people just by the way he pronounced 'Mesopotamia'. Henry Venn recorded of Whitefield: 'He no sooner opened his mouth as a preacher, than God commanded an extraordinary blessing upon his word.' Benjamin Franklin once emptied his pockets for Whitefield's Orphan House in Georgia after first determining to give nothing because he thought it should have been built in less remote Philadelphia.

In his preaching, Whitefield wounded before he healed, and refused to give comfort too soon. Yet no man could plead with sinners in so heartfelt a way as Whitefield. In 1755 John Newton went to hear him a number of times, and recorded that 'the power, the experience, the warmth with which he treated it I can by no means express, though I hope I feel the influence of it.' For all that, his sermon preparation was scanty – mostly he read the Bible and Matthew Henry's commentary.

By the end of his life Whitefield had preached in England, Wales, Scotland, Ireland, Bermuda and America – with seven trips to America and fifteen to Scotland. In so doing he united the whole revival in the English-speaking world as no other man did. In delivering Whitefield's funeral sermon in 1770, Wesley asked: 'Have we read or heard of any person since the apostles, who testified the gospel of the grace of God, through so widely extended a space, through so large a part of the habitable world?'

In his convictions and his manner, Whitefield was both firm and peace-loving. He declared: 'I embrace the Calvinistic scheme, not because Calvin, but Jesus Christ has taught it to me.' 'Man is nothing; he hath a free will to go to hell, but none to go to heaven, till God worketh in him to will and to do of His good pleasure.' Yet he did not want to argue with Wesley over election: 'I think it best not to dispute when there is no possibility of convincing.' He thought that in glory, Wesley would be so close to the throne that he (Whitefield) would not see him. Whitefield also told the Calvinistic but cantankerous Associate Presbytery who wanted him to separate from any contact with the Church of Scotland that if the pope offered him his pulpit, he would proclaim the righteousness of Christ from it.

Whitefield was humble and Christ-centred: 'I want to bring souls, not to a party ... but to a sense of their undone condition by nature, and to true faith in Jesus Christ ... But what is Calvin, or what is Luther? Let us look above names and parties; let Jesus Christ be our all in all ... I want not to have a people called after my name.' His prayer was: 'God give me a deep humility, a well-guided zeal, a burning love, and a single eye.' In 1748 he gave up his position as head of Calvinistic Methodism, and refused to head any party.

A play entitled *Doctor Squintum* satirized him – he had a squint. Many churches were shut to him because of his clear teaching on the need for regeneration. In 1742 at London, Whitefield recorded: 'I was honoured with having a few stones, dirt, rotten eggs, and pieces of dead cats thrown at me.' His journal for 30 December 1738 records: 'Preached nine times this week, and expounded near eighteen times ... I am every moment employed from morning till midnight.' He maintained that 'the best preparation for preaching on Sundays is to preach every day of the week.'

Indeed, he died after preaching halfway up the stairs of Jonathan Parsons's manse at Newburyport in Massachusetts in September 1770, after a crowd had gathered there and begged him to give them another sermon before he retired for the night. The weary Whitefield obliged, and, opening up 2 Corinthians 13:5 as his text, proclaimed: 'Works! works! A man gets to heaven by works! I would as soon think of climbing to the moon on a rope of sand.' Later that night an asthma attack took his life. Without doubt, he was the preacher whom God used most extensively in the Evangelical revival.

51

JONATHAN EDWARDS
(1703–1758)

Religious affections of the godly

*Now, to the King eternal, immortal, invisible, to God who
alone is wise, be honour and glory forever and ever.
Amen (1 Tim. 1:17).*

*For the moth will eat them up like a garment, and the
worm will eat them like wool; but My righteousness will
be forever, and My salvation from generation
to generation (Isa. 51:8).*

*For of Him and through Him and to Him are all things, to
whom be glory forever. Amen (Rom. 11:36).*

*[Jesus Christ] whom having not seen, you love. Though
now you do not see Him, yet believing, you rejoice with
joy inexpressible and full of glory (1 Pet. 1:8).*

Like John Wesley, Jonathan Edwards was born in 1703 to a
clerical father. Although Edwards never seems to have been
particularly worldly, his conversion was deep, the instrument
being 1 Timothy 1:17. He wrote:

> As I read the words, there came into my soul, and was as it were
> diffused through it, a sense of the glory of the divine Being; a
> new sense, quite different from any thing I ever experienced
> before. I thought with myself, how excellent a Being that was,

and how happy I should be, if I might enjoy that God, and be
wrapt up to God in heaven, and be swallowed up in him.

Edwards had beheld the holy beauty of God and for the rest of
his life he was governed by a sense of what might be called the
awful sweetness of the grace of God.

After going to Yale at age thirteen, Edwards was licensed
for the work of the ministry in 1722. He wrote regarding the
Scriptures: 'I felt a harmony between something in my heart,
and those sweet and powerful words.' He became the supply
preacher at a small breakaway Presbyterian church in New
York, then a city of 7,000–10,000 inhabitants, but in 1727 moved
to New England, to Northampton parish. In the same year he
married the beautiful, pious and capable Sarah Pierpont, and
they eventually became the parents of eleven children.

A tall and quiet man, Edwards was not particularly robust, but
he gained his exercise by chopping wood or riding horseback.
Except for emergencies, he was not in the habit of making
pastoral calls. If he were engaged in divine contemplation, he
would forgo dinner. He preached with quiet and reasoned
intensity; he said himself that he had 'a very plain, unfashionable
way of preaching'. Early in his career, he would read the small,
almost illegible handwriting of his manuscripts while staring at
the bell-rope at the back of the church, although after about
1741 he ceased to write his sermons out in full. Except in
theology, he was nothing like Whitefield. He made few gestures
– in fact, he rarely moved – and he made little appeal to elegance
of style or to the imagination.

Yet in December 1734 and in 1735 revival came after a
series of sermons on 'Justification by Faith'. Northampton had
a population of only about 200 families, but perhaps 300 or
more persons were converted in six months. Edwards later
recalled the situation in Northampton at that time: 'The town
seemed to be full of the presence of God; it never was so full

of love, nor of joy, and yet so full of distress, as it was then. There were remarkable tokens of God's presence in almost every house.' Then, on 1 June 1735, Edwards's uncle, Joseph Hawley, committed suicide by cutting his own throat, and the revival was suddenly stopped in its tracks.

Edwards preached a lengthy sermon series in 1739 on *A History of the Work of Redemption*, based on Isaiah 51:8. Edwards divided history into three great epochs of salvation – the Fall to the Incarnation; the Incarnation to the Resurrection; and the Resurrection to the end of the world. These cover the preparation, the purchase and the application of Christ's redemption. The third epoch consists of seven ages:

(a) the Resurrection to the destruction of Jerusalem;
(b) the destruction of Jerusalem to the reign of Constantine;
(c) Constantine to the rise of Antichrist (the papacy);
(d) the rise of Antichrist to the Reformation;
(e) the Reformation to the modern day;
(f) from the modern day to the fall of Antichrist;
(g) from the fall of Antichrist to the end of the world.

Edwards's vision was that 'All nations, in all parts of the world, on every side of the globe, shall ... be knit together in sweet harmony.' All comes from God and returns to Him to His glory. God, whose Trinitarian essence is love, is the beginning, the middle and the end of all history. Faith thus 'abases men, and exalts God', leading to the doxology of Romans 11:36.

In 1740 George Whitefield visited America and the revival fire came to life again. There were dangers on all sides in the revival, but Edwards sought to avoid both rationalism and hysteria. In 1746 he published his magnum opus, *Concerning the Nature of the Affections* and *Their Importance in Religion*, where he listed signs that proved nothing and signs that indicated the presence of true faith in Christ. To Edwards, faith was necessarily accompanied by emotion. Indeed, 'True religion, in great part, consists in holy affections.' 1 Peter 1:8 was his text, and he pointed out that 'the most superlative expressions are used which language will afford.'

As a pastor, Edwards could be clumsy. Some young people giggled over a handbook for midwives, and Edwards read their names out in church. George Marsden shrewdly observes of Edwards: 'Although he was a Calvinist in theology, he was a perfectionist by nature.' By 1750, by a majority of one in the church council, his own congregation dismissed Edwards, at the instigation of Joseph Hawley, a son of the man who committed suicide in 1735. Hawley later apologized, but Edwards bore it with magnanimity and held no grudges.

Edwards went to Stockbridge in 1751 to preach law and grace to the drunken Indians, the Housatunnocks. His main interpreter was a man called John Wauwaumppequunnaunt! Then in 1757 Edwards was called to become the president of the College of New Jersey. However, when he was inoculated against smallpox, he actually caught the disease and died on 22 March 1758. When Sarah heard the news, she wrote to her daughter Esther: 'A holy and good God has covered us with a dark cloud.' Edwards's last words were 'Trust in God and you need not fear.'

52

SELINA, COUNTESS OF HUNTINGDON
(1707–1791)

Not many nobles chosen

For you see your calling, brethren, that not many wise
according to the flesh, not many mighty, not many noble,
are called. But God has chosen the foolish things of the
world to put to shame the wise, and God has chosen
the weak things of the world to put to shame the things
which are mighty; and the base things of the world and
the things which are despised God has chosen, and the
things which are not, to bring to nothing the things
that are, that no flesh should glory in
His presence (1 Cor. 1:26-29).

Like John Wesley, Selina, who became the Countess of Huntingdon, lived through most of the eighteenth century. She was born in Stanton Harold, Leicestershire on 24 August 1707, and she died in London on 17 June 1791. She grew up to be a tall woman, who had a reputation for not having much dress sense. When her father died, Selina inherited a third part of his estate and a title.

From her youth she seemed to possess piety, ability and a strong temper. She became a cultured woman who also

186

followed the politics of the day. In 1728 she married Theophilus Hastings, the ninth Earl of Huntingdon, and moved to Donnington Park, Leicestershire. Selina gave birth to four sons and three daughters, but the mother outlived all her children, except for one daughter, Elizabeth, who did not sympathize with her mother's religious faith.

At the age of nine, Selina was deeply affected by a funeral of a child of her own age. This made her very aware of death, and she would often go to the grave of this little girl and pray there. Yet she seems to have received no positive religious instruction as a child. The Countess first heard evangelical teachings from her sister-in-law, Lady Margaret Hastings, who wrote to Selina: 'Since I have known and believed in the Lord Jesus Christ for salvation, I have been as happy as an angel.' Selina knew that she did not possess this, and so sought after God. She also became ill, and her conversion came about the same time as her restoration to health. In 1738 or early in 1739, Selina herself accepted the message, and, as she phrased it later, 'cast herself fully upon Christ for life and for salvation.'

Her husband asked the Bishop of Gloucester to dissuade her but, being a strong-minded woman, Selina refused to listen to the bishop. She joined the Fetter Lane Society, and took John Wesley's side in the fairly amicable split with the Moravians (Wesley opposed the 'stillness' doctrine and thought that faith did not require assurance).

Theophilus died in 1746, and never became a Christian so far as we know. He wrote: 'I greatly admire the morality of the Bible, but the doctrine of the atonement, I cannot comprehend.' In the initial dispute between Wesley and Whitefield, Selina had denounced predestination, but in 1748 she came to side with the Calvinistic Methodists. From the time of her conversion, she invited leaders of the social world to hear Methodist exhortations in her London apartment, and later in her Chelsea residence. She was the first giver of evangelical coffee mornings!

George Whitefield became her chaplain, and the Countess recalled his sermons as 'close, searching, experimental, awful and awakening'. Some aristocrats were converted, notably Lord Dartmouth and Lady Gertrude Hotham, but many others mocked, notably Bolingbroke, Chesterfield and David Hume.

The Duchess of Buckingham was decidedly hostile: 'It is monstrous to be told that you have a heart as sinful as the common wretches that crawl on the earth. This is highly offensive and insulting, and I cannot but wonder that your ladyship should relish any sentiments so much at variance with high rank and good breeding.' Later, when dying, she refused to allow the Countess of Huntingdon to visit her. It is small wonder that Lady Huntingdon used to say that she was very glad of the letter *m* in the text, 'Not many wise, not many mighty, not many noble are called' (1 Cor. 1:26).

As a peeress, Lady Huntingdon sponsored public evangelical Anglican services and appointed large numbers of evangelical clergy as personal chaplains on assignment throughout the south of England. In 1761 she sold her jewels to pay for the erection of a chapel at the popular resort of Brighton. Further chapels were opened – at Oat Hall, at Lewes, at Tunbridge Wells in Kent, in Bath, and elsewhere. Her aim appears to have been to provide an evangelical ministry where the parish clergy were not sympathetic. The chapel in Bath had a 'Nicodemus Corner' where bishops and clergy could hear Whitefield and others without being seen!

In addition, she sought to have ungodly behaviour suppressed on the stage and in public life, and would intervene to seek relief for dissenting clergy. In 1768, after evangelicals were excluded from Oxford, Lady Huntingdon established a training college at Trevecca in Wales. Tuition was free, the course was for three years, and the students were to have a new suit of clothes every year. After opening a huge chapel in Spa Fields in 1779, she was taken to court, and denied unlimited right to build chapels. She responded, reluctantly, by licensing all her chapels under the Toleration Act, which made all her chaplains Dissenters.

Her remarkable ministry was paid for from her personal fortune. After Whitefield willed her his orphanage in Georgia, she inherited its debts after it was destroyed by fire. Thereafter she struggled financially. Over her lifetime, when many parishes paid their clergy about £40 a year, Lady Huntingdon donated over £100,000 to the cause of Calvinistic Methodism. She outlived most of her friends, and was ready for her death, which occurred in 1791: 'As a stranger and pilgrim I look forward to the termination of my long journey with satisfaction. For then I shall see my Saviour as He is and meet all my friends and companions with whom I have so often taken sweet counsel on earth.'

53

Dr SAMUEL JOHNSON
(1709–1784)

After the Fall in the light of eternity

The night is coming when no one can work (John 9:4b).

*In this is love, not that we loved God, but that He loved
us and sent His Son to be the propitiation for
our sins* (1 John 4:10).

Vanity of vanities, all is vanity (Eccles. 1:2).

Samuel Johnson was born in Lichfield in England in 1709. At
school his natural laziness was curbed by strict discipline, and
this experience perhaps led him later to comment that 'There
is now less flogging in our great schools than formerly, but then
less is learned there; so that what the boys get at one end they
lose at the other.' He left Oxford University without taking a
degree in 1731 although the same university granted him the
degree of Doctor in Civil Law in 1775. All his life he was a man
of letters, who loved literature. A physically big, ungainly, sickly
and rather slovenly man, who was nicknamed the 'Great Bear',
he was a formidable figure both at the dinner table and in the
debating chamber. He was, to use his own word, a 'clubbable'
man who loved company, and whose laughter could be quite
loud and raucous.

Dr Johnson lived his life in time while looking to eternity. When the clergyman, Dr William Dodd, was hanged for fraud, Johnson made his well-known comment that 'When a man is going to be hanged in a fortnight it concentrates his mind wonderfully.' On Johnson's watch there was inscribed, in Greek, 'the night comes' – to remind him that time will eventually give way to eternity.

Johnson's world view was characterized by a robust grasp of the doctrine of original sin. He regarded the schemes and ambitions of men as a delusion – hence his long poem, *The Vanity of Human Wishes*. It is the message of Ecclesiastes – or at least the initial message: 'Vanity of vanities, all is vanity' As Johnson put it: 'Year chases year, decay pursues decay.' This pessimism about human nature led him to become a political Tory, who regarded 'Whiggism' as 'the negation of all principle'. Indeed, his view was that 'most schemes of political improvement are very laughable things.' Yet he was personally most compassionate and generous, and his house was usually full of the down-and-outs of society.

In his philosophical novella *The History of Rasselas*, Johnson portrays Rasselas as one who searches for happiness, but ultimately finds that the deepest wishes of mankind cannot be met in this life. Rasselas comes to embrace enough wisdom to tell young men: 'Let us live as men who are sometime to grow old' – but they drive him away with their laughter. He finds a man who believes in reason but cannot cope when his daughter dies; he also finds a wealthy man who is fearful precisely because his wealth makes him a target for thieves; and he listens to a philosopher but he understands him less as he hears him more. The poor are petty, the rich are treacherous. Rasselas laments: 'the more we enquire, the less we can resolve'.

Unlike his biographer, James Boswell, Johnson was appalled by the slave trade. In his political pamphlet *Taxation No Tyranny*, he made the memorable inquiry: 'How is it that we hear the loudest yelps for liberty among the drivers of negroes?' He combined hard-headed common sense with compassion in a remarkable Christian way. His home was a shelter for a number of poor down-and-outs in society.

Johnson regarded the evidences for the truth of Christianity as strong indeed – stronger than the evidence that the British had taken Canada from the French in the Seven Years War of 1756–63. Hence he declared: 'I know not any crime so great that a man could contrive to commit, as poisoning the sources of eternal truth.'

Throughout his life, Johnson was a man who knew spiritual anxieties and depression, but for some time before his death – which occurred on 13 December 1784 – his fears were calmed through his contemplation of the merits and propitiation of Christ. As he prepared to receive the sacrament for the last time on his deathbed, he prayed:

> Almighty and most merciful Father, I am now as to human eyes it seems, about to commemorate, for the last time, the death of thy Son Jesus Christ, our Saviour and Redeemer. Grant, O Lord, that my whole hope and confidence may be in his merits, and thy mercy; enforce and accept my imperfect repentance; make this commemoration available to the confirmation of my faith, the establishment of my hope, and the enlargement of my charity; and make the death of thy Son Jesus Christ effectual to my redemption.

54

WILLIAM GRIMSHAW
(1708–1763)

Living and dying in Christ

For to me, to live is Christ, and to die is gain
(Phil. 1:21).

William Grimshaw lived and died in Yorkshire in the north of England, and never visited London. Virtually nothing is known of his family, except that they were poor. Later in life he seems to have considered that his father was a true Christian but his mother was not. He suffered from smallpox as a child, which left his face with the characteristic pockmarks, but he grew up to be tall and well built. Later, his physical exertions in the cause of the gospel were to prompt Henry Venn to comment that 'William Grimshaw used his body with less compassion than a merciful man would use his beast.' He dared all weather in the bleak mountains of Yorkshire.

In 1726 he went as a sizar (poor student) to Christ's College, Cambridge, and for the first two years was sober and diligent, but then learned how, in his words, to 'drink, swear, and what not'. His academic work suffered and he only just managed to scrape through his degree. In 1731 he was ordained deacon, in order to gain a respectable profession and obtain a good living.

He worked at Rochdale for a brief time, then at Todmorden. In 1732 he was ordained priest by Bishop Peploe of Chester.

As a priest, he initially made some attempt to hide his university habits but soon came to drink and be merry with his parishioners. He engaged in some bizarre pranks. He once dressed up as the devil to frighten a man into marrying the girl he had seduced. He also felt his own inadequacy when he tried to counsel a woman whose infant daughter had just died. He advised the grieving parents: 'Put away all gloomy thoughts, and go into merry company and divert yourselves, and all will soon be right.' However, he did add: 'To despair of the mercy of God would be the worst thing of all.'

About 1734 he began to forsake hunting, fishing, card-playing and revelling, and took up visiting in a serious way. He also began to pray in secret four times a day. Also, he married a widow in 1735 (she had proposed to him!) but she died in 1739, leaving him with two young children – John and Jane. He was plunged into despair, and once at Todmorden told the congregation: 'My friends, we are all in a damnable state, and I scarcely know how we are to get out of it!' He began to read the works of the Puritans, Thomas Brooks and John Owen, but, initially at least, he knew nothing of Wesley and Whitefield. He married again in 1741, but his second wife died in 1746 and he never remarried.

In 1742 he became the minister of Haworth in Yorkshire, and was to remain there for 21 years. It was a rough and uncivilized place, with a high infant mortality rate and a life expectancy of little more than twenty-five. Mainly through reading John Owen's works, Grimshaw came to evangelical views. He later told Henry Venn: 'I was now willing to renounce myself, every degree of fancied merit and ability, and to embrace Christ only for my all in all. O what light and comfort did I now enjoy in my own soul, and what a taste of the pardoning love of God!' Not all appreciated the change in him, and his nickname became 'Mad Grimshaw'.

Revival broke out in 1742. People crowded the church, and many were obliged to stand outdoors. Grimshaw began to preach in a kind of Methodist circuit consisting of twelve separate centres. He once wrote: 'By the grace of God, I'm resolved never to flag while I can ride, walk, creep or crawl.' In 1742 there were twelve regular communicants at Haworth, but by 1748 he could count 400–500 in the winter and up to 1200 in the summer. He declared: 'When I die I shall then have my greatest grief and my greatest joy – my greatest grief that I have done so little for Jesus, and my greatest joy that Jesus has done so much for me.'

Doctrinally, he was a moderate Calvinist, but he had no love of controversy. When a number of his converts became Baptists, he commented: 'So many of my chickens turn ducks!' He once wrote to John Wesley to rebuke him for his teaching on sinless perfection. A rather boisterous character, Grimshaw aimed to speak very plainly, sometimes for two hours, in what he called 'market language'. He travelled widely, preached twenty to thirty times a week, and ordinary people heard him gladly. To Grimshaw, preaching consisted of 'debasing man and exalting my dear Lord in all his offices.'

Once he prayed for rain so that the Haworth races would not be held, and there was a deluge. On another occasion he disguised himself as a poor beggar and went to the house of a couple who made extravagant claims about their holiness. The man refused to help him, and after a time Grimshaw removed his disguise and gave them a lecture on covetousness and hard-heartedness. When a woman expressed her admiration for a minister with more talents than grace, Grimshaw was blunt: 'I am glad you never saw the devil.' There is something inimitable about him.

While visiting, he caught a fever and died in 1763, aged 54. Henry Venn, of Huddersfield, came to see his dying friend, and asked him how he felt. Grimshaw's reply was 'I am as happy as

I can be on earth, and as sure of glory as if I were in it.' He had Philippians 1:21 inscribed on his coffin, and Venn preached his funeral sermon.

Grimshaw only ever had two children. Jane died at the age of twelve when at Wesley's Kingswood School in 1750. His son, John, was careless about spiritual matters but came to see his father as he lay dying in 1763. The father bluntly told the son that he (John) was not fit to die. The startled son was so shaken that he sought after God and was soon converted. But he was to die himself just three years later, and as he was dying, he asked: 'What will my old father say when he sees I have got to heaven?' John Wesley paid old Grimshaw a fitting tribute: 'A few such as him would make a nation tremble. He carries fire wherever he goes.'

55

HENRY VENN
(1724–1797)

The Lord our righteousness

*Behold, the days are coming, says the Lord, that I will raise
to David a Branch of righteousness; a King shall reign and
prosper, and execute judgment and righteousness in the
earth. In His days Judah will be saved, and Israel will dwell
safely; now this is His name by which He will be called:
The Lord our righteousness* (Jer. 23:5-6).

*Set your mind on things above, not on things
on the earth* (Col. 3:2).

Henry Venn was the vicar of Huddersfield in Yorkshire, then
vicar of Yelling in Huntingdonshire. He was born at Barnes in
Surrey in 1724, a descendant of a long line of clergymen reaching
back to the Reformation (his father was Rev. Richard Venn).

A vigorous and high-spirited youth, he went off in 1742 to
St John's College, Cambridge, but soon went to Jesus College
on obtaining a scholarship there. He graduated B.A. in 1745
and M.A. in 1749. He was ordained deacon by Bishop Gibson
in 1747. By 1749 he was ministering in various places around
Cambridge, then in 1750 in London and Horsley. In 1754 he
became curate of Clapham, near London.

Venn was a fine cricketer, but played his last game just
before he was ordained. At first his ministry was zealous without

being evangelical. He read William Law's *Serious Call to a Devout and Holy Life*, which had much influenced the Wesleys. He prayed and fasted, and preached six sermons a week at Clapham. In 1756 he was laid aside sick for eight months, but recovered by 1757 to marry Miss Bishop, the daughter of an Anglican clergyman and a pious and congenial companion. He also met John Thornton, Dr Thomas Haweis, and later Whitefield, Wesley, Grimshaw, Romaine and Lady Huntingdon. Lady Huntingdon wrote him a letter on 'The Lord our righteousness', and it had the desired effect. He took to the Scriptures with renewed eagerness, and came to see clearly its teachings on justification by faith. Venn's conversion is probably to be dated in 1758.

In 1759 Venn was appointed vicar of Huddersfield. John Wesley had visited there in 1757, and commented: 'A wilder people I never saw in England.' Venn was to remain there until 1771. Numbers swelled, and he preached some eight to ten times a week. The revival began to break out, and Venn's outdoor preaching was especially useful. In the one sermon, he would look stern as he preached the law, smile as he spoke of grace, and sometimes weep as he entreated people to believe in Christ. During a three-year period at Huddersfield, Venn himself reckoned that there were about 900 conversions.

However, Venn's health began to collapse – he was racked by a cough, he spat up blood, and suffered from consumption (tuberculosis). Any effort at preaching and he was laid aside for days. In 1767 his wife died, leaving him with five young children. There was no choice but for him to move. His last sermon at Huddersfield was on Colossians 3:2. In 1771, because his voice had broken down, Venn had to move to a small country living called, ironically enough, Yelling! He did so reluctantly: 'No human being can tell how keenly I feel this separation from a people I have dearly loved.' It was all the worse because a stridently anti-evangelical cleric succeeded him at Huddersfield. Most of his converts became Dissenters.

Venn met and married a widow at this time. Throughout his life, despite his failing health, he would rise at 5.00 a.m. to pray and read the Scriptures, and later catechize his family. No doubt remembering his conversion, he defined saving faith as 'a dependence upon Christ for righteousness and strength, as having paid to the justice of God full satisfaction of his broken law, and obtained acceptance for all believers in his name, to the reward of eternal life.'

It was as a correspondent that Venn shone, and he maintained an extensive correspondence in the days when letters were truly epistles. As a letter writer and wise counsellor, he can be compared to John Newton. He once wrote to a rich widow in London: 'In the day when the eternal state of man is determined, the greater part of those who are lost will perish, not through any gross and scandalous iniquity, but through a deadness to God and his love, an ignorance of their own sinfulness, and, in consequence of that, through reigning pride and self-sufficiency.'

In his family Venn was wise, diligent and successful. He wrote with honesty and affection to his children. One of his daughters married a widower with young children, and Venn gently but firmly cured one of them of his fear of the dark. He told one of his grandsons: 'Remember, little John, if anything could make heaven not heaven to me, it would be the not having you with me there.' Venn's influence was felt in his descendants. Henry's son, John Venn (1759–1813), became the Rector of Clapham in 1792. The so-called Clapham Sect did much to encourage the cause of missions and to fight the slave trade. John's son, Henry (1796–1873), named after his grandfather, was the secretary of the Church Missionary Society from 1841 to 1872. He urged 'the euthanasia of a mission', meaning that churches were to be led by indigenous Christians, not missionaries.

As his health slipped away, Henry Venn the elder declared: 'I have a great work before me, to suffer and to die to his glory.' He was happy in life and happy in death, passing away at the age of seventy-three in 1797. Charles Simeon recalled of him: 'In all the twenty-four years that I knew him, I never remember him to have spoken unkindly of any one but once; and then I was struck with the humiliation he expressed for it in prayer next day.'

56

JOHN NEWTON
(1725–1807)

Conviction by the Word of God

*Because I have called and you refused, I have stretched
out my hand and no one regarded, because you disdained
all my counsel, and would have none of my rebuke, I also
will laugh at your calamity ... Then they will call on me,
but I will not answer ... Because they hated knowledge
and did not choose the fear of the Lord ... Therefore they
shall eat the fruit of their own way* (Prov. 1:24-31).

*If you, then, being evil, know how to give good gifts to
your children, how much more will your heavenly Father
give the Holy Spirit to those who ask Him!* (Luke 11:13).

*If anyone wills to do His will, he shall know concerning
the doctrine, whether it is from God or whether I speak
on My own authority* (John 7:17).

*Behold! The Lamb of God who takes away the
sin of the world!* (John 1:29b).

Dr Johnson once described being on a ship as like being in a gaol,
'with the chance of being drowned'. This should have meant something to John Newton, for he never learnt to swim. Despite that
handicap, at age eleven he went to sea as his father's cabin boy.

Newton's mother died of tuberculosis in 1732, two weeks
before John's seventh birthday. But she had taught John from the

201

Bible and from Isaac Watts's songs. As Newton later testified: 'She stored my memory, which was then very retentive, with many valuable pieces, chapters and portions of Scripture, catechism, hymns and poems.' Four years later, Newton joined his father as his cabin boy. Despite a number of brushes with death – being thrown from a horse and nearly being impaled, as well as just missing a longboat which overturned, drowning a friend of Newton's – he thought little of the precariousness of life or claims of Christ. Instead, he devoured the writings of the Deists, who believed that God existed, but that He had not revealed Himself in Christ. He fell in love with Mary Catlett, whom he usually called Polly, but he continued to lead a life that he later lamented was one of 'licentiousness and folly'.

In 1744 he was pressed into the Navy, but the following year saw him exchanged for a seaman. As a result, he sailed to Sierra Leone on the *Pegasus*, a slave trader. Newton led such a degraded lifestyle that he composed bawdy ballads, made up blasphemous oaths and even took to worshipping the moon. On one occasion he nearly lost his life retrieving his hat while intoxicated after a drinking contest. Later, on board the *Greyhound*, he found a copy of Thomas à Kempis' *The Imitation of Christ*, which seems to have prepared him for what was to follow.

On 10 March 1748 (in the Julian calendar, which became 21 March when the Gregorian calendar was adopted in 1752) he was on board the *Greyhound* when it was caught in a fierce storm. The storm was so terrifying that Newton was lashed shirtless to the helm. For sixteen years he had lived a dissolute, rebellious and hardened lifestyle, but in this crisis the seeds sown by his godly mother bore fruit. He recalled to mind the words of Proverbs 1:24-31, and was convicted that they applied to him.

Newton wondered whether he was a spiritual castaway, without hope. However, Christ was drawing him to Himself, and Newton was encouraged by reading the New Testament, especially Luke 11:13 and John 7:17. He also read a powerful sermon by William Beveridge on John 1:29. For four frightening weeks, the *Greyhound* struggled across the Atlantic towards the coast of Ireland. On land at Londonderry, Newton attended public worship twice daily, and prepared himself to take Holy Communion. Ever afterwards, Newton would remember 21 March each year: 'On that day the Lord sent from on high and delivered me out of deep waters.' This day should not be regarded as the day of Newton's conversion but his awakening that would lead to his coming to saving faith in Christ. The reality of sin, death and judgment struck Newton so that he became serious about his relationship with God.

After marrying his beloved Mary in 1750, Newton bought a succession of lottery tickets in the hope of winning enough money so that he would not have to go to sea again. Not surprisingly, he won nothing. In the years from 1750 to 1754 he went to sea three times and, while collecting slaves, he wrote in his logbook: '*Soli Deo Gloria*'. Later he was to say that 'Custom, example, and interest, had blinded my eyes.' By July 1754, however, he was writing: 'I need no one to pronounce an absolution on me; I can tell myself that my sins are forgiven me, because I know in whom I have believed.' Conviction of sin and judgment had become conviction of the saving grace of the Saviour.

57

JOHN NEWTON
(1725–1807)

Grateful for grace

*Since you were precious in My sight, you have
been honoured* (Isa. 43:4a).

*You shall remember that you were a slave in the land of
Egypt, and the Lord your God redeemed
you* (Deut. 15:15a).

*I have set the Lord always before me; because He is at
my right hand I shall not be moved* (Ps. 16:8).

*Then King David went in and sat before the Lord; and
said: 'Who am I, O Lord God? And what is my house, that
You have brought me this far? And yet this was a small
thing in Your sight, O God; and You have also spoken
of Your servant's house for a great while to come, and
have regarded me according to the rank of a man of high
degree, O Lord God'* (1 Chron. 17:16-17).

Bless the Lord, O my soul, and forget not all His benefits
(Ps. 103:2).

*Therefore, whatever you want men to do to you, do also
to them, for this is the Law and the Prophets*
(Matt. 7:12).

*Though the fig tree may not blossom, nor fruit be on the
vines; though the labour of the olive may fail, and the
fields yield no food; though the flock may be cut off from
the fold, and there be no herd in the stalls — yet I will
rejoice in the Lord, I will joy in the God of my salvation*
(Hab. 3:17-18).

And the Lord said, 'Who then is that faithful and wise
steward, whom his master will make ruler over his
household, to give them their portion of food in due
season? Blessed is that servant whom his master will find
so doing when he comes' (Luke 12:42-43).

Above the fireplace in his study at Olney, John Newton painted on the bare plaster two texts, Isaiah 43:4 and Deuteronomy 15:15, in the King James Version. Newton is not only the man who wrote the hymn 'Amazing Grace', but was one who sought to never lose the wonder of what it means to be saved through God's undeserved favour. A seizure threatened his life, and ended his career as a sailor, so in 1755 he took up the job of Surveyor of the Tides at Liverpool. After being converted almost without human means, Newton now sought the fellowship of evangelical leaders and preachers, including William Romaine, William Grimshaw and George Whitefield. In five days he heard Whitefield preach nine times.

In 1758 he suffered two disappointments. First, he preached in the Independent White Chapel at Leeds, his text being Psalm 16:8. He took no notes with him into the pulpit, lost his place and became so confused that he had to ask the pastor to finish the sermon for him. In the light of this, the second disappointment is perhaps not such a shock: he applied to the Archbishop of York for ordination, but was refused. However, Lord Dartmouth prevailed upon the Bishop of Lincoln to ordain him to Olney in 1764; and in 1780 he moved to St Mary Woolnoth Church in London.

In 1779, together with William Cowper, Newton produced the *Olney Hymns*. Newton's best-known hymn is undoubtedly 'Amazing Grace', which was based on a sermon he preached at New Year on David's response to God's promises to him in 1 Chronicles 17:16-17. Grace always amazed him, and so Psalm 103:2 was another verse that he often pondered. One day the Nonconformist pastor of Bath, William Jay, visited him, and Newton mentioned the name of a man who had once attended Jay's church, but later immersed himself 'almost in all evil'. He had written a very penitent letter to Newton. Jay's response was: 'He may be such; but, if he be, I should never despair of the conversion of any one again.' To which Newton replied: 'Oh, I never did, since God saved me.'

Newton also took a part in attacking the slave trade, which in his unbelieving days had been his livelihood. In 1788, he published his remorseful *Thoughts Upon the African Slave Trade*, based on the Golden Rule of Matthew 7:12. He confessed: 'I hope it will always be a subject of humiliating reflection to me, that I was once an active instrument in a business at which my heart now shudders.' Love and humility pervaded all that he did and said. As a pastor, a letter writer and a counsellor, Newton was a man with few equals in the history of the Church. Saving grace blossomed into sanctifying grace.

On 15 December 1790 Mary died, and a distraught Newton wrote: 'The world seemed to die with her.' Newton's next sermon, characteristically, was on Habakkuk 3:17-18. In the most bitter of circumstances, he had learned to look to the undeserved goodness of God. His pulpit ministry finished not unlike the way it started. At his last service in late 1806, his curate had to remind him what he was preaching about. By December 1807 he was virtually blind, and was writing: 'My memory is nearly gone; but I remember two things: that I am a great sinner, and that Christ is a great Saviour.' Four days before Christmas in that same year, Newton died, having first composed his own epitaph. The first half of it reads: 'John Newton, clerk, once an infidel and libertine, a servant of slaves in Africa, was, by the rich mercy of our Lord and Saviour Jesus Christ, preserved, restored, pardoned, and appointed to preach the faith he had long laboured to destroy.' At his funeral service, Richard Cecil, on Newton's own instructions, preached on Luke 12:42-43.

58

WILLIAM COWPER
(1731–1800)

The struggles of the 'stricken deer'

Jesus said to her, 'I am the resurrection and the life. He who believes in Me, though he may die, he shall live' (John 11:25).

[Christ Jesus] whom God set forth as a propitiation by His blood, through faith, to demonstrate His righteousness, because in His forbearance God had passed over the sins that were previously committed (Rom. 3:25).

But I discipline my body and bring it into subjection, lest, when I have preached to others, I myself should become disqualified (1 Cor. 9:27; for 'disqualified', the KJV has 'castaway').

William Cowper (pronounced 'Cooper') was born in 1731 at Berkhamsted, Hertfordshire. He was the son of John Cowper, a depressive poet and a chaplain. His mother was Anne Donne, a descendant of John Donne (the poet and Dean of St Paul's), but she died when William was only six. The maids foolishly tried to keep the news of her death from young William – which probably made his grief all the greater.

Cowper suffered from weak eyesight – which only improved after he contracted smallpox – and did not fit in with many boyish activities. His childhood was not a happy one, and he wrote of one bullying fifteen-year-old: 'I knew him by his shoe-buckles, better than any other part of his dress.' From 1741 to 1749 he studied at Westminster School and received a thorough grounding in the classics: Homer, Addison, Steele, Milton, Dryden, Swift, Johnson and Gray. He also translated Voltaire.

One night a gravedigger threw up a skull which hit him on the leg, and had the effect of reminding him of his mortality. He gave way to melancholy, but it suddenly lifted at Southampton by the sea. George Herbert's poetry also helped him. This proved to be his first bout of serious depression. Cowper's father pushed him into law, and in 1754 Cowper was called to the bar. However, he seems never to have taken a case. In 1757 he had to cope with two losses in his life – he courted his first cousin, Theodora Cowper, but her father objected and the romance ended; and his friend Sir William Russell drowned.

Facing a public examination, the fragile Cowper tried to hang himself, but the garter broke. He then thought that he had committed the unpardonable sin – of not killing himself! He continued to decline, and he was sent to the evangelical Dr Nathaniel Cotton's House for Madmen at St Albans. For six months, Cowper was in despair: 'Conviction of sin and expectation of instant judgment never left me.' He described himself as living in 'a fleshly tomb ... buried above ground'.

Cowper's sanity was restored for a time through conversion, which came in 1764 when he picked up a Bible and read John 11 on the raising of Lazarus from the dead. This, said Cowper, 'melted my heart'. Walking in a garden, he found a Bible and read Romans 3:25. The impact was immediate: 'I saw the sufficiency of the atonement He had made, my pardon sealed in His blood, and all the fullness and completeness of His justification.'

After becoming friends with a young theological student, William Unwin, Cowper took up residence with the Unwin family, and Mrs Mary Unwin, who was only seven years older than Cowper, was destined to look after him until she died in 1796.

After the Unwin family moved to Olney, Cowper was encouraged by the ministry and friendship of John Newton. In 1779 Newton published the *Olney Hymns* with Cowper. There were 67 hymns by Cowper and 281 by Newton. Cowper saw himself as a damned advocate for the evangelical revival. Ironically enough, Cowper has been called 'the real father of whimsical writing' – although it is difficult to imagine anyone less whimsical in personality.

Slavery aroused Cowper's indignation, and he wrote against it in *Charity* and *The Task* (Book III). He also wrote the ballad *The Negro's Complaint*. He was wary of science, and thought that ballooning, for example, was contrary to nature and God's will. In 1785 Cowper wrote to Newton: 'I am like a slug or snail, that has fallen into a deep well.' He died quietly in Norfolk in 1800, amidst various attempts to assure him of his salvation, either through concocted dreams or a voice speaking through a tube behind his bed.

Cowper's best-known hymns are 'O for a closer walk with God'; 'Hark my Soul! It is the Lord'; 'There is a fountain filled with blood'; 'Jesus, where'er thy people meet'; and the marvellous 'God moves in a mysterious way', first published in 1774. Yet in his life he often seemed far removed from what he was describing. He described himself as 'a stricken deer that left the herd', trailing an arrow in its side. His sad final poem was *The Castaway,* the story of a mariner lost overboard. Based on 1 Corinthians 9:27, its conclusion is:

> *We perish'd, each alone;*
> *But I beneath a rougher sea,*
> *And whelm'd in deeper gulphs than he.*

When Newton was told of Cowper's death, he wrote most movingly of Christian friendship, and of reunion in the life to come:

My friend, my friend! and have we met again,
Far from the home of woe, the home of men;
And has thou taken thy glad harp once more,
Twined with far lovelier wreaths than e'er before;
And is thy strain more joyous and more loud,
While circle round thee heaven's attentive crowd?

Oh! let thy memory wake! I told thee so;
I told thee thus would end thy heaviest woe;
I told thee that thy God would bring thee here,
And God's own hand would wipe away thy tear
While I should claim a mansion by thy side,
I told thee so – for our Emmanuel died.

Newton preached the funeral sermon on Ecclesiastes 2:2-3.

59

THOMAS SCOTT
(1747–1821)

The force of Truth

Then Saul, who also is called Paul, filled with the Holy Spirit, looked intently at him and said, 'O full of all deceit and all fraud, you son of the devil, you enemy of all righteousness, will you not cease perverting the straight ways of the Lord?' (Acts 13:9-10).

All we like sheep have gone astray; we have turned, every one, to his own way; and the Lord has laid on Him the iniquity of us all (Isa. 53:6).

And the tax collector, standing afar off, would not so much as raise his eyes to heaven, but beat his breast, saying, 'God, be merciful to me a sinner!' (Luke 18:13).

When Thomas Scott was ordained as an Anglican deacon in September 1772, he held to no evangelical beliefs. He had been born the son of a grazier, and had met his wife at a christening where he had won her money at cards, but was attracted to her by the way she took her defeat well. She proved to be a sweet-tempered woman. At one stage, he had been apprenticed to a surgeon, but sent home in disgrace for some misconduct. After a long stint as a shepherd, he decided to become a clergyman.

At this stage, Scott believed that he could save himself, that Christ was not divine, and that the Holy Spirit was of no consequence, even assuming that He existed. Like a number of other great evangelical leaders – notably Abraham Kuyper, Thomas Chalmers and John Wesley – Scott was a Christian pastor before he was a Christian. In his autobiography, *The Force of Truth*, he was to admit: 'As a minister, I attended just enough to the public duties of my station to support a decent character.'

Out of curiosity, Scott sneaked in to hear John Newton preach. To his horror, Newton's text was Acts 13:9-10. Arriving curious, Scott went home startled and disgusted. Although he was in the neighbouring parish to Newton and although he never read their books, Scott despised 'Methodism'. However, Newton's care for two of Scott's dying parishioners and then Scott himself during a time of illness softened Scott's attitude towards evangelicalism. Newton clearly possessed something that Scott did not.

On Good Friday 1777 he preached on Isaiah 53:6, and publicly renounced all his previous convictions and perversions of Scripture. Scott had embraced the evangelical and biblical faith that men and women, as sinners, could never save themselves from sin and death and judgment, but that Christ was sufficient. Scott proclaimed that 'Christ indeed bore the sins of all who should ever believe, in all their guilt, condemnation, and deserved punishment, in his own body on the tree.'

In the providence of God it was Scott who succeeded Newton at Olney – after a short interlude when Newton's immediate successor came and went. Like Matthew Henry, Scott wrote a much-respected commentary on the whole Bible – which took him thirty-three years to complete. Men as far apart as William Carey and John Henry Newman expressed their indebtedness to him. Hannah More recalled hearing Thomas Scott preach: 'With the worst voice, the most northern accent, and very plain manners, sound sense and sound piety were yet so predominant that like Aaron's serpent, they swallowed up the rest.'

Scott lived as a pilgrim for the rest of his life. He warned: 'Whatever we idolize or grow proud of, God will generally take from us, or else convert it into a cross.' His message was: 'Time how short! eternity, how long! life how precarious and vanishing! death how certain! the pursuits and employments of this present life how vain, unsatisfying, trifling, and vexatious! God's favour and eternal life how unspeakably precious! His wrath, the never-quenched fire, the never-dying worm, how dreadful!'

When Scott was dying in 1821, Daniel Wilson tried to comfort him by telling him what a great benefit he had been to the Church. Scott stopped him: 'Now this is doing me harm. "God be merciful to me a sinner" is the only ground on which I can rest.'

60

HANNAH MORE
(1745–1833)

Educating the poor in love

How can I give you up, Ephraim? (Hosea 11:8a).

And now abide faith, hope, love, these three; but the greatest of these is love (1 Cor. 13:13).

Now concerning things offered to idols: We know that we all have knowledge. Knowledge puffs up, but love edifies (1 Cor. 8:1).

And God will wipe away every tear from their eyes; there shall be no more death, nor sorrow, nor crying. There shall be no more pain, for the former things have passed away (Rev. 21:4).

Hannah More was one of five children, all daughters, who enjoyed a happy childhood and a close relationship with her father, Jacob More. When Hannah was just thirteen years of age, the sisters opened a school in Bristol, with Martha (known as Mary) being the principal, at all of nineteen years of age. Hannah was writing plays and poems from an early age, but increasingly came under the influence of Dr James Stonehouse, her clergyman neighbour who had turned from Deism to Evangelicalism. Yet she remained an ardent admirer of the actor David Garrick until his death in 1779.

Hannah mixed with many literary and political figures – her local Member of Parliament was Edmund Burke; she introduced the ageing Charles Wesley to William Wilberforce; and she knew Dr Samuel Johnson well enough for him to chide her for reading Henry Fielding's somewhat racy novel *Tom Jones*. Increasingly, the world failed to satisfy her.

In 1789 the More sisters sold their Bristol school. At Bath, Hannah attended the evening services of the evangelical Nonconformist William Jay for about twelve years. At a time when high society lived by the quip of Horace Walpole, who declared that the Fourth Commandment did not apply to persons of status and fashion as they did nothing on the other six days of the week, Hannah wrote essays and treatises to teach that being virtuous is more significant than being fashionable.

She was coming to see how God works in His people: 'Affliction is the school in which great virtues are acquired, in which great characters are formed. It is a kind of moral Gymnasium, in which the disciples of Christ are trained to robust exercise, hardy exertion, and severe conflict.' By 1788 Hannah was involved in boycotting West Indian sugar in her tea as a protest against the slave trade. She fought for the welfare of the slaves as those created in the 'sacred image' of God, but also saw that the French Revolution was ushering in a different kind of slavery. She contrasted evangelical liberty with what she called 'that unlicensed monster of the crowd':

> *Clamouring for peace, she rends the air with noise,*
> *And to reform a part, the whole destroys.*
> *Reviles oppression only to oppress,*
> *And in the act of murder, breathes redress.*

Her convictions were settled: 'I know of no way of teaching morals but by infusing principles of Christianity, nor of teaching Christianity without a thorough knowledge of Scripture.'

Hannah and Patty More began to open a number of schools in poor areas, starting with the small village of Cheddar in 1789. Girls were taught reading, sewing, knitting, spinning and Scripture, for 'God has promised His blessing on His Word.' At Blagdon the local curate organized a campaign against Hannah but she refused to back down, citing: 'How shall I give thee up, Ephraim?' Her confession, somewhat confusingly, was neither Calvinistic nor Arminian: 'Bible Christianity is what I love; that does not insist on opinions indifferent in themselves; – a Christianity practical and pure, which teaches holiness, humility, repentance and faith in Christ; and which after summing up all the evangelical graces, declares that the greatest of these is charity.'

Hannah opened up her home in Bath to exiled French Roman Catholic priests, and donated the proceeds of her *Village Politics*, published in 1793, to their welfare. Tracts flowed from her pen, to be sold for a halfpenny up to a penny-halfpenny. She mocked those who philosophized about helping the millions while having so little compassion for individuals. I Corinthians 8:1 was a verse that she would cite as she sought to make religion 'a part of our common life'. She viewed the Christian faith not as 'a beautiful theory but a soul-sustaining truth'.

William Cobbett was a Radical who favoured slavery, and he accused Wilberforce: 'You seem to have a great affection for the fat and lazy and laughing and singing and dancing negroes.' While he was at it, Cobbett ridiculed Hannah as the 'Old Bishop in Petticoats'. William Jay was closer to the truth when he said that 'upon her lips was the law of kindness.'

Hannah's four sisters died in steady succession, from 1813 to 1819, and in old age she thought of Revelation 21:4, and where the Lamb shall be the light.

61

WILLIAM CAREY
(1761–1834)

Expecting great things

*Therefore let us go forth to Him, outside the camp,
bearing His reproach* (Heb. 13:13).

*Go therefore and make disciples of all the nations,
baptizing them in the name of the Father and of the Son
and of the Holy Spirit* (Matt. 28:19).

*Enlarge the place of your tent ... for you shall expand to
the right and to the left, and your descendants will inherit
the nations, and make the desolate cities
inhabited* (Isa. 54:2-3).

William Carey was born in 1761, the son of a weaver who was
also the village schoolmaster in the obscure rural community
of Paulerspury, buried in the middle of England. He took up
an indoor trade – shoemaking – because of allergies which he
developed at the age of seven. His uncle, Peter Carey, returned
from Canada with tales of travel, and Carey read so much about
Columbus that it became his nickname.

Carey was raised an Anglican, but was converted through
the witness of a fellow cobbler, John Warr, a Dissenter, who
lent him books. He was convicted of his sin after he lied about a
counterfeit shilling; and convicted of the claims of Dissent after

hearing a sermon on 10 January 1779 on Hebrews 13:13. In 1783 he was baptized into the Baptist Church by John Ryland Jr, but he joined John Sutcliff's church at Olney, where John Newton and then Thomas Scott ministered. In 1785 he preached a trial sermon which was received less than enthusiastically. Despite this, he was called as pastor at Moulton (on £10 a year), where he laboured for four years, making shoes and teaching school as well as preaching.

Carey learnt Latin, Greek, Hebrew, Dutch and French, and claimed that 'It is well known to require no very extraordinary talents to learn, in the space of a year, or two at most, the language of any people upon earth, so much of it, at least, as to be able to convey any sentiments we wish to their understandings.' From Moulton, Carey moved in 1789 to Harvey Lane in Leicester, where he found the church under the reign of antinomianism (the rejection of God's law), due partly to the doctrinal underpinning of Hyper-Calvinism (the view that the gospel should only be preached to the elect). He tackled the problem by sending the church membership back to scratch, and starting again.

In 1781 Carey married Dorothy (Dolly) Plackett, who was five years his senior and illiterate, although he later taught her to read and write. Reading a borrowed copy of Captain James Cook's *Voyages* had an impact on Carey. Cook himself had no particular interest in Christianity, and had written rather provocatively concerning missions: 'It is very unlikely, that any measure of this kind should ever be seriously thought of, as it can neither serve the purposes of public ambition, nor of private avarice; and, without such inducements, I may pronounce, that it will never be undertaken.' About the same time, Andrew Fuller's book, *The Gospel Worthy of All Acceptation,* caused much controversy, but it helped Carey to see that Hyper-Calvinism is contrary to Scripture.

In 1792 Carey published his *Enquiry into the Obligations of Christians to use Means for the Conversion of the Heathens,* which sold for one shilling and sixpence. This sought to dismantle the notion that the Great Commission was only for the apostles, not for the universal Church. It challenged Christians: 'It only requires that we should have as much love for the souls of our fellow-creatures and fellow-sinners as they have for the profits arising from a few otter-skins.' On Matthew 28:19, he wrote: 'This commission was as extensive as possible, and laid them under obligation to disperse themselves into every country of the habitable globe, and preach to all the inhabitants, without exception, or limitation.'

In the same year Carey also preached his so-called 'deathless sermon' on Isaiah 54:2-3 to the Northamptonshire Baptist Association under the headings: 'Expect great things. Attempt great things.' Later, 'from God' was added to the first heading, and 'for God' added to the second heading. The result was the formation of the (Particular) Baptist Missionary Society, with thirteen pounds, two shillings and sixpence collected in Andrew Fuller's snuff box, some of it in promises, to be used for the work.

Originally, Carey thought of going to Tahiti, but the return to England from India of the erratic surgeon-missionary John Thomas turned Carey's thoughts to the sub-continent. Carey told the Baptist Society of John Ryland Jr, John Sutcliff, Andrew Fuller and Samuel Pearce: 'I will go down [the gold mine] but remember that you must hold the ropes.' By 1793 Carey was preparing to sail from England for India. Just before the ship left, Thomas, Carey and one other were forced to leave as they did not possess permits. Carey was shattered, but in the subsequent turmoil Thomas was able to prevail on a reluctant Dorothy to agree to go to India, provided her unmarried sister, Katherine, went too. She did. On 13 June 1793 Carey sailed to India with his wife Dorothy and their four children on a Danish ship, *Krön Princessa Maria*. Carey never returned. From quite inauspicious beginnings, a great missionary work would emerge.

62

WILLIAM CAREY
(1761–1834)

Great things through grace

*Wash me thoroughly from my iniquity, and cleanse
me from my sin* (Ps. 51:2).

The second half of Carey's life was spent in India. The early
months were trying. On 23 January 1794 he wrote: 'All my
friends are but One, but He is all-sufficient.' The letters of the
'rope-holders' at home never arrived during Carey's first two
years in India. Carey and his family were forced to make a
number of moves, including to an indigo plant at Mudnabatti, a
lonely place if ever there was one. His five-year-old son Peter
died of malaria. Dorothy went insane, ranted and raved, made
wild accusations against Carey, and tried to kill him. She died
in 1807, and six weeks later Carey announced that he would
be marrying Lady Charlotte von Rumohr, a petite, elegant and
cultured Dane. She died in 1821, and the following year Carey
married Grace Hughes, who outlived him.

Carey struggled spiritually in an unbelieving environment, and
his pundit, Ram Ram Basu (a high-caste Brahmin), was helpful
linguistically but erratic in his Christian life. Carey dismissed him
because he went back to the idols, engaged in embezzlement,

committed adultery and procured an abortion. Carey wrote back to England with honesty, saying of the Indians: 'Never was a people more willing to hear, yet more slow to understand.' Hinduism is a religion of demons. There were Jagannath shrines where pilgrims watched devotees 'swinging', forty feet above the ground, held by two iron flesh hooks. In 1794 Carey and Thomas came across an exposed infant, mostly devoured by white ants. Children were sacrificed to the River Ganges, while the sick and the aged were left to die. In 1799 Carey witnessed a case of sati (widow-burning), 'exclaiming loudly against the murder, and full of horror at what we had seen.'

Eventually, in 1800, a missionary community was set up at Serampore, a Danish settlement near Calcutta. It was to be a community of honesty, intimacy and equality. Twice a day they gathered together for Scripture and prayer, and on Saturday night they aired any differences. The Serampore Trio were William Ward (a printer, who died of cholera in 1823), Joshua Marshman (a sharp-tongued schoolmaster, who ran a Bengali weekly newspaper after 1818), and Carey. Henry Martyn was to write: 'Three such men as Carey, Marshman, and Ward, so suited to one another and their work, are not to be found, I think, in the whole world.'

Success came, and in 1800 Krishna Pal and Felix Carey were baptized. Dorothy and Thomas both missed the occasion, being afflicted by bouts of madness (Thomas died of malaria in 1801). By 1821 some 1,400 Indians had been baptized. These first-generation Christians, like their counterparts in the New Testament era, retained their 'pagan' names and did not adopt 'Christian' names. Also, as Ward put it: 'We carefully avoid whatever might Anglicise our students and converts.' There was no compromise whatsoever with the caste system – all converts had to share together in the Lord's Supper.

Free schools were established – by 1817 there were 103 schools with 6,703 pupils. In 1818 Serampore College was founded, with Carey as professor of divinity and lecturer on botany and zoology. It was designed not just for Christians and not just for theology. Carey corresponded with the famous botanists of the world, and several Indian plant species were named after him, e.g. *carea saulea*. Not so Marshman, of whom Carey said that he appreciated a garden as an ox does grass.

Carey's primary task was that of Bible translation. In 1801 the first edition of the New Testament in Bengali appeared. Carey was delighted: 'To give a man a New Testament who never saw it, who has been reading lies as the Word of God; to give him these everlasting lines which angels would be glad to read – this, this is my blessed work.' Ultimately, Carey was involved in the translation of the Bible into Bengali, Ooriya, Marathi, Hinki, Assamese, and Sanskrit (the language of the Brahmins), as well as portions of twenty-nine other tongues. As a translator, he ranks with Jerome, Wyclif, Luther, Tyndale and Erasmus. As he said in 1804: 'I am more in my element translating the Word of God than in any other employment.'

Yet there were still many setbacks and trials. In 1812 a fire broke out which destroyed the printing house, with presses, paper, books and manuscripts. It seems to have been an accident and not a case of arson. Carey responded: 'The Lord has laid me low, that I might look more simply to him.' As his sister commented: 'Whatever he began he finished: difficulties never seemed to discourage his mind.' Back in England, the clerical wit, Sydney Smith, caricatured Carey and his associates as 'a nest of consecrated cobblers' who 'benefit us much more by their absence than the Hindus by their advice.' More serious was the accusation, arising from Carey's belief that missionaries ought to support themselves, that 'the spirit of the missionary is swallowed up in the pursuits of the merchant.' Fuller was also concerned that Carey translated many of the great Hindu epics.

Relations with home base deteriorated, and in 1828 the Serampore Mission severed ties with the Baptist Missionary

Society. After suffering a series of strokes, Carey died peacefully on 9 June 1834. When he thought he was dying in 1823, he said that he wanted Psalm 51:2 to form the text for his funeral sermon. On his grave, next to his second wife, he had engraved words from a hymn by Isaac Watts:

> *A wretched, poor, and helpless worm,*
> *On thy kind arms I fall.*

He depended utterly on grace: 'If I ever get to heaven, it must be owing to divine grace from first to last.' This governed his relationship with God and with his fellow human beings, as can be seen in a letter that he wrote in 1807 to his son Felix, who was going to Burma: 'Preach the never-failing word of the cross. Do not be above sitting down to the patient instruction even of one solitary native ... Cultivate the utmost friendship and cordiality [with the native], as your equals, and never let European pride or superiority be felt by the natives in the mission house at Rangoon.'

63

CHARLES SIMEON
(1759–1836)

Saved by substitution to know
the love of Christ

*Then he [the high priest] shall kill the goat of the sin
offering, which is for the people, bring its blood inside
the veil, do with that blood as he did with the blood of
the bull, and sprinkle it on the mercy seat and before the
mercy seat ... Aaron shall lay both his hands on the head
of the live goat, confess over it all the iniquities of the
children of Israel, and all their transgressions, concerning
all their sins, putting them on the head of the goat,
and shall send it away into the wilderness by the hand
of a suitable man. The goat shall bear on itself all their
iniquities (Lev. 16:15, 21-22a).*

*Now as they came out, they found a man of Cyrene,
Simon by name. Him they compelled to bear His cross
(Matt. 27:32).*

*Then I said, 'I will not make mention of Him, nor speak
anymore in His name.' But His word was in my heart like
a burning fire shut up in my bones; I was weary of holding
it back, and I could not (Jer. 20:9).*

*[That you] may be able to comprehend with all the saints
what is the width and length and depth and height – to
know the love of Christ which passes knowledge; that you
may be filled with all the fullness of God (Eph. 3:18-19).*

224

Charles Simeon laboured as the minister of Holy Trinity Church, Cambridge, for fifty-four years, and came to wield a powerful influence for evangelicalism in his day. Handley Moule records that even in the 1860s an evangelical was known as a 'Sim', so dominant was his influence. Simeon was born at Reading on 24 September 1759, the son of a rich and successful attorney with little liking for 'Methodism'. After surviving the birch, fagging system, irreligion and vice of Eton, Simeon went to King's College, Cambridge in 1779.

At this stage, Simeon seems to have had little concept of true religion. Later, Simeon was to write: 'Never can I review my early life without the deepest shame and sorrow.' By nature, he was hot-tempered and, to compensate for a lack of good looks, would dress extravagantly. He had visited Newmarket for the races, loved dancing, and once heard of a drunken man who was killed from a fall from his horse. The latter event – being drunk and falling from a horse – was not unknown to Simeon, and he asked himself: 'Why not me?'

On 2 February 1779, the porter brought a note from the Provost, Dr William Cooke, informing him that Holy Communion would be celebrated in three weeks' time, and attendance was compulsory. Simeon was mortified: 'Satan himself was as fit to attend as I.' He later saw the spiritual folly of such a practice: 'I am far from considering it a good thing that young men in the university should be compelled to go to the table of the Lord: for it has an evident tendency to lower in their estimation that sacred ordinance, and to harden them in their iniquities.' To prepare himself, Simeon read the anonymous *The Whole Duty of Man*, but this was not much help.

Simeon felt miserable: 'I frequently looked upon the dogs with envy.' Thankfully, he turned to Bishop Thomas Wilson's book on the Lord's Supper, and the effect was life-changing. He read that the Jews knew what they were doing when they transferred their sin to the head of their offering. He continued:

'The thought rushed into my mind, What! may I transfer all my guilt to another? Has God provided an offering for me, that I may lay my sins on his head? Then, God willing, I will not bear them on my soul a moment longer. Accordingly I sought to lay my sins upon the sacred head of Jesus.' On the Sunday morning of 4 April he awoke with praise: 'Jesus Christ is risen to-day! Hallelujah! Hallelujah!' His testimony was that 'From that hour peace flowed in rich abundance into my soul; and at the Lord's table in our chapel I had the sweetest access to God through my blessed Saviour.'

In 1783 Simeon was ordained priest to Holy Trinity, Cambridge. However, he faced fierce opposition. His eldest brother, John, thought that Charles, when he was converted, had lost 'that valuable gift called common-sense'. Many of his congregation were no keener. The churchwardens threw pews out into the churchyard. When he tried to hold an evening service, the churchwardens bolted the doors. So isolated was Simeon that when a poor man in the street took his hat off to him, Simeon was so touched that he hurried back to his rooms to weep.

A naturally fastidious man, famously armed with his umbrella, Simeon never married. By a number of means, he was able to endure and to overcome opposition. Once, he was strengthened through reading of Simon of Cyrene's carrying of Jesus' cross. Simeon recognized the similarities in name, and was filled with delight: 'Now I could leap and sing for joy as one whom Jesus was honouring with a participation of His sufferings.' In his pocket Bible, he made a special mark next to Jeremiah 20:9.

Firmness of resolve went hand-in-hand with humility: 'My enemy, whatever evil he says of me, does not reduce me so low as he would if he knew all concerning me that God knows.' He added: 'The tender heart, the broken and contrite spirit, are to me far above all the joys that I could ever hope for in this vale of tears. I long to be in my proper place, my hand on my mouth, and my mouth in the dust.' To a woman who was depressed, he wrote: 'You are too much occupied in looking at yourself, and too little in beholding the Lord Jesus Christ. It is by the former you are to be humbled; but it is by the latter that you are to be changed into the divine image.'

By September 1836 Simeon was dying. He had, in fact, already delivered what proved to be his last sermon, but he wanted to at least prepare another set of sermons on what he called 'that grand subject of Ephesians, 3rd Chapter, 18th and 19th verses'. William Carus asked the bedridden Simeon what he was thinking, and Simeon replied: 'I don't think now – I am enjoying.' He died on 13 November 1836, having spent his last weeks on earth contemplating the love of Christ. He declared of the four magnitudes: 'This is the grandest subject I can conceive of for a course of Sermons; – I should think a life well spent, even out of heaven, to write and deliver four Sermons upon it in a manner worthy of it.'

64

HENRY MARTYN
(1781–1812)

Burning out for God

Struck down but not destroyed (2 Cor. 4:9b).

*Casting all your care upon Him, for He cares
for you* (1 Pet. 5:7).

*And Jesus answered and said to her, 'Martha, Martha, you
are worried and troubled about many things'* (Luke 10:41).

*There are many plans in a man's heart. Nevertheless the
Lord's counsel – that will stand* (Prov. 19:21).

*And He put all things under His feet, and gave Him to be
head over all things to the church, which is His body, the
fullness of Him who fills all in all* (Eph. 1:22-23).

*Likewise, I say to you, there is joy in the presence of the
angels of God over one sinner who repents* (Luke 15:10).

Henry Martyn was born on 18 February 1781 in Truro in Cornwall, England. His father had been converted in revival times under Rev. Samuel Walker. A plain-looking youngster, with warts on his hands and few athletic skills, Henry did not immediately stand out as a scholar. In 1797 he was received into St John's College, Cambridge, two years after Oxford had rejected him.

News reached him of the death of his father in January 1800, and he regretted how opinionated and short-tempered he had been towards him. He began to read the Bible in earnest and to attend church where Charles Simeon was the preacher. By 1801 Martyn had performed extremely well at university, and was Senior Wrangler at Cambridge, but it meant little: 'I obtained my highest wishes, but was surprised to find that I had grasped a shadow.' For a time he worked as Charles Simeon's assistant, and in 1804 met Charles Grant (a Member of Parliament and the Chairman of the Board of Directors of the East India Company), William Wilberforce and John Newton (who was just about deaf by this time). On 15 April 1804 Martyn wrote: 'I solemnly renounced the world, and the comforts, even the lawful comforts of it, before God this night, that I might be entirely his servant.'

Life was becoming more complicated for Martyn. In 1805 he was ordained as a priest in the Church of England. However, before this, he had become attracted to Lydia Grenfell, who was six years his senior. Charles Simeon – a bachelor himself – counselled celibacy, but Richard Cecil urged marriage. Martyn recorded: 'My dear Lydia and my duty call me different ways; yet God hath not forsaken me.' He struggled inwardly, but two verses which helped to sustain him came from 2 Corinthians 4:9 and 1 Peter 5:7. There was no romantic conclusion – Lydia refused his offer of marriage and missionary life in India.

Simeon's congregation gave Martyn a compass and a Bible, and off he went on the long sea voyage, via San Salvador in order to avoid the French, to reach India in May 1806. His first sermon on land was based on Luke 10:41. Here he wrote: 'Now let me burn out for God.' He opened schools, preached and set about the translation of the Scriptures, which he regarded as 'the grand point'. Opposition could be severe: one convert was decapitated and another executed by drowning.

Martyn's two sisters died of tuberculosis, from which he also suffered. Lydia wrote to him, offering to correspond with him. He often thought of her as 'my dearest Lydia', and he thought also of Proverbs 19:21. By 1810 the Hindustani New Testament was completed, although it was not published until 1812 because of a fire. He also worked on Persian and Arabic translations. Never of a strong constitution, Martyn's health was obviously breaking down by this time, but he wrote: 'This is my bliss, that Christ is all.' Hence it is not surprising that he wrote of Ephesians 1: 'It is a chapter I keep in mind every day in prayer.'

In 1811 he made a terrible journey in the oppressive heat to Shiraz in Persia. Here he preached to Muslims a confronting message: Muhammad was not foretold; he worked no miracles; he spread his religion by merely human means; he gratified his sensuality; the Qur'an is full of contradictions; and Islam proclaims an inefficacious way of salvation. He once heard of Jesus, supposedly in the fourth heaven, bowing down and clinging to the robes of Muhammad. He wept at this, and said: 'I could not endure existence if Jesus was not glorified – it would be hell to me, if He were to be always thus dishonoured.' To one inquiring Muslim, he gave a Persian New Testament, and wrote words based on Luke 15:10 on the flyleaf.

Martyn died on 16 October 1812, aged 31, while on the way to Constantinople, hoping to return to England. Lydia never married, and died in 1829. Back in Cambridge, Simeon kept a portrait of his missionary friend, and imagined it saying to him, 'Be serious – be in earnest – Don't trifle – don't trifle.' Simeon's response was 'And I won't trifle – I won't trifle.'

65

WILLIAM WILBERFORCE
(1759–1833)

Grateful prayerfulness in adversity

Be anxious for nothing, but in everything by prayer and supplication, with thanksgiving, let your requests be made known to God; and the peace of God, which surpasses all understanding, will guard your hearts and minds through Christ Jesus (Phil. 4:6-7).

I am not worthy of the least of all the mercies and of all the truth which You have shown Your servant (Gen. 32:10a).

Where there is neither Greek nor Jew, circumcised nor uncircumcised, barbarian, Scythian, slave nor free, but Christ is all and in all (Col. 3:11).

And He has made from one blood every nation of men to dwell on all the face of the earth (Acts 17:26a).

Woe to him who builds his house by unrighteousness and his chambers by injustice, who uses his neighbour's service without wages and gives him nothing for his work (Jer. 22:13).

He has shown you, O man, what is good; and what does the Lord require of you but to do justly, to love mercy, and to walk humbly with your God? (Micah 6:8).

William Wilberforce is known as the parliamentary leader of the opposition to the slave trade, which was abolished in the British colonies in 1807. On 26 July 1833, when Wilberforce had long retired from Parliament and was in fact on his deathbed, the slaves themselves were set free in all colonies answerable to

Britain. Wilberforce heard the news and was overjoyed: 'Thank God! Thank God that I have lived to see this day!' Three days later he died.

Wilberforce was born on 24 August 1759 at Hull, England's fourth port, behind Liverpool, Bristol and London. It engaged in whaling and so looked to the Baltic region. Hence it was the only port not to participate in the slave trade.

Wilberforce was a sickly child, and later reflected that in less civilized times and places, his parents would not have taken care of him. There was little in his youth to indicate what he would become. In 1776 he went off to Cambridge University, but there he played cards and billiards instead of attending lectures. A short, somewhat misshapen man who suffered from eye trouble, he nevertheless possessed a fine speaking and singing voice and had the gift of mimicry. Hence he was in some demand as an entertainer. After leaving Cambridge in 1779, he entered Parliament in 1780, and remained there until his retirement forty-five years later.

It was on the Continent with Isaac Milner that Wilberforce read Philip Doddridge's *Rise and Progress of Religion in the Soul* and the Bible. What he called the 'shapeless idleness' of his past struck him, and in 1785 he reluctantly went to visit John Newton, who gave him wise counsel. Newton steered him away from any thoughts of the ministry and kept Wilberforce focused on public life. By 1787 he had declared: 'God Almighty has set before me two great objects, the suppression of the Slave Trade and the Reformation of Manners' (as in Shakespeare's day, 'manners' meant 'morals').

In 1797 Wilberforce married Barbara Ann Spooner. It was a happy marriage, which produced four sons and two daughters, and Barbara looked after him in his many illnesses. He only ever published three works. The first one came in the year of his marriage, with the explanatory, if not concise, title: *A Practical View of the Prevailing Religious System of Professed Christians in*

232

the Higher and Middle Classes in This Country, Contrasted with Real Christianity. It proved to be an instant success. He also wrote A Letter on the Abolition of the Slave Trade in 1807, and the much shorter Appeal to the Religion, Justice, and Humanity of the Inhabitants of the British Empire, in Behalf of the Negro Slaves in the West Indies in 1823.

James Stephen wrote of Wilberforce: 'His presence was as fatal to dullness as to immorality. His mirth was as irresistible as the first laughter of childhood.' A witty and charming man, he possessed considerable gifts of sarcasm but tried to curb this tendency whenever he spoke in the House of Commons. He always maintained that it was the second blow that makes the battle. He had come to see that 'The genuine Christian strives not to prove himself guiltless but humbles himself in the dust and acknowledges that he is not worthy of the least of all God's mercies.'

Wilberforce outlived both of his daughters, and at the age of seventy suffered a severe financial loss. Yet he was a man who lived by what he had written in 1797: 'The grand characteristic mark of the true Christian ... is his desiring to please God in all his thoughts, and words, and actions; to take the revealed Word to be the rule of his belief and practice; to "let his light shine before men" and in all things to adorn the doctrine which he professes.' Always, he sought to devote at least an hour a day to prayer and the study of Scripture. In all his troubles, Philippians 4:6-7 became his favourite text.

In combating the slave trade, Wilberforce cooperated with all and sundry, but he was driven by his Christian convictions, and he appealed frequently to Christian truth. In his Letter on the Abolition of the Slave Trade, he cited Colossians 3:11-12 and Acts 17:26. The Appeal, published in 1823, cited Jeremiah's denunciation of those who used their neighbour's services without paying for them (Jer. 22:13) and Micah's call to do justice and love mercy (Micah 6:8). He also argued for the unity of humanity in Adam; the principle of freedom; the great commandment to love one's neighbour; and that national sin would provoke divine judgment. As he himself put it: 'A man who acts from the principles I profess reflects that he is to give an account of his political conduct at the Judgement seat of Christ.'

66

RICHARD JOHNSON
(1755–1827)

With thanks to God and
kindness to all

*What shall I render to the Lord for all His
benefits toward me?* (Ps. 116:12).

*You shall not curse the deaf, nor put a stumbling block
before the blind, but shall fear your God:
I am the Lord* (Lev. 19:14).

European settlement in Australia began with the arrival of the First Fleet in 1788. Whereas America was settled mainly as colonies of Puritans, Australia was settled as a colony of convicts – about 750 of them. However, on board one of the eleven ships that made up the First Fleet was Rev. Richard Johnson, an evangelical Anglican and the official chaplain to Botany Bay.

Johnson had been raised in Yorkshire where William Grimshaw and Henry Venn had proclaimed the gospel, and where Joseph Milner (the brother of Isaac Milner, who greatly helped William Wilberforce) was the Headmaster of Hull Grammar School which Johnson attended. He then went off to Cambridge University in 1780, and on the last day of 1784 was ordained as priest by the Bishop of Oxford.

Evangelicals had formed the Eclectic Society in 1783, and this had discussed the Botany Bay project. William Pitt, the Prime Minister, was Wilberforce's close friend, and it was he who decided to found a penal colony on the other side of the world. It was probably John Newton's idea that the new colony should have a chaplain, and William Wilberforce who used his influence to bring it about. Newton rather grandly referred to Johnson as the 'Patriarch of the Southern Hemisphere', but Johnson had an onerous task in front of him.

On Saturday 26 January 1788, after a voyage of eight months, the convicts were landed, and the British flag unfurled. It was a most unpromising congregation to minister to – mainly male convicts who did not want to be there. Nevertheless, on Sunday, 3 February 1788, Johnson preached his first sermon to his captive congregation. His text was Psalm 116:12, 'What shall I render unto the Lord for all his benefits toward me?' We have no record of the sermon, but Captain Watkin Tench thought that troops and convicts were attentive.

Johnson and his wife Mary battled on in trying conditions. Their first child was stillborn; their first house was, in Johnson's own words, 'a most miserable hut'; and his first hearers gave little evidence of regeneration. Johnson went on to labour in the gospel for twelve years – preaching, baptizing, conducting marriages and funerals, running a school, battling official indifference and convict depravity, as well as acting as a magistrate on occasions and farming his property known as Canterbury Vale. To preach at Rose Hill (Parramatta), Johnson rose at 4.00 a.m. to get there by boat by 9.00 a.m.

Governor Arthur Phillip never viewed the erection of a place of public worship as one of his priorities, and his successor Francis Grose had a particular dislike for the 'methodist' chaplain. Hence Johnson had the first church building in the colony erected at his own expense, with the first service taking place on 25 August 1793. The total cost, amounting to over £67, was reimbursed to Johnson only in 1797. When Governor John Hunter tried to enforce earlier decrees requiring convicts to attend church services, the building was burnt to the ground early in October 1798. The culprits were never found, despite the fact that Hunter offered any informer a free pardon and passage home, plus a reward of £30. Small wonder that Johnson would engage in soliloquy: 'Hold out faith and patience!' In declining health, Johnson left the colony in 1800, leaving his mantle to Samuel Marsden who had arrived in Botany Bay in 1794.

As an evangelical pastor, Johnson described the Scriptures as 'our only sure and infallible guide'. He was kindly to all, including the convicts and the Aborigines. He preached to all, 'as mortals and yet immortals', as one who was certain that 'unless the gospel is made the power of God to your souls, you must be miserable in time, and to eternity.' His message was: 'That you are sinners, that Jesus Christ is an all-sufficient and willing Saviour, and that the word of God both warrants and commands you to look to him for salvation.' He pleaded that the convicts desist from sin, partly for the sake of the Aborigines: 'Oh beware of laying stumbling-blocks in the way of these blind people (Lev. 19:14), lest the blood of their souls be one day required at your hands.' Indeed, the Johnsons had given their second child, a girl, an Aboriginal name, Milbah, and they had looked after an Aboriginal girl, Abaroo.

Back in England, Johnson served in a number of parishes, and as he came to die in 1827 almost his last words were, 'Christ is precious.'

67
ASAHEL NETTLETON
(1783–1844)

Eternity in our hearts

He has made everything beautiful in its time. Also He has put eternity in their hearts, except that no one can find out the work that God does from beginning to end (Eccles. 3:11).

But as many as received Him, to them He gave the right to become children of God, to those who believe in His name: who were born, not of blood, nor of the will of the flesh, nor of the will of man, but of God (John 1:12-13).

Asahel Nettleton remained a bachelor all his life, and is remembered as a Calvinistic Congregational evangelist who might be ranked next to George Whitefield. As a youth, Nettleton had never been outwardly wild or extravagant in his unconverted days, but one day he watched the sun go down, and the thought that everyone would die caused him to stand and weep. In 1800, during Connecticut's Second Great Awakening, he came to see his need of regeneration, but also rebelled against this. This new seriousness with regard to his salvation came about not after a sermon, as is sometimes said, but after he had attended a ball and found that all his happiness and amusement were overtaken by gloom, with thoughts of death, judgment and eternity.

Nettleton entered a kind of spiritual torture chamber: 'I searched the Scriptures daily, hoping to find inconsistencies in them, to condemn the Bible, because it was against me; and while I was diligently pursuing my purpose, everything I read, and every sermon I heard, condemned me. Christian conversation gave me the most painful sensations.' All his experience testified to Calvinistic views of total depravity and of regeneration: 'I tried to repent, but I could not feel the least sorrow for my innumerable sins ... All self-righteousness failed me; and, having no confidence in God, I was left in deep despondency.'

Nothing gave Nettleton any relief. He saw his own wretchedness and the justice of God. Then: 'Eternity – the word *Eternity* – sounded louder than any voice I ever heard; and every moment of time seemed more valuable than all the wealth of the world.' He came to love the character of God, to see the preciousness of the Saviour, and to delight in spiritual meetings and duties. For about ten months, Nettleton had struggled with God and his own soul, and even after that remained cautious about his own spiritual condition. The deceitfulness of the human heart appalled him, and so he wrote: 'But my unfaithfulness often makes me fear my sincerity; and should I at last be raised to glory, all the praise will be to God for the exhibition of His sovereign grace.' Nevertheless, as he himself was converted, so he also preached and lived. Eternity was his salvation – both the means and the goal.

Nettleton enrolled at Yale in 1805, and graduated in 1809, with the intention of preparing for overseas missionary work. He was licensed in 1811, but circumstances led him to continue preaching in Connecticut where thousands were converted under his ministry. He never held a settled pastorate. His sermons were searching efforts, and revealed a deep knowledge of the human heart, election and divine sovereignty. At the same time he was eloquent on the importance of unity and brotherly love in promoting the cause of God's kingdom. By 1820 he was the leading evangelist of the east, but from 1822 until his death twenty-two years later he suffered from ill health.

Nettleton has become known in some circles only as the Calvinist who vigorously opposed the 'new measures' associated with the evangelism of Charles Finney. These were ultimately based on a new theology, but it was the practices which drew attention to the beliefs behind them. Finney used an 'anxious seat' for souls under conviction of sin; sinners were sometimes publicly named; meetings became protracted; women were allowed to pray and even to speak in mixed public meetings; and new 'converts' were admitted very quickly to church membership. Theologically, Finney held to a number of heterodox views, namely that revival 'is as naturally a result of the use of the appropriate means as a crop is of the use of its appropriate means'; that even since the Fall human nature is not sinful of itself; that God 'has no right to command unless we have power to obey'; and that 'the sinner has all the faculties and natural abilities requisite to render perfect obedience to God.' Against this, Nettleton cited John 1:12-13, and asserted that 'every real Christian becomes one by a special exertion of almighty power to change his heart.' The sinner is born again, not by means of any human decision but through the power of the Holy Spirit.

Nettleton recognized that the 'new measures' were based on a new theology; and so he called the new evangelism 'the illusion of a new era'. On 4 March 1827 Finney preached provocatively in the Presbyterian Church of Troy on *Can Two Walk Together Except They Be Agreed?* (Amos 3:3). He argued that the difference between the two approaches was a difference between a dull and dry spiritual life and a spiritual life animated by warmth and vigour. Finally, a convention was held, with eighteen participants – nine from each side – to discuss the matter for a week in July 1827. As Nettleton feared, Finney's reputation seemed to emerge enhanced after the conference.

Nettleton was not a born controversialist: 'Somebody must speak, or silence will prove our ruin. Fire is an excellent thing in its place, and I am not afraid to see it blaze among briers and thorns; but when I see it kindling where it will ruin fences, and gardens, and houses, and burn up my friends, I cannot be silent.' Nor was he malicious: 'I heartily pity brother Finney for I believe him to be a good man, and wishing to do good.' Nettleton spoke because he was convinced that the adoption of the new measures would have disastrous consequences for the Church.

By the time that Nettleton died in 1844, the 'new measures' were widely accepted amongst evangelists. Nettleton is often portrayed as a crabby, old man fighting vainly for the status quo. Nevertheless, for all his disregard of too much emphasis on visible signs of success, it is estimated that perhaps 30,000 souls were awakened under Nettleton's labours. On the day before he died, he confessed: 'It is sweet to trust in the Lord.'

68

THOMAS CHALMERS
(1780–1847)

A minister justified by faith

*So they said, 'Believe on the Lord Jesus Christ, and you will
be saved, you and your household' (Acts 16:31).*

*All that the Father gives Me will come to Me, and the one
who comes to Me I will by no means cast out (John 6:37).*

*Do not love the world or the things in the world. If
anyone loves the world, the love of the Father
is not in him (1 John 2:15).*

Born in 1780, Thomas Chalmers was raised in a devout Calvinistic household. Aged eleven, he matriculated to St Andrews University, and by 1799 was licensed to preach. He was athletic, jocular, subject to depression, filled with enthusiasm for science and a member of St Vigean's lodge of Freemasons. While minister at Kilmany from 1803 to 1811, Chalmers offered private mathematics and chemistry classes at St Andrews, and preached moral judgments against sin. He later recorded that this had 'not the weight of a feather on the moral habits of my parishioners.'

Chalmers had begun his ministerial career as a Moderate, as opposed to being an Evangelical. He became well known for the comment he made in 1805 that 'after the satisfactory discharge of his parish duties, a minister may enjoy five days in the week of uninterrupted leisure, for the prosecution of any science in which his taste may dispose him to engage.' However, such an approach was disowned when he was converted to the Evangelical faith. In 1825 an opponent cited Chalmers's own words of 1805, and Chalmers was quick to confess his former ignorance and pride: 'I had forgotten two magnitudes – I thought not of the littleness of time – I recklessly thought not of the greatness of eternity!'

Chalmers had come to know Rev. Andrew Thomson, the Evangelical minister of St George's, Edinburgh, from 1814 to 1831, and had suffered the deaths, by tuberculosis (then known as consumption), of a brother in 1806 and of two sisters in 1808 and 1810. He himself had been bedridden with the disease, and had read Blaise Pascal's *Pensées*, and then William Wilberforce's *A Practical View*. He had also been through a broken engagement. By 1811 his preaching was decidedly evangelical, although his appearance remained somewhat dishevelled and his gestures clumsy. He always read his sermons, delivered in a heavy Fife accent and following his manuscript with one finger. But he was a new man! He had learned that 'to preach Christ is the only effective way of preaching morality in all its branches.'

Chalmers summed up his experience: 'I am now most thoroughly of the opinion, and it is an opinion founded on experience, that on the system of "Do this and live", no peace, and even no true, and worthy obedience, can ever be attained. It is "Believe on the Lord Jesus Christ and thou shalt be saved." When this belief enters the heart, joy and confidence enter along with it.' Justification by faith goes hand-in-hand with the free offer of grace: 'I plead His own promise, that "Him that cometh unto me I will in no wise cast out." I come to Him with my heart such as it is; and I pray that the operation of His Spirit, and the power of His sanctifying faith, would make it such as it should be.'

Despite a few setbacks, Chalmers increasingly became recognized as the leader of the Evangelical party within the Church of Scotland. In late 1814 he was called to the Tron at Glasgow. He began to visit all, including Roman Catholics and Dissenters, and organized Sabbath schools in each district. He maintained his interest in astronomy, although some of his suggestions are less than convincing. For example, he argued for the 'Gap theory' (that there is a gap of millions of years between Genesis 1:1 and Genesis 1:2), and he thought that there are a multiplicity of inhabited planets, each with sin and redemption through Christ.

In 1819, after some hesitation, he moved to St John's in Glasgow where he revived the office of deacon. The parish was divided up into twenty-five districts, and poor relief was administered by a deacon in each district. He also opened parish schools, which were an immense success. In 1823 he accepted the Chair of Moral Philosophy at St Andrews, the centre of Scottish Moderatism. Four years later he accepted the Edinburgh Divinity Chair.

Patronage was an issue in the Church at this time. A patron might nominate his chosen minister to a parish, despite the wishes of the congregation. Evangelicals usually opposed this. In 1834 congregations gained the right to veto an unwanted nominee, and so began what is called 'the Ten Years' Conflict'. However, the result was often wrangling in the law courts. Evangelical frustration increased. Chalmers stood firm: 'They may force the ejection of us from our places: they shall never, never force us to the surrender of our principles.' Lord Melbourne, an indifferent Whig in religion, thought Chalmers a madman and a rogue.

This culminated in the Disruption of 1843 when 451 ministers, out of a total of 1,203, walked out of the Established Church to form the Free Church of Scotland. What followed was a remarkable story – for a generation at least. Those ministers who walked out of the Church of Scotland left manses, stipends and churches – in short, all ecclesiastical security – behind them. Yet within a year the Free Church had erected, or nearly completed, some 470 church buildings, and on 1 November 1843 New College, Edinburgh, was opened as a showpiece of Reformed theology.

Chalmers's life and doctrine work together to illustrate what he described in a sermon on 1 John 2:15, as 'the expulsive power of a new affection'.

69

ADONIRAM JUDSON
(1788–1850)

Sowing in sorrow

*It was right that we should make merry and be glad, for
your brother was dead and is alive again, and was lost
and is found* (Luke 15:32).

*For if we believe that Jesus died and rose again, even so
God will bring with Him those who sleep
in Jesus* (1 Thess. 4:14).

*The kingdoms of this world have become the kingdoms of
our Lord and of His Christ, and He shall reign
forever and ever!* (Rev. 11:15b).

Adoniram Judson was born at Malden in the USA in 1788, the
son of an austere Congregational minister of the same name.
A precocious and gifted child, young Adoniram is reputed to
have learnt to read in a week at the age of three. His nickname
at school was 'Virgil', and he was to leapfrog the Freshman year
at Brown University on Rhode Island and go straight into the
Sophomore class. However, here he succumbed to Deism and
unbelief, and his parents were heartbroken. The student who
most influenced him in this was a Jacob Eames. Judson topped
his class, and gave his valedictory address on 'Free Enquiry'.

Later, he took a steamboat from Albany to New York where
he was hoping to write for the stage, but he actually found

a tawdry world of delusion and bombast. Within five weeks Judson was returning home in some turmoil of soul. One night he stayed at an inn, where he slept in a room next to a young man whose awful groans indicated that he was dying in utter hopelessness. The next morning he found out that his next-door neighbour had died, and that his name was Jacob Eames – his unbelieving mentor at Brown University! Judson was shattered, and one word tolled in his mind, the word that described the prodigal son in the pig sty: 'Lost!'

After arriving home, he read Thomas Boston's *Human Nature in its Fourfold State*. By 2 December 1808 he had made 'a solemn declaration of himself to God' and had become a Christian, and by 1810 he had resolved to become a Congregational missionary. On 5 February 1812 he married Ann Hasseltine (often known as Nancy), and was ordained the next day. Later that month the newly married couple left on a 114-day voyage to India. There they were welcomed by William Carey and the Serampore missionaries, but ordered home by the East India Company. At Serampore, the Judsons announced their new-found baptistic convictions, and were baptized by immersion on 6 September 1812 by William Ward.

Despite many misgivings about 'the Golden Kingdom', they moved to Rangoon in Burma, arriving on 13 July 1813, after losing their first child – a stillbirth – on the voyage. Dominating the dirty and dreary landscape was the Shwedagon Pagoda, which was 400 feet high, and which was built over eight hairs of the Buddha himself. Judson began to translate the Gospel of Matthew, which was finished in 1817, with the whole New Testament being finished in 1823, to be followed by the Old Testament in 1834.

It was a struggle to present the gospel to the Burmese, for whom the notion of an eternal God was incomprehensible. Children under eight were naked except for bangles and neck-laces, but they smoked cigars. Animals could not be killed in order to be eaten. On 11 September 1815 Roger Williams Judson was born, but he died of fever in May 1816. His death did arouse some sympathy on the part of the Burmese, and the wife of the Viceroy tried to console the grieving Judsons by granting them an elephant ride and a picnic. Like Carey in India, Judson had to wait years to see his first convert, Maung Nau, who professed faith in 1819.

About this time, persecution began to increase. Judson decided to sail 350 miles up the Irrawaddy to Ava, to appeal to 'the Golden Feet' of the emperor on behalf of the mission. However, the emperor dismissed the missionaries. In 1824 the British conquered Rangoon, and Judson, although an American, was seen as British, and so was imprisoned in what the English called 'the Death Prison'. The conditions were appalling beyond all description. The feet of the fifty prisoners were tied to a bamboo pole at night which was raised above their heads, so that a prisoner could only sleep, if at all, with his head and shoulder on the ground.

When the British began to win the war, the emperor had his commander trampled to death by elephants. On 5 November 1825 Judson was suddenly released as the government needed a translator in its negotiations with Britain. Ann, however, was dying and on 24 October 1826 she succumbed to spinal meningitis. Her favourite motto was 'On earth we serve God – in heaven we praise Him.' To his sister and parents, Judson cited 1 Thessalonians 4 as a comfort.

For a time, Judson himself almost went mad with grief and spiritual depression. He destroyed all his letters and personal papers, and went through a terrible period of self-loathing and self-mortification. For forty days he lived in dangerous seclusion in what was called 'the Hermitage', eating only a little rice. He even dug a grave beside which he would sit. In his spiritual deso-lation, he wrote: 'God is to me the Great Unknown. I believe in him, but I find him not.' He only seems to have revived when he heard that his brother had become a Christian and died in the faith.

The number of inquirers and converts increased. In the meantime, Judson married Sarah Boardman, and, after her death, Emily Chubbock. When asked how bright were the prospects for the conversion of the heathen, he replied: 'As bright as the promises of God.' Revelation 11:15 often sustained him, and he wrote on the cover of a book that he used to compile his dictionary:

> In joy or sorrow, health or pain,
> Our course be onward still;
> We sow on Burmah's barren plain,
> We reap on Zion's hill.

Judson died at sea on 12 April 1850. Francis Wayland has recorded that in his letters Judson referred most frequently to the nearness of the heavenly glory. It was now even nearer, awaiting the resurrection of the dead.

70

RAFARAVAVY
(d.1848)

Seeing the folly of idolatry

*The craftsman ... cuts down cedars for himself ... He
burns half of it in the fire; with this half he eats meat; he
roasts a roast, and is satisfied. He even warms himself ...
And the rest of it he makes into a god, his carved image.
He falls down before it and worships it, prays to it and
says, 'Deliver me, for you are my god!'* (Isa. 44:13-17).

*Do not be afraid of sudden terror, nor of trouble from
the wicked when it comes; for the Lord will be your
confidence, and will keep your foot from
being caught* (Prov. 3:25-26).

The Gospel came rather late to the island of Madagascar, and
when it did come, it met with intense persecution. In 1818 David
Jones and Thomas Bevan were sent from Wales to Mauritius,
with the intention of going on to Madagascar. By the end of the
year, however, Mrs Jones and her baby were dead, and the new
year saw the deaths of Bevan, his wife and his child. In spite of all
missionary labours, Madagascar remained steeped in taboos and
divination. If an infant was born on an unlucky day, he would be
left at a cattle pen. Should he survive that, he was regarded as
having been freed from his bad luck.

On 8 December 1820 David Jones began work in Madagascar, and in 1821 David Griffiths arrived to help him. Yet there was no flood of converts, and in 1828 Queen Ranavalona, one of the wives of the previous king, came to power in Madagascar. She dressed in Paris fashion, was devoted to the idols, and was considered too divine to be approached by her people. She soon began to persecute the fledgling Church. Remarkably enough, James Cameron was able to delay this somewhat by producing bars of soap, which delighted the queen. She also appreciated the artisan skills of the missionaries.

Despite the tensions, twenty new Christians were baptized on 29 May 1831, and another eight the following Sunday. This led to the decree that no Malagasy could be baptized or participate in the Lord's Supper. About this time, a married couple went to a maker of idols to have a household god made. There was some delay, and the couple were obliged to wait until evening. The maker brought home a branch of a tree from the forest, and began to prepare the god. He used the one piece of wood to make the idol, and to fuel the fire that was boiling his rice. The couple paid for the idol, and returned home.

Soon afterwards, a young Christian visited the couple and read Isaiah 44 to them, and the woman, whose name was Rafaravavy, was convicted of the folly of idol worship and came to trust in Christ. At her baptism, she took the name Mary. Her new faith was to be tested by policies of the queen. Ranavalona recalled all Christian books, and by July 1836 there were supposed to be no missionaries left on the island.

In this same year – 1836 – Rafaravavy was denounced by three of her servants for praying and reading the Scriptures. She gave her Bible and other books to the two remaining missionaries in Madagascar for safe keeping. She was sentenced to death, but this was commuted to a fine, together with a warning that her next offence would mean death. When interrogated, she refused to give the names of Christians to the queen. Her property was forfeited, and a mob seized all that it could.

After imprisonment and a further threat of death, Rafaravavy escaped to Mauritius, then on to England, before returning to Madagascar to help Malagasy exiles. She died there in 1848. Once, while hiding from the soldiers, she took comfort and strength in recalling the words of Proverbs 3:25-26. There were waves of persecution, especially in 1840 and 1849, and Christians were beheaded, burnt at the stake, thrown off cliffs, banished, flogged and sold into slavery. But in 1862 Queen Ranavalona died, and the suffering Church was left to marvel that its numbers had actually grown from about 200 baptized believers in 1835 to about 7,000 in 1861.

71

ALLEN GARDINER
(1794–1851)

Hungering, yet hungering more for God

*They shall neither hunger anymore nor thirst anymore;
the sun shall not strike them, nor any heat; for the Lamb
who is in the midst of the throne will shepherd them and
lead them to living fountains of waters. And God will wipe
away every tear from their eyes (Rev. 7:16-17).*

*Wait on the Lord; be of good courage, and He shall
strengthen your heart; wait, I say, on
the Lord! (Ps. 27:14).*

*He shall regard the prayer of the destitute, and shall
not despise their prayer (Ps. 102:17).*

*The young lions lack and suffer hunger; but those who
seek the Lord shall not lack any good thing (Ps. 34:10).*

*Cast your burden on the Lord, and He shall sustain you;
He shall never permit the righteous to
be moved (Ps. 55:22).*

*My soul, wait silently for God alone, for my expectation is
from Him. He only is my rock and my salvation; He is my
defence; I shall not be moved. In God is my salvation and
my glory; the rock of my strength, and my refuge, is in
God. Trust in Him at all times, you people; pour out your
heart before Him; God is a refuge for us (Ps. 62:5-8).*

Allen Francis Gardiner was born to godly parents in 1794 in
Lower Basildon in the English county of Berkshire. As a youngster,
he seemed to love adventure more than the things of God, and

early set his heart upon a career in the Navy. After studying at the naval college at Portsmouth, he went to sea in 1810. He acquitted himself well, and was promoted to the rank of lieutenant, then commander. The deaths of a number of his colleagues, then his mother, prompted him to think on the coming judgment, and he finally mustered up enough courage to buy a Bible in Portsmouth.

Joining the British Navy was a good way to see the world, and he visited India, China and South America. To Gardiner, the idolatry of China and the superstitions of Roman Catholicism appalled while the Christian natives in Tahiti impressed him, and he began to think of becoming a missionary or a minister. He married in 1823, but his wife died ten years later. From 1834, he devoted himself for a time to the Zulus in Natal, and in 1836 returned to England to recruit some helpers, and to remarry. In 1837 he was back in Africa, but hostility between the Boers and the Zulus led him to think of South America. He sailed to Chile, was frustrated, then went to New Guinea, was again frustrated, and finally concluded in 1841 that the Falkland Islands could prove to be the key to reach the natives at the very southern end of South America, in Patagonia and Tierra del Fuego.

Gardiner returned to Britain to appeal for help directly to Christians: 'Let us remember Him who, though He was rich, yet for our sakes became poor, who willeth that all men should be saved and come to the knowledge of the truth, and who will not be satisfied until He has received the fullness of that harvest which the travail of His soul is still ripening.' The Patagonian Mission resulted, and in 1844 Gardiner was back in Patagonia to recommence the gospel work. However, he was driven out and had to return to England. Failure hurt him but did not crush him.

By September 1845 he was back in Montevideo, east of Buenos Aires. Bolivia, which was further inland, also looked promising for a time, but Roman Catholic opposition caused Gardiner to turn towards Tierra del Fuego. In September 1850 he and six companions left Liverpool for Tierra del Fuego. There, their goods were stolen and they came down with scurvy. Provisions from England did not arrive in time, and the men were perishing of hunger. One by one they died of starvation. Gardiner reports that he was kept in perfect peace, without any pain, and his last journal entry reads: 'Great and marvellous are the lovingkindnesses of my gracious God.' By the time the relief ship arrived, on 21 October 1851, Gardiner and his companions were all dead. Later, this led his biographers, John Marsh and Waite Stirling, to think of Revelation 7:16-17.

During those last months, Gardiner turned frequently to the Psalms – to Psalm 27:14; 102:17; 34:10; 55:22, for example – a mixture of yearning and trust. Psalm 62:5-8 was painted on a rock which pointed to where Gardiner lived, and was marked in his Bible. Charles Darwin was to be shocked by the success of missionary work among the Fuegians, whom he regarded as 'the very lowest of the human race'. What Darwin did not realize was that faithfulness unto death was to lead ultimately to blessing and renewed evangelical missionary interest in South America. Until it was wrecked in 1893, the South American Missionary Society's vessel was named, appropriately enough, the *Allen Gardiner*. The work continued.

72

ROBERT FLOCKHART
(1778–1857)

A voice like a trumpet in the streets of Edinburgh

Their sorrows shall be multiplied who hasten after another god (Ps. 16:4).

For every creature of God is good, and nothing is to be refused if it is received with thanksgiving (1 Tim. 4:4).

Therefore, having been justified by faith, we have peace with God through our Lord Jesus Christ (Rom. 5:1).

According to the glorious gospel of the blessed God which was committed to my trust (1 Tim. 1:11).

Cry aloud, spare not; lift up your voice like a trumpet; tell My people their transgression, and the house of Jacob their sins (Isa. 58:1).

The wicked shall be turned into hell, and all the nations that forget God (Ps. 9:17).

Upon the wicked He will rain coals; fire and brimstone and a burning wind shall be the portion of their cup (Ps. 11:6).

'Come now, and let us reason together,' says the Lord, 'though your sins are like scarlet, they shall be as white as snow; though they are red like crimson, they shall be as wool' (Isa. 1:18).

Robert Flockhart was certainly a great sinner who came to know the great grace of God in Christ Jesus. Born on 4 February 1778 in Dalnottar, near Glasgow, he went to school, and then served an apprenticeship in nail-making. In adult life, he was short and rather ungainly, but capable of smart repartee. For some reason, his father made him learn the Mother's and the Shorter Catechisms, but, for the most part, he was raised without any Christian influences. From 1797, he was to spend sixteen years in the Army, at the Cape of Good Hope and then in India and the East Indies.

Flockhart was guilty of virtually every sin, he says, except murder. He lived a life of drunkenness, swearing and sexual immorality. A man who was shot in a duel, but lingered for two weeks before dying, left a Bible, and Flockhart lied to the captain in saying that he had left it to him. By this means, Flockhart acquired a Bible. The superstitions of the Hindus had an effect on him, and he remembered Psalm 16:4, which he had read as a boy. The Baptist missionaries around Calcutta, associated with William Carey, would preach to the troops despite the prohibitions of the officers.

The testimony of a sergeant also affected him, and in 1807 Flockhart told him that he would like to become a Christian. The sergeant replied that the life of a Christian was a continual warfare. Flockhart tried hard to be a Christian, by confessing, fasting and praying. So severe was his fasting that he had to eat with his finger on 1 Timothy 4:1-5 in order to recover his health (the passage in 1 Timothy assures us that all things may be eaten, with thanksgiving). He recognized later that 'It was as impossible for me to believe at that time, as it would have been for me to lift Edinburgh Castle and cast it into the sea.' His conversion came through a number of influences, including singing Isaac Watts's edition of Psalm 32:4-5, and contemplating Romans 5:1 and a number of other verses. He resolved, God willing, to be as long and as zealous in God's service as he had been in the devil's.

At his baptism in Calcutta on 26 August 1810, although William Carey was not present, William Ward preached what Flockhart regarded as a delightful sermon from 1 Timothy 1:11.

After taking part in battles against the French army of Napoleon, Flockhart returned to Glasgow, then Edinburgh. In the same year, 1813, he married – the fourth girl whom he had asked! For the next forty-three years he preached through the city of Edinburgh, come wind, come weather. Isaiah 58:1 was a verse he often cited, and one which clearly motivated him. His approach lacked nothing in boldness. He would preach Psalm 9:17 and 11:6, and when his audience was thoroughly awakened, he would preach Christ crucified and risen.

Once he was locked up in a lunatic asylum, and his Bible was confiscated. He escaped through a window one rainy night, and evaded the police who were after him. In fact, he was arrested about nine or ten times for street preaching, but he found that the police were usually keen to release him. Yet he was able to set up a school in Lauriston, being driven by the fact that he had remembered Isaiah 1:18 for twenty years. The lesson that he drew from this was: 'Thus, judging from my own case, I thought that portions of God's Word, instilled into the children's young hearts, might afterwards be productive of great good, though I might not live to see it.' Over the years, he ministered to all kinds of ruffians and sinners, including a number of men sentenced to death, as well as a woman who had murdered her own illegitimate child, then cut her own throat, but survived.

By God's grace, Flockhart served for longer in God's service than in the devil's.

73

ALEXANDER DUFF

(1806–1878)

Trusting Christ in the dangers of mission

I am a debtor both to Greeks and to barbarians, both to wise and to unwise (Rom. 1:14).

God be merciful to us and bless us, and cause His face to shine upon us, that Your way may be known on earth, Your salvation among all nations (Ps. 67:1-2).

For the law was given through Moses, but grace and truth came through Jesus Christ (John 1:17).

I lay down and slept; I awoke, for the Lord sustained me. I will not be afraid of ten thousands of people Who have set themselves against me all around. Arise, O Lord; Save me, O my God! (Ps. 3:5-7a).

Alexander Duff was born in the Perthshire highlands of Scotland, the son of a farmer who was deeply affected, along with his parish minister, by the preaching of Charles Simeon, along with James Haldane, when they visited the area in 1796. Respect for his pious father kept young Alexander from many youthful follies, and one night he dreamed that God said to him: 'Come up hither; I have work for thee to do.' After being dux at Perth Grammar School, the studious Duff went on to St Andrews

University. He came to be greatly moved by Thomas Chalmers's conviction that all knowledge is unified in God. During his eight years at St Andrews he borrowed more books from the library than any other student, and even devoured authors who were hostile to Christianity. Early in 1829 he decided, before God alone, that he would offer for work in India, and, after marrying Anne Scott Drysdale in July, was ordained on 12 August 1829, with Thomas Chalmers officiating.

At Leuchars, Duff preached on Romans 1:14 where he affirmed the connection between conversion and missionary endeavour: 'There was a time when I had no care or concern for the heathen: there was a time when I had no care or concern for my own soul. When by the grace of God I was led to care for my own soul, then it was that I began to care for the heathen abroad.'

The Duffs sailed for Calcutta on 14 October 1829 on the *Lady Holland*. In February of the following year, however, the ship ran aground on Dassen Island, near Cape Town. No lives were lost, but virtually all the cargo perished. Duff was left with his Bible and Psalter and not much else out of his 800 books. Grateful, he led the ship's company in Psalm 107. In May there was a second shipwreck, in the estuary of Hooghly River in the Bay of Bengal. Again, no lives were lost.

Duff arrived in Calcutta in 1830, and ignored the home committee's instruction not to open a school there. In the land where the East India Company protected caste, idolatry and human sacrifice, Duff worked hard to reach high-caste Indians for Christ. Although Duff learnt the Bengali language, he did not regularly preach in it. Instead, he worked in English – rather than Bengali, Persian, Arabic or Sanskrit – on the 'downward filtration' approach, hoping to undermine Hinduism, which he regarded as 'a stupendous system of error' animated by 'malignant energy'. His intention was to saturate education with the teaching of the Scriptures, especially the Lord's Prayer, the parable of the prodigal son, 1 Corinthians 13 and the Sermon on the Mount. He always sought to carry out the principles of Matthew 18:21-35 in all his dealings with people, including those who were most difficult.

His view was: 'Give me the school books and the schoolmasters of a country, and I will let any one else make not only its songs and its laws, but its literature, sciences and philosophy too!' He regarded education without religion as 'a blind, suicidal policy'. This proved to be a remarkably successful approach, and similar schools were set up in Bombay and Madras. Later he was to be the driving force behind the establishment of Calcutta University. One of his first converts recorded after his baptism: 'In spite of myself I became a Christian.'

In 1834 Duff had returned to Scotland on furlough. Despite his ill health, he made a powerful impact on the Church of Scotland, and in 1839 he published *Missions the Chief End of the Christian Church*, based on Psalm 67:1-2 (although the published edition mistakenly identified it as Psalm 47:1-2). His opening words were: 'The Royal Psalmist, in the spirit of inspiration, personating the Church of the redeemed in every age, and more especially under its last and most perfect dispensation, here offers up a sublime prayer for its inward prosperity, and outward universal extension.'

On the way back to India in 1839, he made the journey to Mount Sinai, which he climbed, and meditated on John 1:17 at the top. In 1843, at the Disruption, Duff and the thirteen other missionaries in India all joined the Free Church of Scotland. For Duff, this meant the loss of the college, but financial support poured in from many sources around the world. Duff's second furlough, in 1850–5, had a similar impact to his first, and included the USA and Canada which he visited in 1854.

In May 1857 Duff, having been allowed by his doctors to return to India provided he took things easily, was not to know that the Indian Mutiny was to break out. Thirty-five missionaries and their wives and children were to lose their lives in the rebellion. Duff's own son, Alexander, was living in Meerut where the uprising was at its fiercest. Naturally, Duff and his wife were very anxious, and Duff wrote to a friend: 'Never before did I realize as now the literality and sweetness of the psalmist's assurance', and he cited Psalm 3:5-7a.

Suffering from dysentery and overwork, he left India in 1864, and in 1867 became Professor of Missions at New College, Edinburgh, and died in 1878. Drawing inspiration from Romans 1–3, he had declared that his only fitting epitaph would be 'Here lies Alexander Duff, by nature and practice a sinful guilty creature, but saved by grace, through faith in the blood and righteousness of his Lord and Saviour Jesus Christ.' His daughter recited John Newton's hymn to him, 'How sweet the name of Jesus sounds'. The dying Duff could only whisper: 'Unspeakable.'

74

JOHN GEDDIE
(1815–1872)

Gentleness and strength in Christ

Son of man, can these bones live? (Ezek. 37:3a).

*And He said to them: 'Go into all the world and preach
the gospel to every creature' (Mark 16:15).*

*Ask of Me, and I will give you the nations for your
inheritance, and the ends of the earth
for your possession (Ps. 2:8).*

*But Jesus looked at them and said to them: 'With men
this is impossible, but with God all things
are possible' (Matt. 19:26).*

*I shall go to him, but he shall not return
to me (2 Sam. 12:23).*

*Father, forgive them, for they do not know
what they do (Luke 23:34).*

*And when His disciples James and John saw this, they
said, 'Lord, do You want us to command fire to come
down from heaven and consume them, just as Elijah did?'
But He turned and rebuked them, and said, 'You do not
know what manner of spirit you are of. For the Son of
Man did not come to destroy men's lives but
to save them.' And they went to another
village (Luke 9:54-56).*

John Geddie was born a Scot in 1815, but raised in Canada after his parents settled in Pictou in Nova Scotia when John was only one year old. A small man with a rather childlike face, Geddie was the son of a clock and watch maker. He went to the Pictou Academy, and by 1837 had been licensed to preach the gospel by the Presbytery of Pictou, which claimed Secessionist ancestry. He only ever held one home pastorate, on Prince Edward Island from 1838–46.

In 1839 Geddie married Charlotte MacDonald, and they volunteered for foreign missionary service; they were undeterred when their house burnt down and when, in 1846, two of their three children died. On 30 November 1846 they left for the South Seas, together with a catechist, Isaac Archibald, and his wife (alas, Archibald was to prove a moral failure). After a stopover in Samoa, Geddie and his family finally arrived at Anelgauhat harbour in Aneityum, the southernmost island of the New Hebrides island group, which since 1980 has become known as Vanuatu. Geddie felt the stern realities of missionary life and asked: 'Can these dry bones live?' He drew comfort from the knowledge that the gospel must be preached to every creature, that Christ shall have the heathen for His inheritance and the uttermost parts of the earth for His possession, and that all things are possible with God.

The native religion consisted mainly of fear of the spirits, ghosts and the sacred men. Geddie's colleague, John Inglis, who arrived in 1852, recorded that the Aneityumese believed in a supreme deity, called Inhujeraing, who created all things, but in practice the Aneityumese feared the natmasses, who were the ghosts of departed ancestors. These natmasses were amoral, and religion consisted mainly of placating them through making feasts and offerings. Priests were feared as disease makers. They would obtain a piece of an intended victim's dress or food (e.g. a banana skin), and then burn it with a special sacred leaf. After the sacred man had prayed to the natmasses, the victim would be afflicted with some kind of disease. Only presents to the sacred man could cure the victim. In addition to such a belief system, there were practices such as infanticide, widow strangulation and cannibalism.

On 29 March 1851 the only child, a son, of Waihit, a chief on Aneityum, died. Geddie comforted him with the realism and hope of resurrection in 2 Samuel 12:23. Waihit, who was very young in the faith, was strengthened and used the verse to witness to his heathen neighbours who had been taunting him. Later that year some heathen natives set fire to the Geddies' house, but this proved a turning point in the evangelization of the island. Two disease makers renounced their cult, and on 13 May 1852 thirteen natives were baptized, and so constituted the first Christian church in the New Hebrides. Less than two months later, Rev. John Inglis and his wife, Jessie, arrived to further the cause on Aneityum.

The gospel expanded, and was the forerunner of civilization on the island. Then the fledgling church was sorely tested: beginning in December 1860 a measles epidemic swept through the island and killed one-third of the population; in March 1861 the fine church and school buildings at Anelgauhat were burned to the ground; a week later a fierce hurricane struck; and on 20 May 1861 George and Ellen Gordon on the island of Erromanga were tomahawked to death. A year later the mission on Tanna was broken up. Tensions appeared amongst the missionaries themselves in 1865 as J.G. Paton, J.D. Gordon (George's brother) and John Inglis sailed on the mission ship *Dayspring* as it accompanied HMS *Curacoa* when it bombarded some Tannese villages. Geddie was horrified and cited Luke 23:34; 9:54-56, declaring that 'Our enterprise is one of mercy and not of judgment, and we forget our high office, when we invoke the vengeance of earthly power on the benighted natives around us.' Yet he refused to let the differences separate him from his fellow missionaries.

Finally, after a series of strokes, Geddie made his way to Geelong in Victoria, Australia, where he died on 14 December 1872. Geddie was the humblest yet strongest of men, one who never lost heart and who sought at great self-sacrifice to bring the New Hebrideans to know the grace of Christ. Mrs Charlotte Geddie, who was of a similar character, survived to the age of 93 and died in 1916.

75

JOHN 'RABBI' DUNCAN
(1796–1870)

Struggling for faith

Whoever believes that Jesus is the Christ is born of God
(1 John 5:1a).

*Truly God is good to Israel, to such as are pure in heart.
But as for me, my feet had almost stumbled; my steps
had nearly slipped. For I was envious of the boastful,
when I saw the prosperity of the wicked ... Until I went
into the sanctuary of God; then I understood their end ...
My flesh and my heart fail; but God is the strength of my
heart and my portion forever* (Ps. 73:1-3, 17, 26).

John Duncan was nicknamed 'Rabbi' Duncan because of his
concern to bring the gospel to the Jews and his teaching as
Professor of Hebrew in New College in Edinburgh. He was
born in Aberdeen, the son of a shoemaker. A restless soul, he
early on embraced some kind of pantheism, and remembered
that he once saw no difference between a horse and himself.
He then took to Sabellianism (which teaches that the Father,
Son and Holy Spirit are not three Persons but one), and then
moved on to liberal Christianity, with no reference to heaven
or hell. His conversion came after a meeting in Aberdeen in
1826 with César Malan from Geneva, who, using a series of
questions based on 1 John 5:1a, pressed him relentlessly on his

relationship with God. Ten years later, in 1836, Duncan was ordained in the Church of Scotland.

In 1841 he went as a missionary to work amongst Hungarian Jews. When the Disruption broke out in 1843, he joined the Free Church and taught Hebrew at New College. He was renowned for his absent-mindedness. In one way, his mind was encyclopaedic, but in another way it was almost chaotic. He thought in terms of aphorisms (pithy sayings), and struggled throughout his Christian life with the issue of assurance. He could remember complex languages, but could not remember the names of flowers or of his students. He once drank fourteen cups of tea while assuring his hostess that he never took more than two. When he came to be married the second time, the guests found that he had fallen asleep reading a Hebrew book and had forgotten he was to be married.

As a Free Churchman, he loved the Psalms but Psalm 73 remained his favourite. It epitomized his own struggles with the faith. When William C. Burns preached at Kilsyth, he invited inquirers to stay behind for counsel. Duncan stayed behind. He once commented that 'Spiritual joy is a delicate thing; it is easily spoiled.' At times he was reluctant to take part in the Lord's Supper. At his best, he recalled: 'As long as I am thinking of Christ I'm happy.' He could resort to utter simplicity, and on retiring to bed, would pray: 'This night when I lie down to sleep, I give my soul to Christ to keep.' He called himself 'a philosophical sceptic who has taken refuge in theology.'

In one of his moments of struggle, he wrote: 'I am sure that Jesus is the Christ, but I am not sure that I am a Christian.' Yet he remained sure of the truth itself, and affirmed that 'The vague, cloudy men are always talking against intolerance. Why, our very calling is to be intolerant; intolerant of proved error and known sin.' He condemned what he called 'cloudification'. Indeed, he once said: 'I cannot love a man and love his sin.' Sin is but 'pleasant poison'.

In 1837 his first wife, Janet, died after the stillbirth of their second daughter. Duncan wrote: 'I can trust even for my unbaptized infant.' Looking at the dead body of his wife, he drew comfort from the solemn words of the Shorter Catechism (Question 37): 'The souls of believers are at their death made perfect in holiness, and do immediately pass into glory; and their bodies, being still united to Christ, do rest in the grave till the resurrection.'

As biblical criticism began to assault the Bible's testimony to itself as the Word of God, Duncan opposed it, and held fast to the historical creeds as biblical and true. He referred to Christ on the cross in terms of 'damnation taken lovingly'. He added: 'There is nothing but Christ between us and hell; and, thanks be to God, we need nothing else.' His thinking was nuanced in its biblical balance. He famously said that 'Hyper-Calvinism is all house and no door: Arminianism is all door and no house.' To Duncan, John Gill (a Hyper-Calvinist) was preferable to John Wesley in intellectual understanding but not in practice. His principles were catholic: 'I'm first a Christian, next a Catholic, then a Calvinist, fourth a Paedo-baptist, and fifth a Presbyterian. I cannot reverse this order.' With his usual perception, he once described all errors as 'abused truths'.

G.K. Chesterton once lamented: 'A man was meant to be doubtful about himself, but undoubting about the truth; this has been exactly reversed.' What Chesterton was commending could well be applied to 'Rabbi' Duncan.

76

JAMES HUDSON TAYLOR
(1832–1905)

Looking to the finished work of Christ

*So when Jesus had received the sour wine, He said, 'It is
finished!' And bowing His head, He gave up
His spirit* (John 19:30).

*And my God shall supply all your need according to His
riches in glory by Christ Jesus* (Phil. 4:19).

*I have become all things to all men, that I might by all
means save some* (1 Cor. 9:22b).

*My grace is sufficient for you, for My strength is made
perfect in weakness* (2 Cor. 12:9a).

James Hudson Taylor was born in Barnsley, Yorkshire, in 1832,
and was usually known as Hudson. His father was a pharmacist
who did some preaching for the Methodists. At fifteen, Hudson
began work at a local bank, but eye trouble forced him back
to his father's pharmacy. Spiritually, he was aimless, angry
and a long way from God at this time. His sister Amelia was a
convinced Christian and prayed for him three times a day. His
mother was also praying for her listless son. In June 1849, at the
age of seventeen, Hudson was home alone and began to read
one of the tracts on his father's bookshelf. He was converted by
its citation of Christ's words on the cross: 'It is finished.'

Within a few months Hudson Taylor was certain that God was calling him to work in China. To prepare himself for the rigours of missionary life in China, he began to learn the Chinese language, gave up his feather-bed mattress and went to work for a surgeon. The Lord tested his faith, and he thought much on Philippians 4:19. One of his famous sayings became: 'God's work, done in God's way, will never lack God's supplies.' On one occasion, after quite a struggle, he gave away his last coin, a half-crown, to an Irishman with a dying wife. But he experienced heavenly joy: 'My heart was as light as my pocket.'

Finally, Hudson Taylor arrived in China in 1854. At this time, some 380 million Chinese in the country's interior had never seen a Westerner nor heard the name of Christ. Only seven of China's eighteen provinces had missionaries. The new missionary was determined that all China would be confronted with the gospel, and maintained that 'The only persons wanted here are those who will rejoice to work – really to labour – not to dream their lives away; to deny themselves; to suffer in order to save.'

At Shanghai, Hudson Taylor was given a singing cricket by a local, with instructions to feed it daily with two grains of boiled rice! In January 1858 he married Maria Dyer, who died in 1870 at the age of thirty-three; in 1871 he married Jennie Faulding. Like his two great predecessors, Robert Morrison (1782–1834) and Karl Gützlaff (1803–51), he came to the view that he would adopt Chinese clothing and grow a pigtail (known as a 'queue'). He wrote:

> I have never heard of anyone who after having *bona fide* attempted to become a Chinese to the Chinese that he might gain the Chinese, either regretted the step he had taken or decided to abandon the course ... We wish to see Christian [Chinese] ... We wish to see churches and Christian Chinese presided over by pastors and officers of their own countrymen,

worshipping the true God in the land of their fathers, in the costume of their fathers, in their own tongue wherein they were born, and in edifices of a thoroughly Chinese style of architecture ... Let us adopt their costume, acquire their language, study to imitate their habits and approximate to their diet as far as health and constitution will allow. Let us live in their house, making no unnecessary alterations in external appearance ... Knives and forks, plates and dishes, cups and saucers, must give place to chopsticks, natives spoons and basins [and food].

The Europeans at Shanghai, for the most part, greeted this decision with scorn. It meant, for example, that Maria had to walk behind her husband. This policy did not mean capitulation to all things Chinese. When a man cried out 'Foreign devil', Hudson Taylor grabbed his hand and showed its similarity to his own. The lesson was that the man must then be a 'native devil'.

After an outpouring of prayer on the sands of Brighton on Sunday, 25 June 1865, Hudson Taylor founded the China Inland Mission (CIM) on six premises:

(a) it would be interdenominational, with a simple doctrinal declaration;

(b) income would be shared, with no debts incurred:

(c) it would never solicit funds from donors, but simply trust God to supply all its needs (based on Matthew 9:38 and 6:33);

(d) work abroad would be directed by those who were abroad;

(e) it would press on into inland China;

(f) missionaries would wear Chinese clothing and worship in Chinese-style buildings.

Mission work was hindered by Britain's disgraceful policy in fighting two wars to maintain the opium trade with China – which led Hudson Taylor to denounce his own country. The

House of Lords even debated whether allowing missionaries into the interior of China was good for British trade. In 1878 he took the unprecedented step of sending unmarried women into the interior. One of the legacies of the CIM was the 'Wordless Book' which was used in evangelism among illiterate people. It originally had four pages – black for sin, red for the blood of Jesus, white for holiness, gold for heaven.

In 1900 the Boxer Rebellion broke out, led by the Society of Harmonious Fists with their red ribbons, yellow sashes, incantations and secret passwords. This saw 188 Protestant missionaries, including children, martyred. In addition, some 30,000 Chinese Christians were also martyred. Many mission societies demanded reparations, but Hudson Taylor refused. In 1866 he had written: 'Utter weakness in ourselves; we should be overwhelmed at the immensity of the work before us, were it not that our very insufficiency gives us a special claim to the fulfilment of His promise, "My grace is sufficient for thee; My strength is made perfect in weakness."' By 1903 he had retired, and he died on 5 June 1905. His life might be summed up in a letter that he had written to his mother: 'We may fail, do fail continually; but He never fails.' His motto was 'Advance, always advance', and he often cited Proverbs 24:11-12.

77

DAVID LIVINGSTONE
(1813–1873)

Being dead, yet still speaking

*I will lift up my eyes to the hills – from whence comes my
help? My help comes from the Lord, who made heaven
and earth ... The Lord shall preserve your going out
and your coming in from this time forth, and
even forevermore* (Ps. 121:1-2, 8).

*For I know that the Lord is great, and our Lord is
above all gods* (Ps. 135:5).

Lo, I am with you always, even to the end of the age
(Matt. 28:20b).

*And so I have made it my aim to preach the gospel, not
where Christ was named, lest I should build on another
man's foundation* (Rom. 15:20; see 2 Cor. 10:13-16).

*And look! The tears of the oppressed, but they have no
comforter – on the side of their oppressors there is power,
but they have no comforter* (Eccles. 4:1b).

*Other sheep I have, which are not of this fold; them also I
must bring, and they shall hear My voice* (John 10:16).

Born in 1813 into a godly home in Blantyre in Lanarkshire in
Scotland (although his mother was in the habit of smoking a
pipe every Sunday!), David Livingstone was raised to know the
Word of God. By the age of nine he could recite all 176 verses
of Psalm 119.

After coming to faith in Christ, Livingstone applied to the London Missionary Society in 1838 to be taken on as a missionary. He was never a scintillating preacher, and once when replacing a sick minister, he lost his train of thought in the pulpit and felt obliged to leave the chapel. Nevertheless, Livingstone studied both theology and medicine at Glasgow, and on 8 December 1840 he sailed for Cape Town to begin work in Africa. On 17 November 1840 as he took leave of his father, mother and sister, he read from Psalms 121 and 135 before the family prayed together for the last time.

In Africa his life was dominated by three impulses: the evangelization of the people, the exploration of the continent and the emancipation of all slaves. Dangers were never far away. He described in graphic terms the trip to Africa on the *George*: 'Imagine if you can a ship in a fit of epilepsy.' Land was equally precarious. On 16 February 1844 he was attacked by a lion, and later recorded that he felt no pain as a kind of dreaminess overtook him. On another occasion a rhinoceros miraculously stopped short of trampling him to death. His missionary journeys were legendary, and he would travel on even when racked with fever and discomforted by haemorrhoids. His wife, Mary, whom he married in 1845, was the daughter of long-term missionary Robert Moffat. She died of cerebral malaria in 1862.

One of Livingstone's favourite verses – one to which he constantly returned – was Jesus' promise in Matthew 28:20 to be with His people even to the end of the age. He underlined it in his journal, and regarded it as the end of all doubting and concern for the future. In 1853 he wrote: 'I will place no value on anything I have or may possess, except in relation to the kingdom of Christ. If anything will advance the interests of that Kingdom, it shall be given away or kept only in reference to whether giving or keeping will most promote the glory of Him to whom I owe all my hopes in time and eternity.' To keep himself humble, he read critics who abused him, and made it a rule not to read anything that praised him. He made a habit of praying that 'we might imitate Christ in all His inimitable perfections.'

Like the apostle Paul, Livingstone always sought to be a true pioneer: 'I hope to be permitted to work as long as I live beyond other men's line of things and plant the seed of the gospel where others have not planted.' There was a human cost to this, for which he was criticized. From 1852 to 1856, for example, he was separated from Mary and their four children, as they returned to Britain while Livingstone stayed on in Africa.

Livingstone is often portrayed as one who was too interested in commerce, but his championing of commercial trade was linked to his detestation of the slave trade. He considered that the opening up of Africa to commerce would kill off the Portuguese and Arabic involvement in what Livingstone called the 'devilish trade in human flesh'. In attacking slavery, he cited Ecclesiastes 4:1 on man's inhumanity to man.

On 1 May 1873 he was found dead, kneeling beside his bed – he had died while praying. His body was preserved in salt and brandy, and carried 1,500 miles to Zanzibar, and then on to Westminster Abbey where he is the only pauper to be buried there with full state honours. On his tomb are the words from John 10:16 which, appropriately enough, tell of Christ's other sheep whom Christ would bring and who would hear His voice.

78

J.C. RYLE
(1816–1900)

What it means to preach the gospel

*My iniquities have overtaken me, so that I am not able to
look up; they are more than the hairs of
my head (Ps. 40:12).*

*For by grace you have been saved through faith, and that
not of yourselves; it is the gift of God (Eph. 2:8).*

Your word is truth (John 17:17).

*For if I preach the gospel, I have nothing to boast of,
for necessity is laid upon me; yes, woe is me if I do not
preach the gospel! (1 Cor. 9:16).*

*I have fought the good fight, I have finished the race,
I have kept the faith (2 Tim. 4:7).*

John Charles Ryle was born into a family that was not particularly religious, although not to the point of disparaging
church attendance. His father owned a silk mill in Macclesfield
in the north of England, and from 1832 to 1837 was a Member
of Parliament. In 1828 young John was sent south to Eton. Here
he learnt little of the evangelical faith, but often God will lodge
just a portion of His Word into the heart of His people. Ryle was
struck by the words of one visiting preacher at Eton who cited
Psalm 40:12, 'My sins are more than the hairs of my head.'

Ryle went on to Christ Church, Oxford where he excelled at cricket, taking ten wickets in a match against Cambridge in 1836. Ryle was converted to the evangelical faith, not by hearing a sermon or reading a tract, but simply by hearing Ephesians 2:8 being read out in an Oxford church. From this time on, he was a man who knew grace, and sought to proclaim it to all who would listen.

Yet grace, though free, brought its own costs. He went on to read William Wilberforce's *A Practical View* (1797), and gave up dancing and billiards which he loved. His own family were not appreciative of his new-found evangelical convictions, but Ryle thought that opposition only strengthened him. As he explained: 'What is won dearly is priced highly and clung to firmly.' Back at Macclesfield, Ryle worked for his father's bank until one fateful day in June 1841 when it went bankrupt. Years later he recalled: 'We got up one summer morning with all the world before us as usual and went to bed that same night completely and entirely ruined.' Such is the uncertainty of this life, and its wealth.

Ryle entered the Anglican ministry and was made a deacon on 21 December 1841. He possessed a strong voice and a clear delivery, and he worked hard to make his preaching, and later his writing, easily comprehensible, 'to arouse, to awaken and to stir careless souls'. One woman expressed disappointment at his preaching because she understood him! He favoured Christian education, declaring that 'a church without a school is like a man with only one arm.'

Ryle knew suffering in his own family. His first wife, Matilda, died in 1847, only two years after they were married; his second wife, Jessie, died in 1860 after ten years' marriage; and in 1861 he married Henrietta Clowes, a musician and photographer, who helped to raise his five young children. In 1880, at a surprisingly advanced age, he was made the Bishop of Liverpool. He chose as his motto the text 'Thy Word is truth'.

The outstanding feature of Ryle's ministry was undoubtedly his undeviating devotion to Scripture as the Word of God. When Ryle became vicar of Stradbroke in Suffolk in 1861, a new pulpit was built for the church. Around the top was carved the text: 'Woe is unto me, if I preach not the Gospel.' After the workmen had carved the letters, he took a chisel and cut a deep groove beneath the word *not*. To Ryle, the inspiration of Scripture was 'the very keel and foundation of Christianity'. He considered that one who held to a partial inspiration of the Bible had his head in a fog and his feet on quicksand. He concluded: 'The view which I maintain is that every book, and chapter, and verse, and syllable of the Bible was originally given by inspiration of God.'

In the aftermath of the appearance of *Essays and Reviews* in 1860, Ryle denounced the biblical critics as 'spiritual robbers' who take away the bread of life and do not even leave a stone. Ryle confronted this unbelief even in his own family. One of his sons, Herbert Edward Ryle, embraced liberal theology, yet was ordained in 1882, and became well-known in the field of Old Testament Higher Criticism. In 1887 Ryle felt obliged to release this son from his post as Examining Chaplain on account of the younger man's acceptance of Higher Criticism. The older Ryle was mystified by the claim that Christians could learn anything worthwhile from liberal German biblical critics.

Always practical, Ryle emphasized that 'a lively Christ-exalting minister will always have a Church-going people.' When he died in 1900, his grave was marked with two very fitting texts – Ephesians 2:8 and 2 Timothy 4:7. Equally fitting are two descriptions of Ryle left by his colleagues. F.J. Chavasse described him as 'that man of granite with the heart of a child', while Richard Hobson considered him to be 'bold as a lion for the truth, the truth of God's Word and his Gospel.'

79

GEORGE MÜLLER
(1805–1898)

To die to self, and trust the Lord

*A father of the fatherless, a defender of widows, is
God in His holy habitation (Ps. 68:5).*

*Give, and it will be given to you; good measure, pressed
down, shaken together, and running over will be put into
your bosom. For with the same measure that you use,
it will be measured back to you (Luke 6:38).*

*And Abraham called the name of the place,
The-Lord-Will-Provide (Gen. 22:14a).*

*For we know that if our earthly house, this tent, is
destroyed, we have a building from God, a house not
made with hands, eternal in the heavens (2 Cor. 5:1).*

*For the love of Christ compels us, because we judge thus:
that if One died for all, then all died; and He died for all,
that those who live should live no longer for themselves
but for Him who died for them and rose again
(2 Cor. 5:14-15).*

Born in Prussia in 1805, George Müller became famous in his
own long lifetime as a prayerful and humble pastor and adminis-
trator of five orphanages that he established in Bristol, England.
As a youngster, Müller gave little indication of the life he would
lead. On the night that his mother lay dying, fourteen-year-old
George was reeling through the streets, drunk. Yet his father had
hopes that he would become a Lutheran clergyman!

In 1825 he was converted after attending a private prayer meeting at Halle, and immediately he set about proclaiming and living out his new-found faith. After being declared unfit for the army, he left for London in 1829, and began to work among the city's Jewish population. He adopted what became known as Brethren views – notably believers' baptism and the weekly celebration of the Lord's Supper – and he renounced any fixed salary.

At Halle University, Müller had lodged for two months in an orphan house built by the Pietist, Auguste Francke. At the time of its construction, the Halle orphanage was the largest building in Europe. This planted a seed in Müller's mind, which flourished when he read the biography of Francke in 1832. From 1832 he was the pastor of Bethesda Chapel in Bristol, and from 1835 he had begun his work amongst orphans. By 1870 there were five orphan houses, catering for 2,000 orphans at any one time, at a cost of about £25,000 annually. Yet each day began with meditation upon God's Word, then with prayer based on that meditation. God spoke to Müller before Müller dared to address his God.

The children would rise at 6.00 a.m. to be ready for knitting at 7.00 a.m. for the girls and reading for the boys. Breakfast was at 8.00 a.m., and the morning service at 8.30 a.m. Then came schoolwork at 10.00 a.m., followed by recreation in the playground. Dinner was served at 12.30 p.m., school recommenced at 1.00 p.m., and finished at 4.00 p.m. when ninety minutes of play was allowed. There was a half-hour service, then a meal was served at 6.00 p.m. After the meal, girls would work with the needle while boys would go back to schoolwork.

After meditating on Psalm 65 ('O Thou that hearest prayer'), Müller wrote down definite prayer petitions. Towards the end of his life, he calculated that he had read the Bible through nearly 200 times, and could find distinct answers to definite prayers in some 50,000 episodes in his life! His five conditions for prevailing prayer were:

(a)   an entire dependence on Christ as mediator
      (John 14:13-14; 15:16);
(b)   separation from all known sin (Ps. 66:18);
(c)   faith in the promises of God (Heb. 11:6; 6:13-20);
(d)   asking according to His will (1 John 5:14; James 4:3);
(e)   importunity in supplication (Luke 18:1-8; James 5:7).

Where these conditions were not met, God would dishonour Himself by answering our prayers, and would do spiritual damage to the suppliant.

The description of God as 'a father of the fatherless' in Psalm 68:5 deeply moved him, and became what A.T. Pierson calls one of his 'life-texts'. Müller wrote: 'By the help of God, this shall be my argument before Him, respecting the orphans, in the hour of need. He is their Father, and therefore has pledged Himself, as it were, to provide for them; and I have only to remind Him of the need of these poor children in order to have it supplied.' Thus he always viewed the orphan work as God's work.

Müller sought to live by faith in the God who supplies the daily needs of His people. Citing Luke 6:38, he explained: 'My aim never was, how much I could obtain, but rather how much I could give.' In 1867 he received a gift from someone who explained that he was making restitution. Müller returned the gift, and told the man to make restitution with the party that he had wronged. He would return any money that was obtained by means of musical entertainment, and did likewise with any funds given for his old age or for illness. When asked whether he possessed a good stock of funds for the orphan houses, Müller replied: 'Our funds are deposited in a bank which cannot break.' A woman once donated a diamond ring to the orphan work. Before selling it, Müller used it to carve in Hebrew 'Jehovah Jireh' ('The Lord will provide') on the window pane of his study. As he explained in 1874: 'I commit the whole work to Him, and He will provide me with what I need.'

The years from 1875 to 1892 were spent in extensive preaching tours to Europe, America, Asia, Africa and Australia. His last sermon at Bethesda Chapel, after a ministry of sixty-six years, was, appropriately enough, on 2 Corinthians 5:1. The tall, slim, erect body of Müller finally breathed its last. All in all, some ten thousand orphans had come under his care.

Before his death, Müller was asked what was the secret of his service. He explained his life's work in terms of his conversion: 'There was a day when I died, utterly died – died to George Müller, his opinions, preferences, tastes and will – died to the world, its approval or censure – died to the approval or blame even of my brethren or friends – and since then I have studied only to show myself approved unto God.'

80

LORD SHAFTESBURY
(1801–1885)

Living before the coming King

Seek first the kingdom of God and His righteousness
(Matt. 6:33a).

*The eternal God is your refuge, and underneath are the
everlasting arms* (Deut. 33:27a).

I will never leave you nor forsake you (Heb. 13:5b;
see Deut. 31:6, 8; Josh. 1:5).

*I am with you always, even to the end of the
age* (Matt. 28:20b).

*Surely I am coming quickly. Amen. Even so,
come, Lord Jesus* (Rev. 22:20).

*Pray for the peace of Jerusalem. May they
prosper who love you* (Ps. 122:6).

For I know that my Redeemer lives (Job 19:25a).

*[They] begged Him that they might just touch the hem of
His garment. And as many as touched Him were
made well* (Mark 6:56b; also Mark 5:27-28).

Lord Shaftesbury was born on 28 April 1801 as Anthony Ashley
Cooper. His father was a Member of Parliament who tended to
neglect his children, so young Anthony's upbringing was largely
left in the hands of a servant, Anna Maria Milles (pronounced
'Millis') who urged him to seek first the kingdom of God and
not to rest until he had found it. She died when Anthony was

only ten – the same year that his uncle died, and he became Lord Ashley.

One of Ashley's younger brothers died after a two-hour fist fight at school. When he was only fifteen, Ashley was further affected by the sight of four or five drunken men burying a pauper. The tall and handsome aristocrat was moved to write: 'I was convinced that God had called me to devote whatever advantages He might have bestowed upon me in the cause of the weak, the helpless, both man and beast, and those who had none to help them.'

In 1826 Lord Ashley entered the House of Commons, and on 18 February 1828 gave his maiden speech. The content was good, but his delivery lacked something – he was almost inaudible to the press gallery. Unlike Wilberforce, he was not a natural orator. Only in 1851 did he become the seventh Earl of Shaftesbury, and so had to vacate his seat in the House of Commons. Back in 1830 he had married the young and beautiful Lady Emily Cooper, and on 6 August 1833 he attended the funeral of William Wilberforce at Westminster Abbey.

In September 1842, in order to experience the conditions of the coalminers, Lord Ashley descended 450 feet into a coalmine in an open bucket, but did not fear as he thought on 'Underneath are the everlasting arms'. Seven years later, in 1849, his second son, Francis, died at the age of sixteen. Before his death, Francis spoke much with his father about the issues of eternity, and Lord Ashley was convinced of his true faith. On his gravestone was inscribed: 'He [i.e. Francis] only sought forgiveness in the free love and mercy of God through the atonement of a crucified Saviour.'

Shaftesbury's two favourite verses were reassurances of the presence of Christ with His people (Heb. 13:5b; Matt. 28:20b), and the next-to-last verse of Revelation became his prayer. In fact, 'Even so, come, Lord Jesus' was embossed in Greek on the flaps of his envelopes. The Protestant Bishop of Jerusalem sent Shaftesbury a ring with Psalm 122:6 engraved on it, and Shaftesbury wore it for the rest of his life. He devoted himself to a multitude of causes – the Jews, chimney-sweeps, children in factories and mines, ragged schools, the mentally ill (known then as lunatics), and the extension of the Church. He opposed the emerging Anglo-Catholic movement, of which his own cousin, E.B. Pusey, was a leader, but he detested theological liberalism even more. When the Education Act of 1870 was passed, he predicted growing secularization and 'the greatest moral change that England has ever known'.

Shaftesbury's convictions were deep: 'I think a man's religion, if it is worth anything, should enter into every sphere of life, and rule his conduct in every relation. I have always been – and, please God, always shall be – an Evangelical of the Evangelicals.' He once declared: 'There are not two hours in the day, but I think of the second advent of our Lord. That is the hope of the church, for Israel and the world. Come, Lord Jesus, come quickly.'

As he was dying, he had the twenty-third psalm read to him, and he prayed: 'Come, Lord Jesus' and 'I know that my Redeemer liveth.' On the day he died – 1 October 1885 – he said: 'I am just touching the hem of His garment.' At Shaftesbury's funeral from Westminster Abbey in 1885, as rain fell, a poor labourer cried: 'Our Earl's gone! God A'mighty knows he loved us, and we loved him. We shan't see his likes again!'

81

D.L. MOODY
(1837–1899)

Tell me the story simply

*Tekel: You have been weighed in the balances,
and found wanting* (Dan. 5:27).
He who does the will of God abides forever
(1 John 2:17b).

Dwight Lyman Moody was born on a small farm in Northfield in rural north-western Massachusetts. He knew poverty, as his father died unexpectedly when Dwight was only four, leaving his mother with seven children and twins on the way. Moody and his siblings had been baptized by the Unitarians, but the link was not strong – more a result of the Unitarian pastor's kindness to the family than any deeply held religious convictions. As a youngster, Moody acquired only four years of formal education, and never mastered spelling or pronunciation. Later, Charles Spurgeon was to say that Moody pronounced 'Mesopotamia' in two syllables! At seventeen Moody moved to Boston to find employment in his uncle's shoe shop.

On 21 April 1855, a Congregationalist Sunday School teacher visited Moody in the shoe shop, and pressed him about his need for the Saviour. Without knowing much, Moody believed, and was admitted into the church in March 1856. Moving to Chicago, Moody read George Müller's *A Life of Trust,* and made a substantial amount of money from wise investments. He also began to minister to the young urchins in the Chicago slums. In 1860 he turned his back on his shoe business and his real estate investments, and devoted himself to full-time evangelism, although deliberately avoiding ordination.

After marrying Emma Revell in 1862, the two of them served as missionaries to the Union soldiers in the American Civil War. Moody took notes from pastors and those educated in theology, and studied the sermons of Charles Spurgeon. By the end of 1865 he was president of the Young Men's Christian Association (YMCA) in Chicago, leader of the Illinois Street Church and director of the Mission School for children. In 1867 he travelled to Great Britain where he met Spurgeon and Müller.

In 1871 Moody's faith was tested when he lost his home, his Illinois Street Church and the YMCA building as he and his family were forced to flee for their lives from the great fire of Chicago, which broke out on Sunday evening, 8 October. More significantly in the long term, two women, W.R. Hawkhurst and Sarah Cooke, encouraged Moody to pray for the anointing of the Holy Spirit. At first he resented the suggestion, but then he solicited their prayers, and sought a greater work of God in his life. While walking along Wall Street in New York City, he was suddenly overcome by God's presence. Finding a place of solitude, he went through an intense second experience, where he cried out to God to withhold His hand, lest he die on the spot for joy.

In 1873 he returned to Britain, and in November even made his way for the first time to Scotland with his musical colleague Ira D. Sankey. Moody's preaching, accompanied by the use of hymns, attracted large crowds and was a remarkable success. There were critics, however. John Kennedy, of Dingwall, took Horatius Bonar to task for supporting the new 'Hyper-Evangelism'. Moody and Sankey returned to America in 1875 as national heroes. In years to come there were two further visits to Britain, as well as visits to Canada and Mexico.

A giant of a man at twenty stone, Moody preached an Arminian gospel in a warm-hearted, anecdotal style without too much concern for doctrinal exactness. He remained less controversial than Charles Finney, who did not believe in original sin; and he avoided the country-yokel excesses of Billy Sunday, who preached in shirtsleeves, broke chairs and declared: 'I don't know any more about theology than a jack-rabbit knows about ping-pong, but I'm on my way to glory.' Yet Moody still proclaimed what he called the 'Three Rs' of the Bible – ruin by the Fall, redemption by the blood and regeneration by the Spirit. His preaching was simple, vigorous and imaginative. For example, in preaching on the Ten Commandments, he made Daniel 5:27 his foundational text, and worked his way through each commandment, asking: 'Now, my friend, are you ready to be weighed by this law of God?' Preachers who are prone to give heavy doctrinal expositions as their sermons would do well to learn from Moody.

Moody emphasized the love of God, as his view was that 'Terror never brought a man in yet.' He could say things that contain truth, but were also capable of misleading people. For example, in his children's stories he said that 'The gospel of Jesus Christ is a gospel of deeds and not of words.' In reality, it is both. Although Moody himself held to the verbal inspiration of Scripture, he cooperated with churchmen who did not. Henry Drummond, for example, wrote: 'There is no more unfortunate word in our Church's vocabulary than "Standard." A Standard is a thing that stands. Theology is a thing that moves.' Yet Moody wrote glowingly that Drummond lived constantly in the thirteenth chapter of First Corinthians, on love. He added: 'All the time we were together he was a Christlike man, and often a rebuke to me.' Moody – unlike Spurgeon – did not fully perceive the trends of the times.

For all that, Moody preached the gospel to something like a hundred million people over his lifetime. His grave is in Northfield, Massachusetts, and his epitaph is taken from the KJV's rendering of 1 John 2:17b, 'He that doeth the will of God abideth forever.'

82

FYODOR DOSTOEVSKY
(1821–1881)

Seeking Salvation for His Children

*I came forth from the Father and have come into the
world. Again, I leave the world and go to
the Father* (John 16:28).

*While they promise them liberty, they themselves are
slaves of corruption* (2 Pet. 2:19).

*But when he was still a great way off, his father saw him
and had compassion, and ran and fell on his
neck and kissed him* (Luke 15:20).

Born in Moscow to a hard-drinking doctor and a devoutly Orthodox mother who succumbed to tuberculosis when Fyodor was
just fifteen, Dostoevsky grew up to become one of the greatest
novelists of all time. While Dostoevsky was studying at the Military Engineering College at St Petersburg, he received the news
that his father had been murdered by some serfs on his estate.
Indeed, Dostoevsky came to know much trauma in his life. He
was afflicted by epileptic fits; he was invariably in financial woes
and struggled to keep ahead of his creditors; he battled with his
great weakness, gambling; his first wife, Maria, died; his brother,
Michael, also died.

Dostoevsky's first novel, *Poor Folk*, was received well in St Petersburg, but Dostoevsky threw in his lot with some revolutionaries, and was soon arrested and sent off to the Peter and Paul Fortress. In 1845 Dostoevsky had written to the revolutionary, Alexander Herzen, in decidedly anti-Christian terms, declaring: 'I have acquired the truth, and in the words "God and religion" I see darkness, obscurity, chains, and the knout whip.'

After eight months in the Fortress, he was sentenced to be shot by a firing squad. In fact, he was actually led out with twenty-two others to be shot when a reprieve was dramatically announced. His sentence was commuted to four years in Omsk penal settlement in Siberia, followed by five years of military service. While in prison, virtually his only companion was a New Testament which he devoured, learning much of it by heart. Job became his favourite book in the Old Testament.

Arriving back in St Petersburg in 1859, Dostoevsky engaged in journalistic work, and also produced his masterpiece *Crime and Punishment*, with its portrayal of the godless and amoral Raskolnikov, who murders an old woman to assert his power. Yet the murderer, Raskolnikov, and the harlot, Sonia, come to find hope and redemption in the New Testament, in the book that tells of the Father's welcome to His prodigal son.

Dostoevsky also came to travel widely. At Basel, he was overcome by Hans Holbein's painting *Christ Taken Down from the Cross*, with its graphic portrayal of Christ's corpse. Accustomed to Eastern Orthodox icons that attempt to express eternity, with passionless figures betraying no expression or emotion, Dostoevsky was almost shattered by Holbein's picture of the terrible reality of the Incarnation – the Word did indeed become flesh. Dostoevsky was in the habit of marking his New Testament, by underlining or writing NB next to what had particularly struck him. The Gospel of John, with its emphasis on Christ as the God-man who brings life, truth and love was especially marked – John 16:28 being one of many examples.

In his novel, *The Devils,* Dostoevsky explored the theme that debauchery would lead to deadened moral sensibilities, and finally to bloodshed on a massive scale. It was Peter Verkhovensky who called virginity 'a stupid prejudice ... an out-of-date convention'. His conclusions were that 'without despotism there has never been any freedom or equality' and 'one or two generations of vice are absolutely essential now.' So it was that the freedom advocated by Rousseau became the tyranny practised by Lenin. Nihilism prepares the way for despotism on an unparalleled scale – if God is dead, everything is permissible. In the words of Dostoevsky's mouthpiece, Elder Zossima: 'Equality is to be found only in the spiritual dignity of man, and that will be understood only among us.' Man without God not only does not know his creator, but he cannot even know himself. Hence, in the words of Zossima: 'They think they are establishing a just order, but, having rejected Christ, they will end by drenching the world in blood.' And so it proved.

Apart from *Crime and Punishment* and *The Devils,* Dostoevsky's other major novels were *The Idiot* and *The Brothers Karamazov* – each one revised again and again, but still bearing the marks of a tortured genius. On his deathbed, Dostoevsky gave instructions that the parable of the prodigal son be read to his children, telling them: 'I love you dearly, but my love is nothing compared with the love of God ... You are His children; humble yourselves before Him, as before your father; implore His pardon, and He will rejoice over your repentance as the father rejoiced over that of the prodigal son.'

83

HORATIUS BONAR
(1808–1889)

ANDREW BONAR
(1810–1892)

Brothers in Christ

The God of all comfort, who comforts us in all our tribulation, that we may be able to comfort those who are in any trouble, with the comfort with which we ourselves are comforted by God (2 Cor. 1:4).

So He said to them, 'This kind can come out by nothing but prayer and fasting' (Mark 9:29).

You must be born again (John 3:7b).

He who wins souls is wise (Prov. 11:30b).

Now as He drew near, He saw the city and wept over it (Luke 19:41).

Then He will also say to those on the left hand, 'Depart from Me, you cursed, into the everlasting fire prepared for the devil and his angels' (Matt. 25:41).

And God will wipe away every tear from their eyes; there shall be no more death, nor sorrow, nor crying. There shall be no more pain, for the former things have passed away (Rev. 21:4).

I will give of the fountain of the water of life freely to him who thirsts (Rev. 21:6b).

You are worthy ... for You were slain, and have redeemed us to God by Your blood ... (Rev. 5:9).

There were four Bonar brothers, born into the godly home of an Edinburgh solicitor, James Bonar, and his wife Marjory, early in the nineteenth century. Three of them entered the Presbyterian ministry, namely John, Horatius (known as Horace to his family) and Andrew. They remained close in every way, and all lived long lives, and only died towards the end of the nineteenth century. Indeed, at one communion service all three brothers preached – one on Christ as prophet, another on Christ as priest and the third on Christ as king. Andrew once cited 2 Corinthians 1:4 as applicable to how they responded to each other's trials and troubles.

Horace became a minister at Leith in 1833, before moving on to the church at Kelso, where in 1837 he preached his first sermon, on Mark 9:29, and took as his motto John 3:7b. From 1866 he was minister of the Chalmers Memorial Church at Grange in Edinburgh, where he remained until his death. He was especially effective with young people, and wrote tracts, hymns and poems to help them. His wonderful communion hymn is 'Here, O my Lord, I see Thee face to face'. All in all, Horatius wrote about 600 hymns that set forth the gospel of substitution in a simple form. For example,

> Not what these hands have done
> Can save this guilty soul;
> Not what this toiling flesh has borne
> Can make my spirit whole...
> Thy work alone, O Christ,
> Can ease this weight of sin;
> Thy blood alone, O Lamb of God,
> Can give me peace within.

Perhaps his most powerful evangelistic lines were:

> Upon a life I did not live,
> Upon a death I did not die;
> Another's life, another's death,
> I stake my whole eternity.

In all his ministry, Horatius's message was that 'God has affirmed *substitution* as the principle on which he means to deal with fallen man.'

Andrew was similar in his spiritual devotion and gifts. He was converted to Christ while he was sitting quietly in his study on 17 October 1830, and reading William Guthrie's *Trial of a Saving Interest in Christ*. He remembered: 'I did nothing but receive.' Following Horatius, he entered the Divinity Hall in 1831, and came to serve at Collace, Perthshire, in 1838. He sought to encourage a school of saints – such as Robert Murray M'Cheyne and John Milne – who promoted experimental Christianity in the Church of Scotland, then in the Free Church after the Disruption of 1843. In 1856 he was called to Finnieston Free Church in Glasgow, where he had 'He who wins souls is wise' carved, in Hebrew, on the church door. It was carved in Hebrew partly due to the hope that it might attract the attention and interest of Jews.

Andrew remained a zealous and compassionate evangelist, and commented with regard to Jesus: 'I think He will weep over the lost as He did over Jerusalem. It will be something to be said for ever in heaven, "Jesus wept as He said: 'Depart, ye cursed.'" But then it was absolutely necessary to say it.' At funerals he loved to preach on Revelation 21:4, 6b. A humble man who took sanctification seriously, Andrew always maintained that 'The best part of all Christian work is that part that only God sees.' In his diary, he wrote: 'Imperfection stamped upon every-thing I ever undertook.'

For better or for worse, both brothers were premillennial in their views of the Second Coming – which was somewhat unusual in Reformed circles. Horatius debated with John Kennedy over whether Reformed Christians ought to support the Arminian Moody-Sankey crusades of 1873-5. Both Kennedy and Bonar made valid points in the controversy, with Bonar being rather too hopeful and Kennedy perhaps overcritical.

The Bonar brothers lived in days when the impact of unbelieving biblical criticism was increasingly being embraced by many leaders in the professing Church. In 1883 Horatius Bonar lamented the trends of the times: 'Man is now thinking out a Bible for himself; framing a religion in harmony with the development of liberal thought; constructing worship on the principles of taste and culture; shaping a god to suit the expanding aspirations of the age.' Andrew too had led the charge against Robertson Smith in 1881, and lived long enough to protest at the vindication of Marcus Dods in 1890.

As Andrew contemplated death, his mind often turned to Revelation 5:9. The gospel of substitution proved to be a sure hope and foundation for the ministries and lives of both Horatius and Andrew Bonar – and John Bonar for that matter.

84

CHARLES HADDON SPURGEON
(1834–1892)

Conversion and controversies

Look to Me, and be saved, all you ends of the earth! For
I am God and there is no other (Isa. 45:22).
Wash me, and I shall be whiter than snow (Ps. 51:7b).
To you who believe, He is precious (1 Pet. 2:7a).
Salvation is of the Lord (Jonah 2:9d; Ps. 3:8a).

Charles Haddon Spurgeon was born on 19 June 1834 into a Christian family living in Tollesbury, near Colchester in England, although because of family hardships, he spent much of his early life with his grandparents at Stambourne in rural Essex. His father and his grandfather were both evangelical Congregational ministers. There have been few figures in Church history that have had so many stories – many of them apocryphal – told about him.

Despite his godly upbringing, Spurgeon as a youth did not know grace: 'I had heard of the plan of salvation by the sacrifice of Jesus from my youth up; but I did not know any more about it in my innermost soul than if I had been born and bred a heathen.' On Sunday 6 January 1850, during a snowstorm in London, Spurgeon attended a Primitive Methodist chapel where there were only about twelve to fifteen present. The preacher failed to turn up, and finally an unknown shoemaker or tailor got up to preach. He had little to say but he stuck to his text, which was Isaiah 45:22. After repeating it many times, he saw Spurgeon looking glum, and spoke bluntly: 'Young man, you look very miserable. Look to Jesus.'

That was all Spurgeon needed, and he knew what it meant to be saved by grace. On the way home Spurgeon remembered Psalm 51: 'Wash me, and I shall be whiter than snow.' It is worth noting that a number of the Lord's most gifted servants – Augustine, Abraham Kuyper and Spurgeon himself – have been converted by very simple means. Spurgeon was baptized in the river Lark at Isleham on 3 May 1850, and later that year at Cambridge he preached his first sermon, which was on the preciousness of Christ, from 1 Peter 2:7. Years later, in 1859, he recalled: 'I do not think I could have said anything upon any other text, but Christ was precious to my soul and I was in the flush of my youthful love, and I could not be silent when a precious Jesus was the subject.' He trusted that he could say in 1859 that Christ was more precious to him than He was in 1850. At an extraordinarily young age, Spurgeon was ordained as pastor of the small Baptist church at Waterbeach. His experience breaks all the rules about laying hands suddenly on no man! From the beginning of his ministry, there was blessing, with his first convert being a poor labourer's wife.

In a Christian sense, he was always his own man, and quite catholic in his affections, and somewhat un-Victorian in his views. He refused to go to a theological college, thought committees were a waste of time and remained staunchly Calvinistic, albeit with a generous heart. He was a speed reader with a photographic memory and a ready wit. He answered something like 500 letters a week. For much of his life, he smoked a cigar and declared: 'I mean to smoke to the glory of God.'

In April 1854 Spurgeon was called to New Park Street, Southwark, in London at the age of nineteen. Within a few years, he had become the most popular preacher of his day, although attacks in the press were common. In 1861 the congregation moved permanently to the Metropolitan Tabernacle at Elephant and Castle, Southwark, with seating for 5,000 people. Besides the church, he also ran the Stockwell Orphanage (opened for boys in 1867 and for girls in 1879; it was bombed in World War II), and a seminary which was set up in 1857 (and renamed Spurgeon's College in 1923). His much-used *Lectures to My Students* come from his Friday-afternoon addresses to his pastoral students, while his massive commentary on the Psalms, *The Treasury of David*, sold 120,000 copies in his lifetime.

On 8 January 1856 Spurgeon married Susannah, and the couple had non-identical twin sons, Charles and Thomas. These were the only children they ever had. Susannah became an invalid although she maintained an invaluable book ministry throughout her life. When Spurgeon began his ministry, newspapers attacked him for being an actor and a nine days' wonder. *The Daily News* on 9 September 1856, for example, had a long article on what it called Spurgeon's 'pulpit buffoonery'. He spoke in the John Ploughman style, and it was regarded as being too direct and plain.

During his ministry, Spurgeon was involved in a number of controversies. He combated Arminianism, declaring that 'The old truth that Calvin preached, that Augustine preached, that Paul preached, is the truth that I must preach today, or else be false to my conscience and my God.' In 1855 a controversy broke out over hyper-Calvinism. While remaining clearly Calvinistic, Spurgeon maintained that the gospel invitations are universal; we are commanded to believe; human beings are responsible before God; and there is a love of God for all humanity.

On 5 June 1864 he preached a sermon on 'Baptismal Regeneration' which strained his relations with Anglican evangelicals. In Spurgeon's view, the Anglican Book of Common Prayer taught baptismal regeneration. However, his most bitter experience was the Downgrade Controversy, which was over the full authority of Scripture, and which led to Spurgeon's leaving the Baptist Union. In August 1887 Spurgeon raised the issue of fellowship between orthodox evangelicals and those who had embraced the higher criticism: 'Christian love has its claims, and divisions are to be shunned as grievous evils; but how far are we justified in being in confederacy with those who are departing from the truth?' On 28 October, Spurgeon withdrew from the Baptist Union, and the resultant controversy isolated him for the remaining years of his life.

Spurgeon regarded modern thought as 'a totally new cult, having no more relation to Christianity than the mist of the evening to the everlasting hills.' He possessed a picturesque way of expressing himself: 'The old gospel is the real wonder-worker; the new stuff would not save a robin.' Just before his death, he wrote: 'I hate the Christianised infidelity of the modern school more than ever.' Indeed: 'If I must be the last of the Puritans, I will not be ashamed of it. My Lord will revive his buried truth as sure as he is God; the present madness will cease with its own short hour.' He considered that Calvinism was epitomized in the text from Jonah 2:9 and Psalm 3:8, 'Salvation is of the Lord.' From this truth, he derived his strength, and he declared: 'This verse contains the sum and substance of Calvinistic doctrine.'

85

CHARLES HADDON SPURGEON
(1834–1892)

Struggles with depression

*Therefore God also has highly exalted Him and given Him
the name which is above every name, that at the name
of Jesus every knee should bow, of those in heaven, and
of those on earth, and of those under the earth, and that
every tongue should confess that Jesus Christ is Lord, to
the glory of God the Father* (Phil. 2:9-11).

*He who dwells in the secret place of the Most High shall
abide under the shadow of the Almighty* (Ps. 91:1).

My grace is sufficient for you (2 Cor. 12:9a).

On 19 October 1856 Charles Spurgeon was preaching at the
Surrey Gardens Music Hall when someone shouted out 'Fire!'
There were thousands in the congregation, and in the ensuing
panic seven were killed and many more were maimed and
injured. At first Spurgeon was not aware of what had happened,
but when he was informed, he collapsed and was unable to
function for many days. For a few days it appeared that he might
never preach again, and he remembered that he was 'pressed
beyond measure and out of bounds with an enormous weight
of misery.' He was brought through this breakdown by contemplating Philippians 2:9-11, that Christ's name would be exalted

by God the Father's determination, no matter what happened to Spurgeon.

In Spurgeon's estimation, 'Fits of depression come over most of us.' Certainly in his own case, he would be overcome by depression, and not be aware of the cause. Often Scripture would arouse him out of the black depths. For example, he was once cured when he saw Psalm 91 in a shoemaker's shop window. On another occasion he arrived home weary and depressed, and thought of the words 'My grace is sufficient for thee' until he burst into laughter. His lesson was: 'Little faith will bring your souls to heaven, but great faith will bring heaven to your souls.'

Regarding our view of God, Spurgeon recommended: 'Never exalt one attribute at the expense of another.' A minister is not to be subject to depression because he is thin-skinned: 'You must be able to bear criticism, or you are not fit to be at the head of a congregation; and you must let the critic go without reckoning him among your deadly foes, or you will prove yourself a mere weakling.' He managed to be both serious and whimsical in his approach to life, but he was emphatic that 'Holiness in a minister is at once his chief necessity and his goodliest ornament.' He thundered to would-be preachers: 'Better to have been a devil than a preacher playing fast and loose with God's Word, and by such means working the ruin of the souls of men.' Yet for all that, he also sought to be a captivating preacher. His basic approach was: 'I take my text and make a beeline to the cross.'

No preacher had a more wonderful capacity for illustration than Spurgeon. For example, in describing the depravity of the human heart, he said that it was like a volcano – not always belching but always a volcano. This grasp of picture language was derived to a considerable degree from his appreciation of the same quality in the writing and preaching of John Bunyan. He could collect illustrations from everywhere. To illustrate our miserable excuses in the Day of Judgment, he recalled where he had read about a man suspected of poaching in the forest.

He had a gun and a dog with him, but lamely tried to argue that he was collecting mushrooms!

Spurgeon has managed to be all things to all men, in death more than life. Yet during his lifetime he stood clearly for a warm-hearted Calvinism anchored in the full revelation of Scripture. Concerning himself, he agreed with the woman who told John Newton: 'Ah! sir, the Lord must have loved me before I was born, or else he would not have seen anything in me to love afterwards.' For all his strong convictions, there was no narrow spirit about him, and he admired the Arminian John Wesley. With reservations, he gave his support to the Moody-Sankey missions in Britain in 1873–5. Indeed, he wrote, referring to the doctrines of grace: 'I believe there are multitudes of men who cannot see these truths, or, at least, cannot see them in the way in which we put them, who nevertheless have received Christ as their Saviour, and are as dear to the heart of the God of grace as the soundest Calvinist in or out of heaven.'

About 1867 his health began to break down. He suffered from rheumatism, gout and Bright's disease, which attacks the kidneys. While seeking to recover in warm and Italianate Menton (often called Mentone), near Nice in France, he died on 31 January 1892. When he died, Susannah sent a telegraph to 'Son Tom': 'Father in heaven. Mother resigned.' His life illustrated his own words: 'Blessed is that ministry of which Christ is all.'

86

MARY SLESSOR
(1848–1915)

Prayer overcoming fear

*He is the living God, and steadfast forever; His kingdom
is the one which shall not be destroyed, and His dominion
shall endure to the end. He delivers and rescues, and He
works signs and wonders in heaven and on earth,
who has delivered Daniel from the power of
the lions* (Dan. 6:26-27).

Mary Slessor was born in Aberdeen in Scotland in 1848. She was
one of seven children born to a shoemaker who was an alcoholic. Her mother was a member of the Belmont Street United
Presbyterian Church of Scotland, and was deeply interested in
the Church's mission on the west coast of Africa. Mary's elder
brother Robert wanted to be a missionary to Calabar (in southern
Nigeria), but he died at an early age. Mary was converted young
– being warned of the fire to come by an old widow – and taught
Sunday School. In the slums of Dundee, she learned how to
handle rough gangs, but not to meditate on God's Word. She
read it avidly, but added: 'If I try to meditate my mind just goes
a' roads.'

By 1874 the news of David Livingstone's death was being
used to stimulate further missionary interest in Scotland. In 1876

Mary left for Calabar, with her salary fixed at £60 per year. She came to live in a mud hut, and managed to send some of her salary back to Scotland. Like the majority of missionaries, she caught malaria. In Calabar she encountered witchcraft, twin-murder, polygamy, slavery, drunkenness and cannibalism – as well as lesser troubles such as lizards, rats and doting fat women. If twins were born, they were killed, and the mother was sent to live alone in the bush. Mary adopted abandoned children, and after twenty-two years had rescued fifty-one twins. She told people who propounded the theory of humanity's natural innocence to go and live for a month in a West African harem.

Her nickname was 'Ma', and she became renowned for running bare-headed and barefoot through the jungle. In her approach, school and gospel went together. But she also set up a medical centre. Yet she was by nature very shy, and in Scotland would refuse to speak at missionary meetings if men were present. She feared being on a steam-launch on the water, and was not naturally courageous. On one occasion she refused to cross a field because there was a cow in it. Every land journey was undertaken with the real threat of attack by wild animals. Mary recalled Daniel 6: 'I did not use to believe the story of Daniel in the lions' den until I had to take some of these awful marches, and then I knew it was true, and that it was written for my comfort.' In all her missionary dealings she recorded: 'My one great consolation and rest is in prayer.' Indeed: 'My life is one long daily, hourly, record of answered prayer.' This life drew its meaning from the next: 'Life is so great and so grand; eternity is so real and so terrible in its issues.' She called life apart from Christ 'a dreadful gift'. Acclaim meant nothing to her: 'If He be glorified that is all, whether I be considered able or not.'

Some Sundays she would speak at ten meetings. Most of her evangelism was conducted most naturally. While out walking one Sunday she came across some government road workers living in booths, so she spoke to them of the parable of the lost sheep. She loved the book of Job, but John was her favourite book. Every page of every Bible she ever owned is packed with annotations.

From 1892 to 1909 she was vice-consul of the Ikotobong Native Court, and she would knit to calm her nerves while the palavers went on and on, while she sought finally to administer what has been called 'essential justice unhampered by legal technicalities'. In all this she was firm as well as gentle, and never allowed anyone under her jurisdiction to sit in her presence. She maintained a surprising grasp of political issues, including the affairs of the nations. She also enjoyed games, such as cricket, and encouraged the Africans to play them. The news of World War I distressed her, and she wrote: 'May our nation be sent from its pleasures to its knees, and the Church be awed and brought back to Him.' The spiritual walk of the Christian remained essential to her: 'The secret of our failures in winning men; they don't find Him with us.'

She died in 1915, at the age of sixty-six, but she was not afraid: 'Don't talk about the cold hand of death – it is the hand of Christ.'

87

FANNY CROSBY
(1820–1915)

Seeing Christ

*Beloved, now we are children of God; and it has not yet
been revealed what we shall be, but we know that when
He is revealed, we shall be like Him, for we shall
see Him as He is* (1 John 3:2).
She did what she could (Mark 14:8a).

At the age of six weeks, in 1820, Fanny Crosby was made blind
by an incompetent doctor in New York. Her father died before
Fanny reached her first birthday, so her mother was left a
widow with a blind baby. Fanny's grandmother, Eunice, looked
after her granddaughter, and would vividly describe the world
of nature to her, with all its shapes, colours, birds and flowers.
Later, she was to learn by heart the Pentateuch, the Gospels,
most of the Psalms, Proverbs, Ruth and the Song of Solomon.
She was also struck by John Milton's autobiographical sonnet
On His Blindness.

From 1835, she began to study at the New York Institution
for the Blind, although she found Braille difficult as her fingertips
were calloused from playing the guitar. A very short woman
who was not physically attractive, Fanny possessed enormous
energy. Despite her blindness, she walked quickly, being easily

recognizable by her out-of-date dresses, the huge cross around her neck and her shiny green glasses. Fanny rarely indulged in self-pity, and at the age of eight wrote:

> *Oh, what a happy child I am,*
> *Although I cannot see!*
> *I am resolved that in this world*
> *Contented I will be!*

She said later that if she ever met the doctor who placed the hot poultices on her inflamed eyes, 'I would tell him that he unwittingly did me the greatest favour in the world.'

On 20 November 1850, in the aftermath of a cholera epidemic that claimed thousands of lives, Fanny went to the Methodist Broadway Tabernacle. Here, she was captivated by Isaac Watts's hymn 'Alas, and Did My Saviour Bleed?' The conclusion especially gripped her heart:

> *But drops of grief can ne'er repay*
> *The debt of love I owe;*
> *Here, Lord, I give myself away;*
> *'Tis all that I can do.*

Fanny recorded; 'For the first time I realized that I had been trying to hold the world in one hand and the Lord in the other.' This was her conversion. Increasingly, she turned her talent for poetry into a gift for hymnody.

In 1858 she married Alexander Van Alstyne (a blind musician) and so is more formally known as Frances Jane Van Alstyne. Their only child, of whom she very rarely spoke, died in infancy. Indeed, the marriage proved to be somewhat disappointing, and when Van (as she called him) died in 1902, Fanny recalled: 'He had his faults – and so have I mine, but notwithstanding these, we loved each other to the last.'

Fanny wrote something like 9,000 hymns, often using pseu-donyms. Their quality is uneven, at times containing more sentimentality than biblical theology. However, her best gospel songs have enduring value: 'Safe in the Arms of Jesus'; 'Pass Me Not, O Gentle Saviour'; 'Blessed Assurance'; 'To God Be the Glory, Great Things He Hath Done'; 'Rescue the Perishing'; and 'Jesus, Keep Me Near the Cross'. Ira Sankey, the singing partner to the evangelist D.L. Moody, made considerable use of Fanny's songs.

Many – even most – of Fanny's hymns yearn for heaven, and tell of seeing Christ. One of them contains the lines:

> *I shall know Him; I shall know Him*
> *And redeemed by His side I shall stand.*
> *I shall know Him; I shall know Him*
> *By the print of the nails in His hand.*

This was her hope:

> *And I shall see Him face to face,*
> *And tell the story – saved by grace.*

In death, at almost 95 rather than her hoped-for 105, she closed her blind eyes, and the first person she ever saw was Christ Himself. On her tombstone were Jesus' words: 'She did what she could.'

88

ABRAHAM KUYPER
(1837–1920)

Christ as Lord of all

All things were created through Him and for Him
(Col. 1:16b).

*Then God blessed them, and God said to them, 'Be
fruitful and multiply; fill the earth and subdue it; have
dominion over the fish of the sea, over the birds of the air,
and over every living thing that moves
on the earth' (Gen. 1:28).*

*God is greatly to be feared in the assembly of the saints,
and to be held in reverence by all those around Him.
O Lord God of hosts, who is mighty like You, O Lord?
Your faithfulness also surrounds You (Ps. 89:7-8).*

Abraham Kuyper (often known as 'Bram') was born in a small
fishing village called Maassluis, in the Netherlands. He was the
son of a pastor who hovered in his theological views between
Reformed orthodoxy and a kind of liberal Modernism. After
being home-schooled, then attending the gymnasium at Leiden,
he went on to the University of Leiden, graduating in 1858.
Without being converted, he decided to follow his father into
the ministry and entered the Leiden Divinity School, which was
dominated by unbelieving biblical critics including Abraham

Keunen, who did his best to demolish any belief in Moses and the prophets. By 1863 Kuyper had earned his doctorate, which was a reworking of some earlier studies on Calvin and à Lasco.

As Kuyper himself recalled, there were three events which contributed to his conversion. First, during his university days he was providentially led to study the works of Calvin and of John à Lasco (1499–1560) on the Church. However, the vigour of this study led to a breakdown in his health and, while recovering, he read Charlotte M. Yonge's High Anglican novel, *The Heir of Redcliffe*. This was the second great influence upon him as it moved him to embrace humility and lowliness. The third and most significant event came after he had married Johanna Schaay and taken up pastoral work in a small village church in Beesd. While visiting a peasant woman of about thirty years of age, Pietronella Baltus, Kuyper was taken aback when she initially refused to shake his hand, and then told him that he was a preacher of false modernistic doctrine. It was just as well that Kuyper had been led to see the virtues of humility! He noted: 'With the meagre Bible knowledge I had picked up at the university I could not measure up to these simple folk.'

A changed man, he moved to Utrecht in 1867, then Amsterdam in 1870. He became an editor of the *Herald*, with its motto 'For a free church and a free school in a free land', preached powerfully and simply, and taught the catechism to children in the orphanages. His life was changed again in 1874 when he was elected to parliament – a decision which is open to some criticism. Apparently a man with little need of sleep – although his health did break down twice – he poured out voluminous writings on an extensive range of subjects. In combating unregenerate liberalism and credal unfaithfulness, Kuyper made many enemies in the State Church, and about 200 congregations were forced out in 1874, seeing themselves as the 'Grieving Ones'. With great clarity, he denounced Modernism as 'a mirage' and liberal biblical criticism as 'biblical vandalism'.

In 1901 Kuyper's Anti-revolutionary Party came to power in coalition with the Roman Catholics, with Kuyper as Prime Minister. In the political realm, Kuyper was involved with the granting of government aid to Christian schools. The Free University was established in 1880, initially with as many disciplines as students, namely five! At its opening he uttered a moving and powerful declaration that Christ is all in all: 'Oh, no single piece of our mental world is to be hermetically sealed off from the rest, and there is not a square inch in the whole domain of our human existence over which Christ, who is Sovereign over *all*, does not cry: "Mine!"'

There are tensions in his thought, and some of it is not altogether realistic. For example, he wanted to see a Christian labour union. He believed most earnestly in the 'cultural mandate' of Genesis 1:28 as something that encouraged human endeavour in every area of life. He greatly emphasized common grace as 'the recognition that in the whole world the curse is restrained by grace, that the life of the world is to be honoured in its independence, and that we must, in every domain, discover the treasures and develop the potencies hidden by God in nature and in human life.' He also emphasized what he called 'sphere sovereignty', which exalted Christ as Lord over every distinct sphere of life. However, if these are not sustained by a clear grasp of special grace and the sufficiency of the Bible, they can easily lead into a splintering of knowledge and to secularism – the very things that Kuyper wished to combat.

His favourite psalm was Psalm 89, on Christ as the Davidic king over all the world, and at his funeral in November 1920 verses 7-8 were sung. It was an appropriate way to bid farewell to Kuyper. What he called the 'ruling passion of my life' was that 'in spite of all worldly opposition, God's holy ordinances shall be established again in the home, in the school and in the State for the good of the people.'

John Henry Newman (1801–90) came to believe that there was no logical ground between Roman Catholicism and pantheism, and so opted for the former. In his view, the future would see these two systems confront one another. A century later, C.S. Lewis predicted a final confrontation between Hinduism and Christianity – Hinduism as a system which tends to absorb all other systems facing Christianity as a system which ultimately excludes all other systems. But Abraham Kuyper saw Christianity and Modernism as the two final antagonists. Unlike Newman, Kuyper saw Calvinism as the safest refuge for the Christian, indeed as 'the only decisive, lawful, and consistent defence for Protestant nations against encroaching, and overwhelming Modernism.'

89

J. GRESHAM MACHEN
(1881–1937)

Mr Valiant for Truth

For I delivered to you first of all that which I also received:
that Christ died for our sins according to the Scriptures,
and that He was buried, and that He rose again
the third day according to the Scriptures
(1 Cor. 15:3-4).
Fight the good fight of faith (1 Tim. 6:12a).
Be faithful unto death (Rev. 2:10b).

John Gresham Machen was a Southern gentleman and a scholar, who came to lead the attack on theological liberalism in the Presbyterian Church in the USA and beyond. Having said that, it must also be said that Machen was no tactician – in fact, Samuel Craig regarded him as 'about the world's worst'.

Machen was born into a scholarly home on 28 July 1881 in Baltimore, Maryland. He trained at Johns Hopkins University as well as Princeton Seminary, Princeton University, and at Marburg and Göttingen in Germany. In 1905 Machen felt the overpowering personality and faith – liberal as it was – of Wilhelm Herrmann, who separated science and history from theology. However, he returned to Princeton Seminary to teach the New Testament.

Machen loved travel, mountain climbing, football and tennis, and apparently never lost at checkers. His nickname was 'Das' or 'Dassie' from the German 'Das Mädchen' ('the Maiden'). His personal kindness is evident from his quiet support of an elderly unemployed alcoholic from 1910 to 1933. In 1917 he left to serve as a YMCA secretary in World War I, which essentially meant that he sold chocolate to the soldiers. Once he was deeply touched by the sight of a wounded American giving his overcoat to a wounded German.

The 1920s saw theological warfare in America. Machen considered that the modern age's leading characteristic was 'a profound satisfaction with human goodness', but Christianity, in contrast, was 'the religion of the broken heart'. On 21 May 1922 the liberal Baptist Harry Emerson Fosdick preached a provocative sermon 'Shall the Fundamentalists Win?' from the pulpit of the First Presbyterian Church of New York. Clarence Macartney responded appropriately with 'Shall Unbelief Win?'

Machen published a number of works, notably *The Origin of Paul's Religion* in 1921 and *The Virgin Birth of Christ* in 1930. However, in 1923 came his clarion call, *Christianity and Liberalism*. This was a lucid and devastating attack on theological liberalism: 'The Church of Rome may represent a perversion of the Christian religion; but naturalistic liberalism is not Christianity at all.' Regarding the liberal view of Christ, Machen asked: 'What shall be thought of a human being who lapsed so far from the path of humility and sanity as to believe that the eternal destinies of the world were committed into His hands?' Hence he saw separation as 'the crying need of the hour'.

Machen was wary of the Church's being too involved in social issues. Like B.B. Warfield, he was hesitant on the subject of evolution, and did not become involved with William Jennings Bryan's crusade against it. He considered that the Bible condemned drunkenness, not moderate drinking, so he opposed Prohibition (1920–33) in an age when most Christians thought

that teetotalism was the only moral option. He urged a 'healthy
hatred of being governed'. He even championed Philadelphia's
jaywalkers!

The General Assembly of the Presbyterian Church reorganized
Princeton Seminary in 1929 to reduce the influence of strict Calvinism. Then came *Re-Thinking Missions,* a Church report of 1932,
which Machen called 'an attack upon the historic Christian Faith'.
At the same time the liberal Presbyterian missionary and novelist
Pearl Buck labelled older views of salvation as 'superstitious',
repudiated the doctrine of original sin and referred to Christ as
'the essence of men's highest dreams'. Machen affirmed:

> From the beginning, the Christian gospel ... consisted in an
> account of something that had happened. And from the
> beginning, the meaning of the happening was set forth; ... then
> there was Christian doctrine. 'Christ died' – that is history;
> 'Christ died for our sins' – that is doctrine. Without these two
> elements joined in an absolutely indissoluble union, there is no
> Christianity.

He emphasized facts: 'It is impossible to think with an empty
mind.' Walter Lippmann was one secular liberal who realized
what was at stake for the evangelicals when he said that the
liberal plea for tolerance and goodwill was tantamount to telling
conservatives to 'smile and commit suicide'.

In 1929 Machen preached his final sermon at Princeton,
appropriately enough, on 'Fight the Good Fight of Faith', where
he declared that 'The Apostle Paul was a great fighter ... It is
impossible to be a true soldier of Jesus Christ and not fight.' He
explained that a deadly enemy to true Christianity had invaded
the Church itself, and Christians needed to learn from the apostle:
'Paul was a great fighter because he was at peace'; he knew Christ's
peace within. Machen's words are full of wisdom: 'I do not mean
that the great issue of the day must be polemically presented in
every sermon that you preach ... You should always endeavour

to build the people up by simple and positive instruction in the Word.' But he prayed that God would save His ministers from neutrality, with the appearance of urbanity and charity.

So isolated did Machen become that the General Assembly suspended him in 1936. The Presbyterian Church had changed beyond recognition since 1893 when Charles Augustus Briggs had been put out of the ministry for denying the verbal inspiration of Scripture. The final result was that in 1936 a new denomination was formed which after a time became known as the Orthodox Presbyterian Church of America. But Machen had little time left for this life. Travelling to North Dakota in late 1936, he caught pneumonia and died in a little Catholic hospital on 1 January 1937. His last recorded words were in a telegram to John Murray: 'I'm so thankful for [the] active obedience of Christ. No hope without it.' Without a firm anchorage in the reality of history, Christian theology would be meaningless.

One of Machen's sayings was: 'To move the world you must have a place to stand.' In his own life he exhibited a heroic honesty. Even Pearl Buck realized this: 'The man was admirable. He never gave in one inch to anyone.' On his tombstone in Baltimore is the inscription: 'Faithful unto death.'

90

ERIC LIDDELL
(1902–1945)

Pursuing the right

Fear not, for I am with you; be not dismayed, for I am your God. I will strengthen you, yes, I will help you. I will uphold you with My righteous right hand (Isa. 41:10).

But now the Lord says: 'Far be it from Me; for those who honour Me I will honour, and those who despise Me shall be lightly esteemed' (1 Sam. 2:30b).

You have heard that it was said, 'You shall love your neighbour and hate your enemy.' But I say to you, love your enemies, bless those who curse you, do good to those who hate you, and pray for those who spitefully use you and persecute you (Matt. 5:43-44).

He who is faithful in what is least is faithful also in much (Luke 16:10a).

Eric Liddell was born as Henry Eric Liddell in Tientsin in China on 16 January 1902, the son of missionary parents. Because his initials would then be HEL, his name was changed to Eric. In 1907 the family returned to Scotland for furlough, and Eric and his older brother Rob were sent to Eltham College, School for the Sons of Missionaries at Blackheath, London. For much of his life until he reached his teens, Eric rarely lived with both of his parents. He was shy and his nickname was 'The Mouse', but he was athletic.

His running style, while effective, was odd – his arm and knee actions were high, and his head was thrown right back. He also played international rugby union for Scotland on seven occasions.

In 1921 Eric went off to the University of Edinburgh, and in 1923 was asked to speak for the Glasgow Students' Evangelistic Union at Armadale, a coal mining town west of Edinburgh. From China, his sister Jenny sent him Isaiah 41:10 to encourage her somewhat timid brother. His Christian convictions grew, and he saw no place for neutrality where Christianity is concerned. The next year – 1924 – Liddell was selected to run for Britain at the Paris Olympics. Because the heats for the 100 metres' sprint were run on Sunday, Liddell simply withdrew, as he did for the relay races for 100 metres and 400 metres, for the same reason.

Liddell ran in the 200 metres' race, and won a bronze medal, but unexpectedly won the gold medal in the 400 metres' race – which was not his favoured event. Before the race, a team masseur had handed him a note which read: 'It says in the Old Book, "Him that honours me, I will honour." Wishing you the best of success always.' Later, Liddell was to remember this as 'perhaps the finest thing I experienced in Paris.'

Back in Scotland, Liddell might have basked in some acclaim and glory, but instead, in 1925, he set off by the Trans-Siberian Railway, as a missionary to China. He noted the motto of his Scottish Congregational College: 'Christ for the world, for the world needs Christ.' In Liddell's view, 'We are all missionaries … Wherever we go, we either bring people nearer to Christ, or we repel them from Christ.' In 1932 he was ordained into the Congregational ministry, and two years later he married Florence MacKenzie, known as Flo. Three daughters were born – Patricia, Heather and Maureen.

The forces of Chiang Kai-shek and of Mao Zedong fought each other until the Japanese invasion of China in 1937. It was a time of danger and uncertainty, but Liddell was encouraged when a Japanese inspector shook his hand on finding that he was a Christian, and when he found a lively group of Chinese believers at Hsin Chi. Finally, in mid-1941 a pregnant Flo (with Maureen) and the two girls left for Toronto in Canada, where Flo had earlier studied nursing.

Liddell was left to ponder the issues of guidance, the Sermon on the Mount and the work of the Holy Spirit, and to pray for an hour a day. The USA entered the war in December 1941, and a month later the Japanese ordered all British and American nationals into the British Concession in Tientsin in north China, near Peking (now called Beijing). Liddell prepared a book of daily readings for the year, later published as *The Disciplines of the Christian Life*. He dealt with Scripture as a whole, but especially wanted to meditate on Romans 8:28, Philippians 4:13 and 2 Corinthians 12:9. In 1943 all enemy nationals were moved to a compound to the south-east, but still in north China, in Weihsien – the so-called 'Courtyard of the Happy Way' – which had been set up by American Presbyterians in 1883. Here, Liddell – often called 'Uncle Eric' – sought to minister to body and soul amidst the disease, the rats, the open cesspools and the ever-present threat of death.

Responding to the Japanese guards was difficult, but Liddell found Matthew 5:43-44 spoke to him, and consequently his attitude changed when he began to pray for his captors. Over sixty years later, Chinese authorities revealed that in a prisoner exchange Liddell give up his place to a pregnant woman. Headaches afflicted him, but the prime cause was far more serious – Liddell was suffering from a brain tumour. After suffering a stroke on 11 February 1945, Liddell died ten days later, at the age of 43. It was 2 May before Flo found out. Liddell lived out the truth of a verse which had once encouraged him when he picked up a wounded Chinese man from a derelict temple, despite fears of reprisal from the Japanese: 'He who is faithful in what is least is faithful also in much' (Luke 16:10a).

91

AMY CARMICHAEL
(1867–1951)

Secret good works

Now if anyone builds on this foundation with gold, silver, precious stones, wood, hay, straw, each one's work will become clear; for the Day will declare it, because it will be revealed by fire; and the fire will test each one's work, of what sort it is. If anyone's work, which he has built on it endures, he will receive a reward (1 Cor. 3:12-14).

Hereby perceive we the love of God, because He laid down His life for us: and we ought to lay down our lives for the brethren (1 John 3:16, KJV).

Then the righteous will answer Him, saying, 'Lord, when did we see You hungry and feed You, or thirsty and give You drink? When did we see You a stranger and take You in, or naked and clothe You? Or when did we see You sick, or in prison, and come to You?' And the King will answer and say to them: 'Assuredly, I say to you, inasmuch as you did it to one of the least of these My brethren, you did it to Me' (Matt. 25:37-40).

Known affectionately as 'Amma' (which is Tamil for 'mother'), Amy Beatrice Carmichael lived a long life, being born on 16 December 1867 in Millisle, on the north coast of Ireland, and dying in India in 1951. Her biography can be told in three stages: From 1867 to 1901 when the work with the Temple children began; from 1901 to 1931 when she was at the height of her powers in the work with the Dohnavur Fellowship; and from 1931 to 1951 when she was a virtual invalid but carried on an active writing and praying ministry.

Amy was born into an Irish Presbyterian family, the daughter of a respected mill owner. She was raised to know God, and at the age of three prayed that she would be given blue eyes. She was bewildered the next morning when they were still brown. She soon recovered from that setback. One bleak, wet Sunday morning in Belfast, as the family were returning home from church, they saw an old woman lugging a heavy bundle. Somewhat embarrassed, Amy and her two brothers helped the poor woman. Passing a fountain, Amy thought she heard the words of I Corinthians 3:12-14, 'Gold, silver, precious stones, wood, hay, stubble – every man's work shall be made manifest; for the day shall declare it, because it shall be declared by fire; and the fire shall try every man's work of what sort it is. If any man's work abide ...' (KJV). On reaching home, Amy shut herself in her room to settle her life with God.

In 1892 Amy felt the call to missionary service. At first she thought that she would go to Ceylon, then to China, only to be thwarted by the doctor, so she thought of Japan. In November 1895, under the auspices of the Church of England Zenana Missionary Society, she made her way to India, which was to become the scene of her life's work. India had long aroused the evangelical conscience with its Hindu idolatry and its associated practices of suttee (widow burning), child marriage, temple prostitution and the rigid caste system. After she finally settled, Amy was never to return home to Europe.

Amy knew that sanctification was a struggle: 'Wings are an illusive fallacy. Some may possess them, but they are not very visible, and as for me, there isn't the least sign of a feather.' At times she could be quite caustic: 'There isn't much of a halo in real life; we save it all up for the missionary meetings.' In 1901 she went to Dohnavur in south India, and so began the work to save girls from temple prostitution. Amy was both loving and strict in dealing with the rescued girls. From 7.00 p.m. to 7.30 p.m. each evening she played with them with toys from her cupboard. The sickest baby always slept in her room. Amy could be innovative, and once tied two girls' pigtails together to teach them how to cooperate. A child who lied might have quinine put on her tongue.

Amy took over the leadership at Dohnavur after the deaths of two senior missionaries, Mrs Hopwood and Thomas Walker, in August 1912. She wrote that she suddenly felt like a weaned child. The Dohnavur ladies took the name the Sisters of the Common Life – an echo of Groote's Brethren of the Common Life which was set up about 1380. They took no vows, but there was to be no marriage. In 1918 the first two boys arrived at Dohnavur to be looked after, but it was the arrival of Godfrey Webb-Peploe in 1926 which saw the boys' work structured in a way that corresponded to Amy's work with the girls.

Life was tough: 'Under the sweetness there is a real Cross.' In 1931 Amy fell into a pit and broke her leg and twisted her spine. For the last twenty years of her life she was confined to her room, incapacitated and in pain. She told her New Zealand nurse: 'When you hear I have gone, jump for joy!' She went on 18 January 1951, and was buried without a headstone although a stone bird-bath was erected beside her grave.

Amy held strong views – she never appealed for funds and never wasted a penny; she opposed using pictures of Christ, claiming that the Church only resorted to pictures when its power had gone; she also disapproved of fairy tales and any kind of fiction as a waste of time and a threat to the foundations of character; and was utterly opposed to teaching her girls any sex education, thinking that it was the task of the husband, not the parents or teachers. Slander was stamped on at Dohnavur through the use of the slogan 'Never about, always to.' When she was included in the Royal Birthday Honours List, she was horrified: 'It troubles me to have an experience so different from His Who was despised and rejected, not kindly honoured.'

In 1922 she cited the words of 1 John 3:16, and commented: 'How often I think of that *ought*.' Her little work, *If,* is incomparable in its devotion and power. Echoing the parable of the sheep and goats in Matthew 25, she wrote: 'If I want to be known as the doer of something that has proved the right thing, or as the one who suggested that it should be done, then I know nothing of Calvary love.'

92

YANG-WON SON
(1902–1950)

Faithfulness before God and the world

*You shall not make for yourself a carved image
... (Exod. 20:4a).*

*But Peter and the other apostles answered and said: 'We
ought to obey God rather than men' (Acts 5:29).*

*And He has on His robe and on His thigh a name written:
King of kings and Lord of lords (Rev. 19:16).*

*Son of man, I have made you a watchman for the house
of Israel; therefore hear a word from My mouth, and give
them warning from Me (Ezek. 3:17).*

*Do not fear any of those things which you are about to
suffer. Indeed, the devil is about to throw some of you
into prison, that you may be tested, and you will have
tribulation ten days. Be faithful until death, and I
will give you the crown of life (Rev. 2:10).*

God is love (1 John 4:8, 16).

Yang-won Son was born in 1902 into a home that knew the
turmoil associated with conversion to Christianity. His father
became a believer, only to earn the ridicule of friends and family,
including his wife. However, the Lord blessed his faithfulness,
and the family became united in looking to Christ. His father
was ordained a Presbyterian deacon, and the young son learned
early what it meant to stand for Christ. In 1910 Japan annexed

Korea, and emperor worship became an issue for all Koreans. The Japanese principal urged Yang-won to worship the emperor, but the young lad cited the second commandment and Acts 5:29 in refusing to engage in idolatry.

From the late sixteenth century, there had been Roman Catholic attempts at evangelizing Korea, but up until the 1880s the country had been known as 'the Hermit Kingdom', and had sought to avoid contact with foreign nations. This changed dramatically in 1882 when Korea entered into treaty relations with the United States. American Presbyterian and Methodist missionaries took advantage of this and soon began to arrive.

According to Rev. Horace G. Underwood, the Koreans did not appear very religious, but their minds were subject either to the ancestor worship of Confucianism or the fear of the spirits in Shamanism. Nevertheless, in 1907 Korea experienced revival as tens of thousands became Christians. Under the sovereignty of God, the biblical book that was much used in the revival was First John. Yet Korea enjoyed great blessing while enduring great hardship. In June 1890 John Nevius visited Seoul from China, and his missionary methods were, for the most part, adopted by the Protestant missionaries. Self-governing, self-propagating and self-supporting churches were established, rather than Western mission stations.

After studying in Seoul and then in Tokyo, Yang-won entered Pyong-yang Theological Seminary in April 1935. His first pastorate was at the Garden of Loving Care, where he was the pastor to the leper church and principal of the leper school. He preached that Christ is the King of kings, and for this he was arrested. There was no trial, and he did not see his family for nine months. When, finally, he was brought to trial, he was sentenced to eighteen months in gaol. Before his sentencing, Pastor Son told his elders: 'If we would greet the spring, we must endure the cold winter.'

During the 1930s the Japanese called on all subject peoples to do obeisance at a Shinto shrine dedicated to the 'divine' founder of the 'divine' empire of Japan. The Japanese emperor, Hirohito, was viewed in the same terms as the Roman emperor of ancient times. The Japanese policy was to target private schools, abolish Sunday as a holiday and set up Shinto shrines in each church. It banned teaching that dealt with the Second Coming and the Last Judgment, and prohibited relations with overseas churches. By 1945 the Japanese government had excised the Old Testament from the theological curriculum.

Yang-won was due for release on 17 May 1943, but instead he was left in prison. He was comforted by the thought that the Lord had been with Joseph and with Paul in prison, and that 'Silence in chains is a more eloquent form of preaching than words.' It was two more years before he was released, by which time World War II was almost over.

Two days after the U.S.A. dropped the atomic bomb on Hiroshima, the U.S.S.R. declared war on Japan, which meant that north of the 38th parallel surrendered to the Soviet regime. The situation was chaotic, with refugees, food shortages and inflation making the task of rebuilding extremely difficult. Communists murdered Yang-won's two eldest sons, Matthew and John, but, with extraordinary grace, Yang-won ended up forgiving and adopting one of his sons' killers, Chai-sun. Within two years, the murderer was professing faith in Christ.

In mid-1950 there was a brutal communist offensive launched by North Korea against the South. Pastor Son refused to flee, feeling convicted that he was called to be a watchman like Ezekiel. He preached on Revelation 2:10 to the congregation of the Garden of Loving Care. Times were testing in the extreme: the church was running short of food, and the communists shot dead one leper – a foretaste of what was to come. On 13 September 1950 Pastor Son was arrested, and soon after was shot. He had long meditated on 'God is love', and wrote that 'All things for me are from the love of God. My tears, my suffering, my life, my death ...' Meanwhile, Chai-sun returned to take up the leper work.

93

JOHN STAM
(1907–1934)

BETTY STAM
(1906–1934)

God is able!

*You will keep him in perfect peace, whose mind is stayed
on You, because he trusts in You* (Isa. 26:3).

For to me, to live is Christ, and to die is gain (Phil. 1:21).

*'Father, glorify Your name.' Then a voice came from
heaven, saying, 'I have both glorified it and will
glorify it again'* (John 12:28).

*Now to Him who is able to do exceedingly abundantly
above all that we ask or think, according to the
power that works in us* (Eph. 3:20).

John Stam was the fifth of six tall brothers, of Dutch extraction, but raised in Paterson, New Jersey. Although raised in a godly home, Stam was only converted through the work of a blind evangelist in 1922. He became a street evangelist, and learnt Greek with three other young men as they commuted to New York. He went off to Moody Bible Institute to study, and once wrote in a letter to an unbeliever: 'I would sooner be the most humble Christian, than have all a man could want of earthly things and yet be without Christ.' He pastored a small county church in Elida, Ohio, for sixteen months, majoring on Scripture memorization. He began with Isaiah 26:3.

Elisabeth Alden Scott, known as Betty, was born in the U.S.A., but her parents were Presbyterian missionaries in China. She attended a summer conference at Keswick, New Jersey, and wrote to her parents: 'It's as clear as daylight to me that the only worthwhile life is one of unconditional surrender to God's will, and of living in His way, trusting His love and guidance.' At the same time she adopted Philippians 1:21 as her life motto.

In 1931 Betty sailed for China to work in the China Inland Mission, and John joined her in the following year. They were married in October 1933, and little Helen Priscilla was born on 11 September 1934. In all his labours for the gospel in China, the words of John 12:28 were often on John's mind. Evangelism was difficult. Many Chinese venerated the weasel. Even church life took some getting used to. With no organ or precentor, the front section of the congregation could easily finish a verse ahead of the back section!

Quite suddenly, on 6 December 1934, the communist forces brutally captured the city of Tsingteh. They were about to kill baby Helen when an old farmer intervened and was shot dead – his life for the baby's. Baby Helen was left unharmed. When relaying to CIM headquarters in Shanghai their captors' demand for a $20,000 ransom, John closed with: 'The Lord bless you and guide you, and as for us, may God be glorified whether by life or by death.' Twice John cited 'He is able.'

On 8 December 1934 John and Betty were marched through the city streets with their hands tied behind their backs. A Christian who spoke up on their behalf was summarily executed. Then the communists cut John's throat, and decapitated Betty with a sword. Their bodies were left on the outskirts of town, where they had fallen. Twenty-four hours later a Chinese evangelist named Lo found out what had happened, and managed to retrieve Helen who was carried to safety. Chinese peasants reattached the heads to the bodies using hemp thread. Helen was to grow up, marry and have children, but remained quite anonymous for the rest of her life.

Clearly, when John Stam wrote those three words, 'He is able', he had Scripture in mind, but it is not certain which particular verse. He may have been thinking of 'God is able to make all grace abound toward you' (2 Cor. 9:8), or 'He is able to aid those who are tempted' (Heb. 2:18), or perhaps 'He is able to save to the uttermost those who come to God through Him' (Heb. 7:25). One might suggest Jude's benediction: 'Now unto Him who is able to keep you from stumbling' (Jude 24).

A more likely candidate is Philippians 3:21 where Paul tells of the resurrection to come 'according to the working by which He is able even to subdue all things to Himself.' Or maybe even 2 Timothy 1:12 which says: 'He is able to keep what I have committed to Him until that Day.' Because of the situation in which John Stam found himself, he may possibly have thought of Shadrach, Meshach and Abed-Nego who declared: 'Our God whom we serve is able to deliver us from the burning fiery furnace, and He will deliver us from your hand, O king' (Dan. 3:17). Indeed, all of these verses are summed up in Paul's benediction at the end of the third chapter of Ephesians: 'Now to Him who is able to do exceedingly abundantly above all that we ask or think, according to the power that works in us' (Eph. 3:20).

John and Betty Stam went to their deaths trusting in the God who is able to do all things in Christ Jesus His Son. He was able to save their baby daughter. He is able to raise the dead because the last enemy has been defeated through Christ's resurrection. And He is able to bring wonderful good out of terrible evil. The deaths of the Stams stimulated missionary interest across the evangelical world. Seeds were sown in the ravaged land of China which was to endure the mad brutality of Mao Zedong. In spite of all the government's power and propaganda, millions of Chinese people have turned to Christ in faith. God is able indeed.

94

DIETRICH BONHOEFFER
(1906–1945)

Speaking for the helpless

Open your mouth for the speechless (Prov. 31:8).
*It is good for me that I have been afflicted, that I may
learn Your statutes* (Ps. 119:71).
Do your utmost to come before winter (2 Tim. 4:21a).

Dietrich Bonhoeffer and his twin sister Sabine were born on 4 February 1906 in Breslau in Silesia, in what is now a part of Poland. There were eight children altogether, born to father Karl who was a director of a mental hospital and a professor of psychiatry and neurology, and to mother Paula who was a teacher and a beautiful singer. The Bonhoeffer family did not attend church regularly although Paula did provide the children with religious instruction. Dietrich grew up to be tall, blond (later balding), strong, friendly and quick in conversation. He loved games, notably tennis, and always played to win. He also played the classical piano so well that he could have made music his career. The cult of the star revolted him, and he wanted society to return from the newspaper and radio to the book.

When Dietrich suddenly announced that he was going to read theology, his family were rather bewildered. A cultured and highly intelligent man, Bonhoeffer did well at his studies at Tübingen and Berlin University, and prepared his doctorate, *Sanctorum Communio*. By 1927 he had become assistant pastor of a German congregation in Barcelona in Spain. He loved preaching, and was diligent in preparing for it, often working up to ten hours on each sermon.

After further studies at Union Theological Seminary, New York, Bonhoeffer came to regard American Protestantism as 'Protestantism without Reformation'. But he attended Abyssinian Baptist Church in Harlem, where, although a highly accomplished musician himself, he nevertheless came to appreciate the simple depth of Negro spirituals. He was a changed man: 'For the first time I discovered the Bible ... I had often preached. I had seen a great deal of the Church, and talked and preached about it – but I had not yet become a Christian.' He was especially drawn to the Sermon on the Mount, and felt his calling was now clear. By 1931 he was back in Berlin, and in November 1931 he was ordained into the Lutheran ministry.

On 30 January 1933 Adolf Hitler became Chancellor of Germany, and almost immediately supported Ludwig Müller, a German Christian, as the Protestant Reich bishop – a new position, designed to be subservient to Nazi authority. Eventually Müller was elected in a rigged election. On 7 April the Aryan Clause was passed, which prohibited Jews from being appointed to any civil service or government positions. Against the German Christians stood the Confessing Church. In September 1933 the Evangelical Church adopted the Aryan Clause which denied the pulpit to ordained ministers of Jewish blood. By 22 April 1934, 5,000 pastors and laypeople had gathered at Ulm to create the Confessing Church. Bonhoeffer advocated a policy of no compromise: 'He who deliberately separates himself from the Confessing Church in Germany, separates himself from salvation.' To Bonhoeffer, the duty of the Christian was clear, and Proverbs 31: 8 was often on his lips.

After a stay in England, Bonhoeffer returned to Germany in April 1935 to head a Confessing Church seminary which ended up at Finkenwalde. Here Bonhoeffer wrote: 'We have learnt here to read the Bible once again prayerfully.' The Psalms became especially dear to him, and in 1939 he referred to Psalm 119:71 as 'one of my favourite verses from my favourite Psalm.' In October 1937 Himmler ordered that Finkenwalde be closed, and arrested the twenty-seven students. Bonhoeffer had come to the view that the Church could not simply bind up the victims under the wheel of the State but needed to jam a spoke in the wheel itself.

Out of this period came *Life Together* and *The Cost of Discipleship*. The latter was dedicated to Martin Niemöller, and was a passionate attack on any notion of 'cheap grace'. In Bonhoeffer's words: 'Cheap grace is the preaching of forgiveness without requiring repentance, baptism without church discipline, communion without confession, absolution without personal confession. Cheap grace is grace without discipleship, grace without the cross, grace without Jesus Christ, living and incarnate.' For all his emphasis on discipleship, Bonhoeffer never lost sight of free grace, and considered that 'A truly evangelical sermon must be like offering a child a beautiful red apple or holding out a glass of water to a thirsty man and asking: "Wouldn't you like it?"'

Due to be called up for military service, Bonhoeffer visited George Bell in England for advice, and then in June 1939 arrived in New York. However, safety brought him no peace, and he explained in a letter:

> I have made a mistake in coming to America ... I will have no right to participate in the reconstruction of Christian life in Germany after the war if I do not share in the trials of this time with my people ... Christians in Germany will face the terrible alternative of either willing the defeat of their nation in order that Christian civilisation may survive, or willing the

victory of their nation and thereby destroying our civilisation. I know which of these alternatives I must choose; but I cannot make the choice in security!

2 Timothy 4:21 gripped him: 'Do your best to come before winter.' He realized the problems with reading too much into the verse, but he wrote that 'it is not a misuse of scripture if I apply that to myself. If God gives me grace to do it.' Hence he returned to Germany in July, only a month after his arrival, and only two months before the outbreak of war. He had always maintained that 'Peace is the opposite of security.'

95

DIETRICH BONHOEFFER
(1906–1945)

Called to die

*'And do you seek great things for yourself? Do not seek
them; for behold, I will bring adversity on all flesh,' says
the Lord. 'But I will give your life to you as a prize in all
places, wherever you go'* (Jer. 45:5).

*But He was wounded for our transgressions, He was
bruised for our iniquities; the chastisement for our
peace was upon Him, and by His stripes we
are healed* (Isa. 53:5).

*Blessed be the God and Father of our Lord Jesus Christ,
who according to His abundant mercy has begotten us
again to a living hope through the resurrection of
Jesus Christ from the dead* (1 Pet. 1:3).

On 1 September 1939 Germany invaded Poland. War meant that
Bonhoeffer came under an increasing number of restrictions: on
4 September 1940 he was forbidden to speak in public and on
27 March 1941 he was forbidden to print or publish any of his
writings. Rumours of euthanasia and Jewish deportations began to
be heard. Christians struggled to respond to very terrible circumstances. Helmuth von Moltke rejected any idea of violence against
Hitler but Bonhoeffer came to favour assassination. A number
of plots and protests against Hitler failed, and in April 1943

Bonhoeffer was arrested and charged with 'subversion of the armed forces', and taken to Tegel prison as the Gestapo closed in on the Abwehr, for whom Bonhoeffer was secretly working.

In the midst of all this, for better or for worse, Bonhoeffer had become engaged to the young and beautiful Maria von Wedemeyer on 17 January 1943, although there was no official announcement at this stage. In prison Bonhoeffer learnt by heart the hymns of Paul Gerhardt, read and studied his Bible as well as other books, prayed and wrote. His final work was his magnum opus, the incomplete *Ethics*, where he recorded: 'The West is becoming hostile towards Christ. This is the peculiar situation of our time, and it is genuine decay.' He feared that he had become so involved in the conspiracy that it would be difficult to find one's way back to simplicity and straightforwardness. His poem *Who am I?* deals with the contradictions which he saw in his own character – outwardly calm, firm and cheerful, but inwardly sick and restless, yearning for nature and friendship. Its last lines are:

> *Who am I? They mock me, these lonely*
> *questions of mine.*
> *Whoever I am, thou knowest O God,*
> *I am Thine.*

In another poem he wrote of freedom being attained by discipline, action, suffering and death.

Bonhoeffer saw a new religionless age dawning, and contemplated the weakness and suffering of God in the world: 'Man is summoned to share in God's suffering in the world.' He wrote to his twin Sabine, who was married to Gerhard Leibholz, a converted Jew: 'It is good to learn early enough that suffering and God are not a contradiction but rather a unity, for the idea that God himself is suffering is one that has always been one of the most convincing teachings of Christianity. I think God is nearer to suffering than to happiness, and to find God in this way gives peace and rest and a strong and courageous heart.' In one of his letters from prison, he wrote: 'I am reading the Bible straight through from cover to cover, and have just got as far as Job, which I am particularly fond of. I read the Psalms every day, as I have done for years; I know them and love them more than any other book.' All worldly aspirations came to mean nothing. From his prison cell in Tegel on 30 April 1944, Bonhoeffer wrote to Eberhard Bethge: 'We shall have to repeat Jer. 45:5 to ourselves every day.' His prayer remained: 'May God in his mercy lead us through these times; but above all may he lead us to himself.'

The situation deteriorated, and on 20 July 1944 the plot against Hitler's life failed. Bonhoeffer had an opportunity to escape in October but he refused as he feared recriminations against his family. His courage seemed extraordinary, and during air raids he was often released to look after frightened prisoners. Maria's cousin, Fabian von Schlabrendorff, recalled Bonhoeffer's kindness and politeness despite the torture he endured. At Buchenwald, where he was transferred on 7 February 1945, Payne Best (an imprisoned British intelligence officer) described him as 'all humility and sweetness'. Bonhoeffer's last sermon was preached from Isaiah 53:5 and 1 Peter 1:3 to a mixed group of Catholics, a few Protestants and one communist (Kokorin, Molotov's nephew) in a classroom in Schönberg. Best recalled: 'He reached the hearts of all, finding just the right words to express the spirit of our imprisonment, and the thoughts and resolutions which it had brought.'

After the service, Bonhoeffer was called for. Drawing Best aside, Bonhoeffer had time to pass him a message for Bishop Bell to assure him of the nature of Christian brotherhood, and concluding with the words: 'This is the end – for me, the beginning of life.' He was hanged at Flossenburg on 9 April 1945 on Hitler's special orders, only about a month before the war ended.

Bonhoeffer remains one of the most thoughtful and inspiring martyrs of the Church in the twentieth century. He was a pacifist who came to support tyrannicide, a revolutionary who wanted to preserve order, a theologian who has been widely regarded as an extreme liberal, yet whom his friend and biographer, Eberhard Bethge, regarded as one who engaged in 'naïve biblicism'. His life and death illustrate his own words from *The Cost of Discipleship*: 'When Christ calls a man, he bids him come and die.'

96

PAUL SCHNEIDER
(1897–1939)

Rejoicing in suffering for Christ

*For this cause I was born, and for this cause I have come
into the world, that I should bear witness to the truth.
Everyone who is of the truth hears
My voice* (John 18:37b).

*Zebulun is a people who jeopardized their lives to the
point of death; Naphtali also, on the heights
of the battlefield* (Judg. 5:18).

*But rejoice to the extent that you partake of Christ's
sufferings, that when His glory is revealed, you may
also be glad with exceeding joy* (1 Pet. 4:13).

*Blessed be the God and Father of our Lord Jesus Christ,
who according to His abundant mercy has begotten us
again to a living hope through the resurrection of Jesus
Christ from the dead, to an inheritance incorruptible and
undefiled and that does not fade away, reserved
in heaven for you* (1 Pet. 1:3-4).

Paul Schneider was the first Protestant pastor to lose his life
through the anti-Christian tyranny of the Nazi regime in
Germany. Whereas Dietrich Bonhoeffer was Lutheran, Schneider was Reformed. They were also different in temperament
and person, but both were musical – Bonhoeffer played the
piano and the guitar, while Schneider played the organ and

the flute. Bonhoeffer was a highly cultured and philosophical thinker, whereas Schneider was a capable yet relatively simple and uncomplicated man of fearless integrity.

Schneider was born on 29 August 1897, the son of a country pastor, who gave John 18:37 to Paul as his confirmation text. His mother, whom he called 'the happiest person in our house', suffered as an invalid, but would sit at the window and sing. She died in 1914, having selected Romans 12:12 as her epitaph. In World War I, on 22 March 1916, Schneider was badly wounded in the stomach. He received the Iron Cross the same day, and began to think of the ministry rather than medicine.

Schneider went on to study at Giessen University, Marburg and Tübingen. At this time, he was theologically liberal, but increasingly coming to submit to Scripture. He once became so depressed that suicide seemed an option, until I Corinthians 10:13 gripped him. On 29 August 1921 he applied to the Rhineland Consistory to be taken on as a ministerial candidate. To identify with the workers, he took a job for three months – from May to August 1922 – at a blast furnace in a factory. His aim was spiritual growth: 'O to be motivated by love in the little battles of life. May God help me.' Yet he struggled: 'I face nothingness, complete and absolute emptiness ... Power from on high fails me and I must, therefore, pray for power.'

By October 1922 he was engaged to Margarete Dieterich (whom he invariably called Gretel), the daughter of a pastor. By the time Schneider moved from Tübingen to Soest Seminary, he had embraced evangelical truth. At the end of October 1923 he wrote to his future in-laws: 'You know that I had to arrive at my current posture by finding my way from a liberal stance.' His position now was: 'In the recognition of our own sinfulness, the deity and redemptive power of Jesus Christ are revealed to us in their absolute sufficiency.'

After working for the Berlin City Mission amongst alcoholics, he then moved back to Hochelheim, and in January 1925 was ordained in the church where he had grown up. On his father's death in January 1926, he was called to succeed him at Hochelheim and Dornholzhausen. Yet he also went through another dark period, and on 14 March 1926 wrote in his diary: 'The Church's stated faith is not my faith. The joy of preaching and preparing to preach has left me. Up to now my prayer life had always been haphazard, and now it is completely barren.' By 8 July 1926, however, he was writing: 'I am now once again able to praise God.'

On 12 August 1926 he married Gretel, and together they produced six children – five boys and one girl. With children, he was like a child himself. He loved to play with them, and could perform feats like doing handsprings and walking on his hands. Schneider used a motorcycle to get around his parishes, and he accordingly dressed in a bright yellow motorcycle riding suit.

With the passing of the Aryan Law in 1933, pastors were expected to run a genealogy check on parishioners. There were 60 million Germans at this time, which included about 500,000 Jews. There were something like 90,000 baptized non-Aryans in the Church, and of the 18,000 Protestant clergy, thirty-seven had Jewish backgrounds, of which twenty-nine were still active in ministry. At a pastors' conference, Schneider cited Ephesians 2:14, 1 Corinthians 12:13 and Galatians 3:28.

When Ernst Röhm (the head of the SA troops, or Brownshirts as they were known, and a homosexual) and a little later the Propaganda Minister, Dr Joseph Goebbels, made fun of Christian morality, which Goebbels called a 'fossilized view of life', Schneider responded. In the aftermath, the Protestant Consistory of the Rhineland panicked, and Schneider was forced to move on. On 8 May 1934 Schneider was inducted into two places: Womrath and Dickenschied. The Nazi government banned the circulation of the Manifesto of the Old Prussian Confessing Synod, which had attacked the new paganism of blood, race, nationalism, honour and freedom, and the language of 'eternal Germany'. Schneider was gaoled along with some 500 Confessing Church pastors at this time.

While he was still recovering from a motorcycle accident, Schneider was arrested on 31 May 1937 and taken into protective custody in Koblenz. There was no charge, no questioning and no trial. After eight weeks, Schneider was released, but was banished from the Rhineland. However, he threw his banishment order into a rubbish bin, caught the next train home and preached the following day, 25 July 1937, on Isaiah 7:9. Schneider had come to a decisive point in his life: 'We can only be ashamed that we trusted God so little ... Let us both pray that we may take hold of the word: "Fear not, only believe".' (from Mark 5:36). He searched the book of Judges, and was struck by Judges 5:18. On 3 October 1937 he urged: 'The churches must not let themselves be frightened.' He was comforted by 1 Peter 4:13, and wrote of 1 Peter 1:3-4, 'Should not that hope be enough to carry us through this earthly life?' It was, for Paul Schneider.

97

PAUL SCHNEIDER
(1897–1939)

Overcoming in death

*You are of God, little children, and have overcome them,
because He who is in you is greater than he who
is in the world* (1 John 4:4).

*For whatever is born of God overcomes the world; And
this is the victory that has overcome the
world – our faith* (1 John 5:4).

*The eyes of all look expectantly to You ... The Lord is
near to all who call upon Him, to all who call upon Him
in truth ... The Lord preserves all who love Him, but all
the wicked He will destroy* (Ps. 145:15a, 18, 20).

*For whom the Lord loves He chastens, and scourges
every son whom He receives* (Heb. 12:6).

*Now then, we are ambassadors for Christ, as though God
were pleading through us: we implore you on Christ's
behalf, be reconciled to God* (2 Cor. 5:20).

As we have seen, Paul Schneider had come to see that the battle was now between the forces of God and the forces of evil. He drew strength from many parts of the Bible, including 1 John 4:4 and 5:4. He also realized that 'Prudence and cleverness will get us nowhere.' It was inevitable that he would be arrested again, and so he was, on Sunday 3 October 1937, after preaching at

Dickenschied on Psalm 145:15-21. He was again thrown into prison at Koblenz. While there, his ministry continued, and he tried to memorize passages from Isaiah and Romans, and slipped papers with prayers and Bible readings to the other prisoners.

On 25 November 1937 Schneider was sent 200 miles away to Buchenwald concentration camp, but he comforted himself and his family with the words: 'We know full well that our fate is in God's hands.' However, he never saw them again. When confronted with a statement which declared that he would not return to the Rhineland, he refused to sign. His attitude was: 'We can do without our clever church politicians unless they are prepared to fight their battles in the local church and from the base of a single congregation.' Before Pastor Schneider left for Buchenwald, Frau Schneider gave him the text: 'The lion of Judah shall break every chain' (Rev. 5:5). Naturally, they discussed God's purposes in all the suffering they were called to endure, and they discussed Hebrews 12:6 together.

After refusing to salute the swastika on Hitler's forty-ninth birthday on 20 April 1938, Schneider received twenty five lashes and was put in solitary confinement in a cell that was four feet wide and ten feet long. For fifteen months he was denied a Bible. Still his ministry continued as he called out memorized words of Scripture to his fellow prisoners. For this he received more lashings, was denied rations and sleep, and suspended by his wrists for hours. His ministry during this time was fearless.

Finally, on 18 July 1939, Paul Schneider was murdered in the camp infirmary with a lethal injection of strophanthin (a poison which induces a cardiac arrest and which in concentrated form can bring down a hippopotamus). Frau Schneider received a telegram which said: 'Paul Schneider, born 29th August 1897, died today. If it is wished to bury at own cost, contact within 24 hours, Registrar of deaths, Weimar. Otherwise, cremation. Camp Commandant, Buchenwald.' She recovered the body. There was strict Gestapo supervision of the funeral, and some misgivings on their part.

Indeed, there were many Roman Catholic mourners who turned up, as well as some 150 Confessing Church pastors. Mourned and respected by all, Schneider was buried on 21 July 1939 at Dickenschied.

When Dietrich Bonhoeffer heard the news, he was in London with his twin sister Sabine. He gathered his nephews and nieces together and told them: 'Listen, children. You must never forget the name of Pastor Paul Schneider. He is our first martyr.'

Margarete and the children moved to Elberfeld to a home provided, illegally, by the Confessing Church. An Allied air raid in 1943 destroyed it, including Schneider's letters which were stored in the attic. Margarete only died on 27 December 2002, not long before what would have been her 100th birthday. She chose the plaque that now hangs in Pastor Schneider's old cell at Buchenwald, which reads: 'We are ... Christ's ambassadors, as though God were making his appeal through us. We implore you on Christ's behalf: Be reconciled to God' (2 Cor. 5:20).

98

SOPHIE SCHOLL
(1921–1943)

A heart of wisdom and justice

But be doers of the word, and not hearers only, deceiving yourselves (James 1:22).

Then I returned and considered all the oppression that is done under the sun: And look! The tears of the oppressed, but they have no comforter – on the side of their oppressors there is power; but they have no comforter (Eccles. 4:1-2).

Lord, You have been our dwelling place in all generations ... Even from everlasting to everlasting, You are God ... The days of our lives .. are soon cut off, and we fly away ... So teach us to number our days, that we may gain a heart of wisdom (see Ps. 90:1-12).

When Sophie Scholl was born, her father, Robert, was the mayor of Forchtenberg am Kocher. By 1932 the family had moved to Ulm in southern Germany. There were six Scholl children: Inge (1917–98), Hans (1918–43), Elisabeth (b.1920), Sophie (1921–43), Werner (1922–44), and Thilde, who was born in 1925 but died the next year. They were raised as Lutherans, but Robert Scholl had worked as a medic in World War I because of his pacifist convictions.

Hitler's rise to power led to tensions in the Scholl household as the father was grieved when Hans carried the banner of the Ulm Hitler Youth section at the Nuremberg party rally of 1936.

However, Hans lost his fervour for National Socialism, and the family became more united. During the war, Hans was half soldier, half medical student. A restless and gifted character, he turned to Augustine, Aquinas, Pascal and Kierkegaard, as well as the Bible. Sophie was not yet twelve when Hitler came to power in 1933. She was a quiet and somewhat reserved personality, who always dressed neatly but wore no make-up. Her diaries and letters reveal that she dreamed of God's renewing the air with His breath. She was artistic, and also quite musical, and played the church organ. In May 1942 she enrolled to study biology and philosophy at the University of Munich, where Hans was studying medicine.

One of Sophie's closest friends was Susanne Hirzel, the daughter of an Ulm pastor in the Confessing Church. Possessing a deep sense of doing what was right, Sophie wrote: 'Doesn't every human being, no matter which era he lives in, always have to reckon with being accountable to God at any moment?' She used to read from Augustine of Hippo under a tall tree, and here she found meaning. She also read the sermons of the English Roman Catholic, John Henry Newman, especially regarding the Christian conscience. She wrote: 'After all, one should have the courage to believe only in what is good.' James became her favourite epistle in the Bible.

In her diary Sophie recorded: 'I cannot understand why today "religious" people are worried about the existence of God just because men attack His works with sword and infamy. As if God didn't have the power (I feel that everything is in His hands) – the *power*. We must fear for the existence of mankind only because men turn away from Him who is their life.' Sophie empathized with those who were oppressed by the Nazis, and wrote: 'I want to share the suffering of these days.' Indeed, she told Susanne Hirzel that she was prepared to shoot Hitler.

In July 1942 Hans and a number of his friends were sent to Russia for a time. Hans later wrote: 'I am grateful to God today that I had to go to Russia.' The Nazi eugenics programme had led to euthanasia. On 3 August 1941 Clemens Graf von Galen, the Roman Catholic Bishop of Münster, preached a vigorous sermon against the euthanasia programme. Hans was one who was greatly encouraged and challenged by the sermon, and Galen's denunciation of what he called the 'terrible doctrine' of 'life which does not deserve to live'. The Nazis were forced to halt the euthanasia programme but the murders continued.

Meanwhile, a group of university students and a university professor operated secretly at Munich University. Its name was The White Rose which may have come from the name of a novel. It printed six leaflets, and it had a seventh in draft form when the Gestapo closed in. Sophie did not actually author or co-author any of them, but she came to identify with the dissident group. The first leaflet referred to 'Western and Christian civilization', and denounced 'this atheistic war machine'. The second leaflet said that Jews were human beings, while the third one called Nazism 'the dictatorship of evil'. The fourth one appealed strongly to Christian motives, and stated: 'Of course man is free, but without God he is defenceless against evil.' Hitler was declared to be a liar, and the Nazis 'the servants of the Antichrist'. The words of Ecclesiastes 4:1-2 were cited. The fifth leaflet asserted that Hitler could not win the war, only prolong it, while the sixth – the one that led to their arrest – decidedly mocked Hitler (it was to be smuggled out of Germany by Helmuth von Moltke, a Protestant member of the Kreisau Circle who was himself hanged by the Nazis in January 1945).

On 13 January 1943 there was a demonstration by the university students at Munich after the gauleiter of Bavaria, Paul Giesler, made some crude remarks about women, whether married or not, bearing children for the Reich. The possibility of a general uprising against the Nazis seemed not totally unlikely. However, on 18 February 1943 Hans and Sophie and their friend, Christoph Probst, were arrested for distributing copies of the sixth leaflet at Munich University. Four days later the People's Court in Munich tried the three of them. The head of the court was Roland Friesler, who was an ex-Bolshevik known for his ferocious rants against prisoners. Robert Scholl arrived in time to cry out: 'There is a higher justice before which we all must stand!' This led to his being escorted from the room. Hans too told Friesler: 'You will soon stand where we stand now!' In fact, Friesler was to perish in an Allied bombing raid over Berlin.

The Scholl siblings and Probst were sentenced to immediate death. Mrs Scholl was distraught, but told her daughter: 'Sophie ... remember Jesus.' Sophie replied: 'Yes, but you too.' The Protestant chaplain, Kurt Alt, encouraged Sophie to read aloud 1 Corinthians 13, which she did. Then she read from Psalm 90, which Hans had read earlier, and they celebrated communion together. The chaplain was a sympathizer, and cited John 15:13 to her. Showing calm courage, the three of them were beheaded at five o'clock that same afternoon – first Sophie, then Hans, then Christoph. With his head on the block, Hans shouted out: 'Long live freedom!'

99

ISOBEL KUHN
(1901–1957)

Earnestly searching, and finding

And you will seek Me and find Me, when you search for Me with all your heart (Jer. 29:13).

Then He said to them all, 'If anyone desires to come after Me, let him deny himself, and take up his cross daily, and follow Me. For whoever desires to save his life will lose it, but whoever loses his life for My sake will save it' (Luke 9:23-24; see also Mark 10:29-30).

But seek first the kingdom of God and His righteousness, and all these things shall be added to you (Matt. 6:33).

Behold, I am with you and will keep you wherever you go, and I will bring you back to this land; for I will not leave you until I have done what I have spoken to you (Gen. 28:15).

We grope for the wall like the blind (Isa. 59:10a).

It is vain for you to rise up early, to sit up late, to eat the bread of sorrows; for so He gives His beloved sleep (Ps. 127:2).

For God has not given us a spirit of fear, but of power and of love and of a sound mind (2 Tim. 1:7).

Lord, now You are letting Your servant depart in peace, according to Your word; for my eyes have seen Your salvation (Luke 2:29-30).

Isobel Kuhn (née Miller) was born in Canada. As a university student, she embraced agnosticism, and went through a broken engagement to a man who proved unfaithful to her. For a time she was suicidal, but she remembered her father's kindness and a quote from Dante: 'In His will is our peace.' Her professor of English at the University of British Columbia was especially fond of using what Isobel called 'the pitying sneer' against the Christian faith, rather than trying to dismantle it by using reasoned argument. She was later to describe this time as the 'slippery ways in the darkness' (Jer. 23:12). She remembered: 'My heart was often like lead, even while my lips were chattering merry nonsense.'

However, 'by searching', as she emphasized, she came to saving faith in Christ, and was determined to serve Him in all things. She saw the question raised in Job 11:7, and the Bible's answers given in Jeremiah 29:13 and in John 14:6; 5:39; 7:17. Although she did not immediately go to church, she began to read and underline the Gospels, and to pray rather immature prayers that God kindly answered. She set about 'extinguishing her tapers', as she put it, in dealing with doubtful issues such as playing cards, going to the theatre, reading novels and dancing. She also played a part in reclaiming a minister to the true gospel after he had embraced its liberal counterfeit.

Isobel heard the tall and self-sacrificing missionary, musician and science graduate, James O. Fraser, at a conference in Washington in 1924, and was particularly struck when, before the fireplace on the last night of the conference, he cited Luke 9:23-24 along with Mark 10:29-30. She was soon leaving for Chicago to study at the Moody Bible Institute. After graduation, she sailed in 1928 for China as a single woman, with 'Let us go on' from Hebrews 6:1 on her lips. Isobel's mother utterly opposed her going to China, initially at least, although she herself was president of the Women's Missionary Society of the Canadian Presbyterian Church.

In 1929 in China, Isobel married John Kuhn, who had been in China already for two years, waiting for her – 'the irresistible force collides with the immovable object' was how Isobel described it. They lived in a remote area, working amongst the Lisu in the far western province of Yunnan – a people who considered the desire for privacy to be the Westerners' queerest trait. Often they were separated for fairly lengthy periods. Yet they lived out the motto they had adopted for their marriage, 'God first', based on Matthew 6:33. They had two children – Kathryn and Danny, born twelve years apart.

Evangelism was a struggle, but God worked in sovereign grace. Isobel was musical and could play the organ and the piano, and also sought to use her Hawaiian guitar to advantage. John would at times engage in all-night prayer meetings. When a convert named Small Pearl was baptized, the local Chinese thought she must have done something terrible to warrant such punishment!

Isobel saw her life as one lived 'in the arena' (1 Cor. 4:9). These were extremely troubled times. By 1937 there was war, with the Kuomintang and the communists cooperating against the common enemy, Japan. In all the turmoil and dislocation, Isobel often rested on Genesis 28:15. Another woman missionary, Gladys Aylward, became famous for her heroic trek whereby she led 100 homeless children to safety across Japanese-held territory. The Chinese civil war recommenced after the ending of World War II, and in October 1949 the (misnamed) People's Democratic Republic of China was declared. Those missionaries who survived the communist revolution were soon expelled: in 1948 there were about 6,000 Protestant missionaries in China, and by 1951 they were all gone. With Kathryn thankfully already in the U.S.A., Isobel had escaped with Danny into Burma (Myanmar), citing Isaiah 59:10, while John stayed on for another eighteen months to help the Church.

In 1952 they were relocated in the mountains of north Thailand, a move which Isobel accepted after reading the words

'Climb or die' in one of Amy Carmichael's writings. However, within a couple of years, Isobel was diagnosed with breast cancer and she died in 1957. She calmed herself with Psalm 127:2, and sought to battle her fears with a number of other verses, including 2 Timothy 1:7. The medical treatment was not successful, but as she was dying, Isobel cited Luke 2:29-30 to two fellow missionaries. Her husband John recorded of Isobel's death: 'If ever I was near heaven, and if ever I was conscious that death had lost its sting, it was then.'

Since the last decades of the twentieth century, China has experienced one of the mightiest and most unexpected revivals in the history of the Church. In 1950 there were about one million Protestant communicants in China, but in fifty years this had grown to almost 100 million evangelicals. And among the Lisus, the Christian presence is particularly notable. Just before she died, Isobel had written: 'I'll be spending my time (in heaven) hanging over the ramparts greedily watching north Thailand, so that all the angels will see of me will be my heels!!! Not allowed? We'll see.' Such was her love for her adopted people, based on the principle of 'God first'.

100

ARTHUR STACE
(1884–1967)

Proclaiming the Lord of eternity

*For thus says the High and Lofty One Who inhabits
eternity, whose name is Holy: 'I dwell in the high and holy
place, with him who has a contrite and humble spirit'*
(Isa. 57:15).

As the year 1999 rolled into 2000, the Sydney Harbour Bridge
was emblazoned with the word 'Eternity'. It was a surprising
way for an avowedly secular nation to celebrate the passing of
time. Humanly speaking, it was meant to be a tribute to Arthur
Stace – known as Mr Eternity – who was converted from a life of
alcoholism and petty crime. His parents were poor drunkards,
and his two sisters and two brothers lived lives of drunkenness
and prostitution. As a boy, Arthur skipped as much school as
possible, became a state ward and spent his first cheque in a
hotel. World War I proved something of an interlude, but he was
soon back into his alcoholic habits, despite signing the pledge a
number of times.

In 1930 Stace dropped into St Barnabas Church on Broadway
in Sydney, and determined that Christianity was the answer to
his decrepit lifestyle. Sometime later, in Burton Street Baptist

Church, Stace heard John Ridley preach on Isaiah 57:15 ('Thus says the High and Lofty One who inhabits eternity'). Ridley cried out: 'Eternity! Eternity! I wish I could sound or shout that word to everyone in the streets of Sydney. Eternity! You have to meet it. Where will you spend eternity?'

Stace was a shy, frail-looking little man who, despite his reputation in some circles, was not illiterate, but who wrote without distinction and spelt with even less. Yet to cite his own words: 'Suddenly I began crying and I felt a powerful call from the Lord to write "Eternity". I had a piece of chalk in my pocket and I bent down right there and wrote it.' He continued to do so for the next thirty-three years, at least fifty times a day. The only change in his practice came when he turned the first 'e' into a capital to thwart a man who tried to deface the word by placing an 'm' in front of it, thus turning it into 'meternity'.

Somehow, Stace managed to write 'Eternity' in chalk on the streets of Sydney in a beautiful copperplate script. Under cover of darkness he carried out his task, and his identity was only discovered in 1956 when his minister, Lisle Thompson, watched him take out his crayon and write his message on the pavement. By the time of his death, Stace had written what Bruce Beaver called 'the one big word' some 500,000 times.

In popular mythology, Stace was an illiterate man who proved capable of writing just one word. Actually, he had some literacy skills, and these developed as he grew in grace. He also possessed a lively wit, and, referring to his stays in gaol, would warn those who came to hear him to 'Beware, your sins will find you *in*.'

To Sir David Griffin, a former Lord Mayor of Sydney, Stace's ministry was just 'a delicious piece of eccentricity', but God used this ill-educated man to proclaim His Word. 'Eternity' is indeed a fitting message to a culture immersed in the here and now, and reluctant to ponder the issues of life and death, of time and eternity. The poet Douglas Stewart summed up Stace's gospel motives:

It moved in him, it struck him deep with sorrow
That men should live in time with all its vanity
Or think they did, and yet were in Eternity.

In his own way, Stace was seeking to say what the distinguished Puritan theologian, Stephen Charnock, said: 'By frequent meditation of God's eternity, we should become more sensible of the trifling nature of the world.'

101

C.S. LEWIS
(1898–1963)

Facing the claims of Jesus

*Be wise as serpents and harmless
as doves* (Matt. 10:16b).

*The heavens declare the glory of God; and the firmament
shows His handiwork ... The law of the Lord is perfect,
converting the soul ... Let the words of my mouth and
the meditation of my heart be acceptable in Your sight, O
Lord, my strength and my Redeemer* (Ps. 19:1, 7a, 14).

*He said to them, 'But who do you say that I am?' Simon
Peter answered and said, 'You are the Christ, the Son
of the living God'* (Matt. 16:15-16).

Clive Staples Lewis was born on 29 November 1898 and died
on 22 November 1963, the same day that President John F.
Kennedy was assassinated. He was born in Belfast, and from an
early age announced that his name was Jack (after 'Jacksie', the
family's dog that had just been run over by a car). It stuck, for
his friends and family, but for later readers he was always C.S.
Lewis. He was to become well-known as a Christian apologist
(e.g. *Mere Christianity*; *The Problem of Pain*; *Miracles*; *Screwtape
Letters*), children's writer (the seven volumes of *The Chronicles
of Narnia*), novelist (e.g. *Out of the Silent Planet*; *Perelandra*; *That
Hideous Strength*), academic, poet, essayist and theologian.

Before Lewis's tenth birthday, his mother died. After initial private tuition, Lewis was sent to boarding schools where he learnt more vulgarity than anything else. He became an atheist, and, like many atheists, lived in what he called 'a whirl of contradictions': 'I maintained that God did not exist. I was also very angry with God for not existing. I was equally angry with Him for creating a world.' In 1916 he won a scholarship to University College, Oxford, but the following year he went off to war, where he was wounded.

Back at Oxford, he did extremely well at his studies, and was developing a delight in literature and in philosophy. The fantasy writings of George MacDonald (1824–1905) moved Lewis in a more Christian direction, although at the time he was scarcely aware of it. As an atheist he would argue, in the words of Lucretius, that the existence of suffering and pain showed that God did not exist:

> Had God designed the world, it would not be
> A world so frail and faulty as we see.

His conversion came in two stages. He became a theist in his room in Magdalen College in 1929, 'the most dejected and reluctant convert in all England'. Although he never became Reformed in his thinking, he admitted that there was no search for God involved. Indeed, said Lewis, 'they might as well have talked about the mouse's search for the cat.' Despite disliking hymns and organ music, Lewis began to attend his parish church. He pondered G.K. Chesterton's *The Everlasting Man*, and thought on the claims of Christ. Two years later, he embraced Christ as the Son of God – while being driven to the zoo.

After teaching at Oxford for nearly thirty years, Lewis became Professor of Medieval and Renaissance English at Cambridge in 1954. In 1956 he married a divorced American Christian, Joy Davidman, who had made the spiritual journey from atheistic communism. This was done in a civil ceremony, and was designed to allow Joy to remain in the United Kingdom. She was soon found to be very ill with cancer, so Lewis married her in a Christian ceremony in hospital on 21 March 1957. Joy recovered for a time but died in 1960, and Lewis poured out his anguish in *A Grief Observed*.

In *Mere Christianity*, Lewis described himself as an Anglican, 'not especially "high", nor especially "low", nor especially anything else'. In his writings, he rarely exegeted Scripture, but explained its teachings in a clear and simple, yet stimulating, way. A humble man, he strove to follow Christ's command in Matthew 10:16, and wrote of the Saviour: 'He wants a child's heart, but a grown-up's head.' Pride was something he abhorred as 'the complete anti-God state of mind'. All his life, he was a keen observer of human nature and of the creation. He regarded Psalm 19 as 'the greatest poem in the Psalter and one of the greatest lyrics in the world.'

Lewis's analysis of the claims of Christ is oft-quoted:

> A man who was merely a man and said the sort of things Jesus said would not be a great moral teacher. He would either be a lunatic – on the level with a man who says he is a poached egg – or else he would be the Devil of Hell. You must make your choice. Either this man was, and is, the Son of God: or else a madman or something worse. You can shut Him up for a fool, you can spit at Him and kill Him as a demon; or you can fall at His feet and call Him Lord and God. But let us not come with any patronising nonsense about His being a great human teacher. He has not left that open to us. He did not intend to.

Indeed, during His earthly life, Christ was viewed in various ways: as insane (Mark 3:20-21); or of the devil (see Mark 3:22-27); or the Christ, the Son of the living God (Matt.16:16). Just before his death, Lewis wrote with touching simplicity to a young correspondent: 'If you continue to love Jesus, nothing much can go wrong with you, and I hope you may always do so.'

Lewis was rather too vague on the workings of the atonement, and was deficient in his appreciation of the inspiration of Scripture. However, he came increasingly to distrust the biblical critics:

> They seem to me to lack literary judgment, to be imperceptive about the very quality of the texts they are reading ... All theology of the liberal type involves at some point – and often involves throughout – the claim that the real behaviour and purpose and teaching of Christ came very rapidly to be misunderstood and misrepresented by His followers, and has been recovered or exhumed only by modern scholars ... 'The assured results of modern scholarship', as to the way in which an old book was written, are 'assured', we may conclude, only because the men who knew the facts are dead and can't blow the gaff.

Rather gloomily, he noted the increasing liberalism of Anglican clerics, and in his own laconic and understated way, made his point with telling power: 'Missionary to the priests of one's own church is an embarrassing role; though I have a horrid feeling that if such mission work is not soon undertaken the future history of the Church of England is likely to be short.'

102

JIM ELLIOT
(1927–1956)

ROGER YOUDERIAN
(1924–1956)

NATE SAINT
(1923–1956)

ED McCULLY
(1927–1956)

PETER FLEMING
(1928–1956)

Looking unto Jesus

And I tell you, make friends for yourselves by means of unrighteous wealth, so that when it fails they may receive you into the eternal dwellings (Luke 16:9; ESV).

Through God we will do valiantly, for it is He who shall tread down our enemies (Ps. 60:12).

For this God is our God for ever and ever: He will be our Guide even unto death (Ps. 48:14; KJV).

For we know that if our earthly house, this tent, is destroyed, we have a building from God, a house not made with hands, eternal in the heavens ... Now He who has prepared us for this very thing is God ... We are confident, yes, well pleased rather to be absent from the body and to be present with the Lord (2 Cor. 5:1, 5, 8).

Whoever loses his life for My sake and the gospel's will save it (Mark 8:35b).

In 1956 these five American men – Jim Elliot, Roger Youderian, Nate Saint, Ed McCully and Peter Fleming – were all martyred together while trying to reach the Waodani Indians (known as the 'Auca' which means 'naked savage') of Ecuador with the gospel. Elisabeth Elliot recalled that all five men held to the Bible as 'the literal and supernatural and perfect word from God to man'. Accordingly, one notes that Jim Elliot's journals are suitably full of Scripture and his meditations on God's Word.

On 28 October 1948 Jim Elliot, reflecting on Luke 16:9, wrote words that were later to become well known in the evangelical world: 'He is no fool who gives what he cannot keep to gain what he cannot lose.' In February 1952, as he left for Ecuador, he called out to his weeping parents on the pier in the words of Psalm 60:12. Pete Fleming was converted at thirteen by means of a blind evangelist. When Jim Elliot read John 19 in Greek, he almost wept, and wrote to his parents: 'Surely it is a wonderful story of love.' Ed McCully was a tall, strapping former football star, while Nate Saint was the pilot for Missionary Aviation Fellowship. Roger Youderian walked like an old man because he had contracted polio when he was nine years old.

The Aucas were a savage people, with a homicide rate of over 60%, according to Nate Saint's son, Steve. They were made more savage by the havoc caused by hunters of rubber from 1875 to 1925. In the 1940s they had killed Shell Oil Company labourers, and were greatly feared by their Indian neighbours. Savagery so often begets savagery, and the oil company replied by bombing the Waodani.

For a number of months, the missionaries had lowered gifts by aeroplane in an attempt to make friendly contact with the Aucas. The first gift was a small aluminium kettle with a lid and about twenty brightly coloured buttons, while the second gift was a machete – almost indispensable in the South American jungle. Using the few Auca words he knew, Jim Elliot called out friendly messages over a loudspeaker. These trips seemed to go smoothly, and the Aucas even attached a gift to the line dangling from the plane – it was a live parrot in a bark bag.

Finally, the men decided to enter the Auca territory on Tuesday, 3 January 1956. Nate Saint wrote: 'Except for forty-seven billion flying insects of every sort, this place is a little paradise.' At first there seemed good reason to be hopeful, and one Auca man, whom they nicknamed 'George', even agreed to go for a short ride in the plane, which became known to the Indians as the 'wood bee'. But at 4.30 p.m. on Sunday, 8 January, planned radio contact was not made. Something had gone very wrong.

As five wives pondered what might have happened, Barbara Youderian remembered Psalm 48:14. Eventually it emerged that all five men had been speared to death. Olive Fleming drew strength from the words of 2 Corinthians 5:1-8, and all five widows looked to Mark 8:35b. The death of God's saints is never in vain, and Christians from all over the world were touched by accounts of the men's faith and heroism. Volunteers for missionary work came forward in direct response to the story of the five martyrs. In 1958 Rachel Saint (sister of Nate, and known as 'Star') and Elisabeth Elliot (widow of Jim) returned to the area to continue the work of medical aid, translation and evangelism. Thirty-eight years later Steve Saint returned to the Amazon to continue the work of his martyred father.

103

GEORGI VINS
(1928–1998)

To serve God alone

*You, who have shown me great and severe troubles, shall
revive me again, and bring me up again from the depths
of the earth. You shall increase my greatness, and
comfort me on every side (Ps. 71:20-21).*

*Then I heard a voice from heaven saying to me, 'Write:
"Blessed are the dead who die in the Lord from now on."
"Yes," says the Spirit, "that they may rest from
their labours, and their works follow
them"' (Rev. 14:13).*

*Behold, how good and how pleasant it is for brethren to
dwell together in unity! (Ps. 133:1).*

*But Peter and the other apostles answered and said: 'We
ought to obey God rather than men' (Acts 5:29).*

In 1917 'Holy Russia', hitherto dominated by Eastern Orthodoxy,
tottered in February (March) under the Provisional Government, and then collapsed completely in October (November)
with the coming to power of the Bolshevik Party. Persecution
broke out on a large scale. In January 1918 Lenin declared that
'Religious and church societies must be completely free unions
of like-minded citizens independent of the authorities.' This was,
of course, a travesty. Lenin's brutal successor, Joseph Stalin, was

to say of the Orthodox clergy: 'The only pity is that they have not been wholly liquidated.' Yet during the period from 1989 to 1991, under Gorbachev, Marxism wavered, then itself collapsed in the U.S.S.R. and across eastern Europe.

The second half of the nineteenth century had witnessed a growth in the evangelical movement, despite the opposition of the Tsars. By the time of Vins's birth, in 1928, the Baptists had grown significantly. From 1962 to 1965 a fearful Nikita Khrushchev sought to gain greater state control over the evangelicals. Baptist children were ordered not to attend church, and no baptisms under the age of thirty were to take place. The Council of Evangelical Christian-Baptist Churches, with Georgi Vins as secretary, broke away from the more compliant United Baptist Council in 1965. Many Baptist leaders ended up in labour camps, but evangelism went on. Birthday parties, for example, would be used as a cover for Sunday School work. In Alexander Solzhenitsyn's novel, *One Day in the Life of Ivan Denisovich*, there is a sympathetic portrayal of an imprisoned Baptist named Alyoshka. The comment is made that 'those Baptists loved to evangelise.' Local Baptists would store up paper until a ton or more had been collected, then a mobile publishing team would arrive and quickly print Bibles. Georgi Vins's view was that had the Russian Baptists tolerated theological or moral liberalism, it would have been the end of the movement.

Georgi Vins's own father, Peter, also a pastor, had worked in the Far East, and been arrested three times – the first time in 1930 when Georgi was aged just two. When he was arrested for the third and last time in 1936 or 1937, young Georgi remembered him waving at the family. Soon after, Peter Vins was executed. Georgi held degrees in economics and engineering, but was ordained into the Baptist ministry in 1962. In February 1967 he was arrested and deprived of sleep as part of his interrogation. He was sent to the northern Urals until his release in May 1969. His health suddenly collapsed in prison, which is not surprising, considering that his cell was only six paces, and the conditions were freezing. He almost died, but resolved: 'I will give myself to Christ with my whole soul.'

In prison, Vins thought of his dear ones, and that 'Christ is unconquerable!' Also, 'Atheism, invested with power, creates tyranny.' He took to writing poetry:

> Not for robbery, not for gold,
> Do we stand before you.
> Today here, as in Pilate's day,
> Christ our Saviour is being judged.

His mother wrote to him and cited Psalm 71:20-21 and Revelation 14:13 to comfort and encourage him. She declared that 'it is a fine thing to remain unembittered by life's sufferings.'

Vins found Psalm 133:1 fulfilled in the Christian brotherhood found in the camps. When he was released, he preached a sermon which offended the authorities, and he was assigned to a Kiev factory. For three years he lived in hiding. On 10 December 1970 he wrote to Kosygin, Brezhnev, Podgorny and Rudenko to protest when he learned that his mother had been imprisoned. About 180 believers from the Kiev church also protested, but the Soviet authorities broke up prayer meetings and beat up participants.

On 30 March 1974 Vins was arrested again, and his trial began on 27 January 1975. The KGB invited him to collaborate but he refused. As a result, he was sentenced to five years in a labour camp, followed by five years in exile in Siberia. His supporters in court threw flowers at him, and about 500 sang. According to Rick Barry, of Russian Gospel Ministries, one of the formal accusations against Vins was that he was the author of the twenty-third Psalm!

Vins wrote: 'In accordance with biblical teaching, we believe that every authority is ultimately from God and that we are obliged to submit ourselves to such authority on all civil matters. To work. To pay taxes. To show respect to the government. But when it is a question of faith, then we submit ourselves to God alone.' In

1979, as part of an exchange agreed to by Leonid Brezhnev and Jimmy Carter, five Russian dissidents were swapped for two Soviet spies. The Supreme Soviet stripped Vins of his Soviet citizenship, and expelled him, to be accompanied six weeks later by his wife, five children and some other relatives. In 1990 Mikhail Gorbachev revoked this decree, and allowed him to return to Russia on preaching tours.

Vins died from a brain tumour in exile in the United States on 11 January 1998 at the age of sixty-nine, having devoted his final years to the work of Russian Gospel Ministries, based in Indiana. His was an uncompromising testimony to the power of the gospel when confronted by tyrannous power.

104

Dr MARTYN LLOYD-JONES
(1899–1981)

Jesus Christ and the true gospel

*For I determined not to know anything among you except
Jesus Christ and Him crucified (1 Cor. 2:2).*

*Being confident of this very thing, that He who has begun
a good work in you will complete it until the day of Jesus
Christ (Phil. 1:6).*

*For when we were still without strength, in due time
Christ died for the ungodly (Rom. 5:6).*

David Martyn Lloyd-Jones was born in Cardiff in Wales on 20
December 1899. After a fire in the family home and shop, the
family relocated to London in 1914. Two years later, Lloyd-
Jones began medical training, and rose to become the chief
clinical assistant to Sir Thomas Horder, the King's personal
physician. However, he had become a Christian, and in 1926
he left to become a missioner in Sandfields, in South Wales.
His only other settled pastorate was at Westminster Chapel,
where he joined the ageing G. Campbell Morgan just before
World War II, and remained until his retirement in 1968. In the
last thirteen years of his life, Lloyd-Jones was kept very active
in preaching, and preparing some of his sermons and lectures
for publication.

For all his massive intellect, Lloyd-Jones saw himself fundamentally as an evangelist. His ministry was based squarely on I Corinthians 2:2. He began his ministry at Sandfields, Aberavon, on 28 November 1926, preaching on that text, and over fifty years later, in 1977, preached on the same text (but without repeating the same sermon). For that matter, this was the same text which was carved into his gravestone.

To Lloyd-Jones, I Corinthians 2:2 clearly shows the apostle Paul's view was that, apart from the gospel, there is only spiritual and moral bankruptcy. To make the same point in his own day, Lloyd-Jones cited the novelist Aldous Huxley, who had embraced some kind of mystical Buddhism, and confessed: 'It is a bit embarrassing to have been concerned with the human problem all one's life and that at the end one has no more to offer by way of advice than "Try to be a little kinder".' Lloyd-Jones never lost the assurance that the gospel alone was the power of God unto salvation. He could be provocative at times, and prone to exaggeration, as when he declared that 'the final enemy of the Christian faith is morality.'

To Lloyd-Jones, it is essential to know and proclaim the full-orbed gospel of salvation by God's electing grace. He once commented that Philippians 1:6 was one of his favourite verses, although he characteristically added that he was uncertain whether we are allowed to have favourite verses. He seems to have had a number of favourite verses, because in his long series on Romans, he referred to Romans 5:6 as 'one of the greatest verses in the whole Bible'.

In July 1951 Lloyd-Jones gave three addresses on 'The Sovereignty of God' at an Inter-Varsity Fellowship conference in Wales. In the third address, he piled up verses for his hearers to think through. These included verses that clearly say that God has set apart a people for Himself (Acts 13:48; Rom. 11:5-6; I Cor. 1:26-29; Eph. 1:3-5; 2 Thess. 2:13; 2 Tim. 1:9; I Pet. 1:2; Rom. 8:28-29; 9:1-24; Matt. 11:25-26). Along with these positive texts – to which more could be added – there are negative ones which emphasize our natural inability to come to Christ: we must be born again (John 3:3); we must be drawn by the Father (John 6:44; Matt. 16:17); the carnal mind is not subject to the law of God (Rom. 8:7); the natural man cannot receive the things of the Spirit of God (1 Cor. 2:14). It was a devastating display of God's plan of salvation. One man at the conference, Geraint Morgan, recorded: 'In that conference I yielded gladly my Arminian views and came to rejoice in the doctrines of sovereign grace. That conference gave me an anchor.'

The weakness of the Church in the modern Western world was, in Lloyd-Jones's view, largely the fault of the Church. Too much of the professing Church put unity and peace above truth. He stated that 'Nothing so surely drives the world away from the truth as uncertainty or confusion in the church with respect to the content of her message.' Only if the local church were truly alive and regenerate, knowing something of the power of the Holy Spirit and committed to gospel truth, could evangelism be effective. Any revival of Calvinistic preaching that took place in the twentieth century owed much to the ministry of Martyn Lloyd-Jones.

105

DR MARTYN LLOYD-JONES
(1899–1981)

Truth married to experience

Nevertheless do not rejoice in this, that the spirits are subject to you, but rather rejoice because your names are written in heaven (Luke 10:20).

Beloved, now we are children of God; and it has not yet been revealed what we shall be, but we know that when He is revealed, we shall be like Him, for we shall see Him as He is (1 John 3:2).

Therefore we do not lose heart. Even though our outward man is perishing, yet the inward man is being renewed day by day. For our light affliction, which is but for a moment, is working for us a far more exceeding and eternal weight of glory, while we do not look at the things which are seen, but at the things which are not seen. For the things which are seen are temporary, but the things which are not seen are eternal (2 Cor. 4:16-18).

Martyn Lloyd-Jones is sometimes viewed only as a preacher of doctrinaire Reformed theology, but that is a lopsided and misleading interpretation. Indeed, he lamented: 'I spend half my time telling Christians to study doctrine and the other half telling them that doctrine is not enough.' To that degree, he thought that the Calvinists needed Methodism to prevent their doctrine from losing warmth and graciousness. He often said that he was a man of the eighteenth century, meaning that the evangelical fervour and emotion of the revival of that century resonated more with him than the doctrinal precision of the Puritans of the seventeenth century. In his lectures on *Preaching and Preachers,* he stated: 'I can forgive the preacher almost anything if he gives me a sense of God.'

For all his belief in preaching, and that the longed-for revival of the Christian cause would only come about through the revival of true preaching, near the end of his life he maintained: 'I did not live for preaching.' In the last year of his life, he pointed to Luke 10:20, and commented solemnly: 'Bear that in mind.' He then went on to say that 'Our greatest danger is to live upon our activity. The ultimate test of a preacher is what he feels like when he cannot preach.' The preacher must be a Christian before he is a preacher.

Truth is vital, but it not only acquits, it also transforms. Hence he told his congregation: 'As you walk the streets of London remember you have the reputation of God in your hands.' In 1971 he declared: 'Life! There is a lack of life amongst us. What is the cause? It is due to a lack of realization that God is a living God. There is a neglect on our part of the living God … Our supreme need is to realize God is alive.' Paper creeds are important, but they are not the same as spiritual life. He once confessed that his greatest defect as a preacher was a lack of powerful love for the congregation. Truth was to be combined with emotion, as it was, say, in George Whitefield, or the apostle Paul, who knew what it was to weep for a people (note Acts 20:31; Rom. 9:1-5; Phil. 3:18).

Looking at the promise that Christians shall be made like Christ when they see Him as He is (1 John 3:2), Lloyd-Jones was so enraptured at the thought that he felt sorry for anyone who has not had to spend a week with such a verse. This was not something that could be explained, yet it was not mystical in the sense of not being logical. Rather, as Lloyd-Jones put it: 'Nothing is more wonderful than to know that God loves you; and no man can truly know that God loves him except in Jesus Christ and Him crucified.'

In 1981 Lloyd-Jones came to die. He had been a Harley Street specialist who had left medicine in order to preach the gospel, but we are all jars of clay. He became frail and had lost his powers of speech, and scribbled on a piece of paper: 'Do not pray for healing. Do not hold me back from the glory.' One of his two daughters, Elizabeth, pointed to 2 Corinthians 4:16-18, and the weak and feeble man nodded with some vigour. In life as in death, and all human inconsistencies, he wholeheartedly embraced the Christian view of the truth of Christ experienced in the very depths of one's soul.

106

HELEN ROSEVEARE
(1925–)

Struggles and triumphs

Now therefore, give me this mountain
(Josh. 14:12a).

Be still, and know that I am God (Ps. 46:10a).

*But on Mount Zion there shall be deliverance, and there
shall be holiness; the house of Jacob shall possess
their possessions* (Obad. 17).

*Therefore, behold, I will allure her, will bring her into the
wilderness, and speak comfort to her. I will give her her
vineyards from there, and the Valley of Achor [Trouble] as
a door of hope; she shall sing there, as in the days of her
youth, as in the day when she came up from the land of
Egypt. And it shall be, in that day, says the Lord, that you
will call Me 'my Husband' and no longer call
Me 'my Baal'* (Hosea 2:14-16).

Make this valley full of ditches (2 Kings 3:16).

Helen Roseveare was born in Haileybury, Hertfordshire (just
north of London) in 1925, and at the time of writing lives
in retirement in Northern Ireland. Her father, Sir Martin
Roseveare, moved to Malawi at the age of 59 and set up its
educational system, living there until his death at 86. Helen's
brother, Robert, also taught for more than ten years in various

parts of southern Africa. The title of her spiritually honest auto-biography, *Give Me This Mountain*, is taken from the words of Caleb recorded in Joshua 14:12-13. As a child, Helen was afraid of water and of heights. As a child, she was desperate to be in the limelight, and so she lied that she had met Hitler at the Berlin Olympics in 1936 (which she had actually attended).

Helen went to an Anglo-Catholic church, and she remembered: 'I was an ardent Anglo-Catholic, regular at the confessional and the Mass, every part of me stretching out after the Unseen Power who could meet all needs.' Yet at the same time she felt empty, and became a fan of the cinema. In July 1944 she began studying medicine in Newnham College of Cambridge University. Here she met members of the Cambridge Inter-Collegiate Christian Union, and began to attend Bible studies and lectures. The evangelicals were sure that she was converted, but in fact Sundays were a three-way struggle for her, between Anglo-Catholicism in the mornings, Communism in the afternoons and Evangelicalism in the evenings.

During the Christmas break in 1944, Helen's younger sister had mumps, so Helen was able to attend Mount Hermon Bible College, Ealing, where she studied Genesis, and then Romans. Without realizing it, she stayed up all night to finish it. The next day she fell asleep for the session on Romans, and was tearful. However, she was greatly comforted by a text on the wall, Psalm 46:10. The following Christmas – 1945 – she was baptized as a believer. Helen had a dream, and opened her Bible at Obadiah 17. She took this as a call to utter dedication. However, she interpreted 1 John 3:8-10 in a perfectionist way, and recorded: 'I feared this chapter, with a strange kind of horror.' She was still living in two worlds – she could play cricket one Sunday and also throw herself into evangelism at West London Hospital. Her lament was that 'I fell into most of the traps possible.'

Helen became convinced that she should go to the Congo, and she arrived there in 1953 (the Kingdom of Congo became the Belgian Congo in 1908; the Congo in 1960 when it gained its independence; Zaire in 1971; and the Democratic Republic of the Congo in 1997). At Opienge she saw revival, powerful singing, much confession of sin and a burden for prayer – but she continued to know spiritual struggles, and came down with malaria. In 1955 she was moved to Nebobongo, where she remained for ten years, and where she worked very long hours, from 5.30 a.m. to 10.30 p.m. She looked after a leprosy centre and children's home, and established forty-eight rural health clinics, a training centre for paramedical workers and a 100-bed hospital, and, for good measure, learned how to work the brick kiln.

Helen's sister, Diana, an Anglo-Catholic nun in a closed order, received permission to write to Helen, and she cited Hosea 2:14-16. After five years, Helen returned to England, and in a rather depressed state she went to a house-party, where the speaker's text was Hosea 2:14-16. Her spirits revived and clarity of thought returned. In mid-1960 Helen returned for a second term, but there was much political unrest in 1960, and most foreigners were evacuated. The Prime Minister was assassinated, and some 100,000 people lost their lives. Independence led, as in so many other places, to a throwing off of all restraints and a mocking of Christianity. Helen, however, stayed. The mission motto was taken from C.T. Studd: 'If Jesus Christ be God and died for me, then no sacrifice can be too great for me to make for Him.'

In 1964 Helen was taken by some rebels (called 'Simbas', meaning 'lions'), and on one terrible night – 29 October – was raped and then arrested. She records that 'the suffering just seemed to highlight His love.' She told a young Italian nun who had also been raped that the Virgin Mary was regarded as an adulteress, and that they had not lost their purity because they never had any. Helen put herself at the front of the other women in an attempt to protect them. Early in 1965, after five months in captivity, she was rescued by the National Army and returned to England.

The next year, 1966, Helen was back in the Congo, and spent the next seven years there. She became the director of the Evangelical Medical Centre of Nyankunde in north-east Zaire. Morale was low and corruption endemic, but the centre was opened on 29 October 1966 (two years to the day after her night of horror), with thirty-six male students and three girl students. She saw the door of hope through the valley of Achor. She had learnt: 'Only as I found my own insufficiency did I realize His sufficiency.' Yet her troubles continued. She went through a three month court case where she was charged with sex discrimination and anti-Party colonialism. Finally, she resigned from the work, thinking it was time for Africans to take it over. In 1973 Helen returned to England to live, although she revisited Africa a number of times. In 2005 she wrote that for the last thirty years of her life, 2 Kings 3:16 had been her inspiration.

Her story is not a straightforward tale of success. One is struck by her honesty with herself, and her genuine love for the Africans, even in facing hatred, ill-treatment and suspicion. Finally, she tells of sharing the wordless book with an illiterate herdsman on an African roadside and with a woman with lung cancer on a British train. 'There was no difference' is her comment.

107

JONI EARECKSON TADA
(1950–)

True healing

*For whom the Lord loves He chastens, and scourges every
son whom He receives … Now no chastening seems
to be joyful for the present, but painful; nevertheless,
afterward it yields the peaceable fruit of righteousness to
those who have been trained by it* (Heb. 12:6, 11).

*Jesus said to him, 'Rise, take up your bed
and walk'* (John 5:8).

*That I may know Him and the power of His resurrection,
and the fellowship of His sufferings, being conformed
to His death* (Phil. 3:10).

*But when you give a banquet, invite the poor, the
crippled, the lame, the blind, and you will be blessed*
(Luke 14:13-14).

*'My gracious favour is all you need. My power works best
in your weakness!' So now I am glad to boast about my
weaknesses, so that the power of Christ may
work through me* (2 Cor. 12:9 NLT).

*And when He comes, He will open the eyes of the blind
and unstop the ears of the deaf. The lame will leap like
a deer, and those who cannot speak will shout and sing!*
(Isa. 35:5-6 NLT).

*Worthy is the Lamb who was slain to receive power and
riches and wisdom, and strength and honour and glory
and blessing!* (Rev. 5:12).

For what is your life? It is even a vapour that appears for a
little time and then vanishes away (James 4:14b).

But none of these things move me; nor do I count my
life dear to myself, so that I may finish my race with joy,
and the ministry which I received from the Lord Jesus, to
testify to the gospel of the grace of God (Acts 20:24).

In 1967, as a typical, happy, energetic seventeen-year-old, Joni Eareckson dived into the shallow waters of Chesapeake Bay, – and broke her neck. It was only because her sister Kathy was bitten by a crab at the same time, then called out to Joni to watch out for crabs and received no answer, that Joni was found in time, before she drowned. As it happened, she almost died of her terrible injuries, spent two years in hospital and was rendered a quadriplegic. Confined to a wheelchair, she developed her talents as a singer and as an artist who drew with a pencil held between her teeth. More vitally, she has been sustained by God who is both loving and sovereign.

As she struggled to come to terms with her new lifestyle, her mind went to the words of Hebrews 12:6,11. Some punishment, she concluded, is retribution and some is restoration. By the grace of God, hers was a matter of restoration. She had been heading down the wrong path – 'sinning big-time', to use her words – but she was led to repent and to thank God for rescuing her through the terrible 'accident'. She had written on a card: 'Dear Box, I am tired of saying I'm a Christian out of one side of my mouth and saying something else out of the other.' When she asked God for forgiveness, she recalled: 'I felt clean and fresh.' As her understanding grew, she became fond of citing the words of John Bunyan: 'Conversion is not the smooth, easy-going process some men seem to think ... It is wounding work, this breaking of the hearts, but without wounding there is no saving.'

After her accident, Joni was naturally drawn to John 5:8 like a magnet, and, in fact, she was taken to a Kathryn Kuhlman crusade in Washington, but, like so many others, was not healed.

Later, she came to consider that John 5:8 had been fulfilled in a different and deeper way. As she put it: 'There are more important things in life than walking.' Joni came to see that 'every day of our short life has eternal consequences for good or ill. Thus, it is only fitting that a merciful and wise God should give us some sense of the stakes involved, some sense of the magnitude of the spiritual battle. He does this by giving us foretastes of heaven in the joys we experience, and foretastes of hell in our suffering.' Suffering is not God's final plan for His people, but it is used by Him to awaken them. With this eternal perspective, Joni could write: 'I'd rather be in this chair, knowing Him, than on my feet without Him.'

At a meeting in Sydney in 2000, Joni read Philippians 3:10. The impact was devastating. The verse became so deep and obvious. Here was a woman of faith in a wheelchair who had experienced both power and suffering in the here and now. At her place of work in Agoura Hills, California, there are three landings, with a Bible passage on each one – Luke 14:13-14, 2 Corinthians 12:9 and Isaiah 35:5-6.

There were other sufferings in her life besides what took place at Chesapeake Bay. Joni's niece died of a cancerous tumour in the brain as a child. The night she died, Joni saw a dazzling form of light, which she considered to be the angels transporting her niece's soul to heaven. After her marriage to Ken Tada, Joni yearned to bring a little girl into the world, and wept that she could not conceive. But, pointing to Revelation 5:12, she was strengthened by the thought that, even in heaven, 'Our Lord will be honoured as the slain Lamb. His sufferings will *never* be forgotten.'

Her perspective on life was partly governed by James 4:14, and she came to see that 'suffering gets us ready for heaven ... It makes us want to go there ... It moves our eyes from this world, which God knows could never satisfy us anyway, and sets them on the life to come.' She adds: 'When I think of heaven, I think of a time when I will be welcomed home. I remember when I was on my feet what a cozy, wonderful feeling it was to come home after hockey practice. For Christians, heaven will be like that ... We'll have new bodies and new minds!'

To the unbeliever, this might be viewed as escapism or a death wish. In 1967 and again in 1991 she knew deep depression, and felt attracted to euthanasia. Later, she began to struggle with chronic pain, and in June 2010 was diagnosed with breast cancer. Yet she has also found that 'the more intense the pain, the closer His embrace.' She has also denounced the encroaching laws favouring eugenics, and regards the abortion of Down's Syndrome and spina bifida babies as 'a more subtle and pervasive kind of genocide than the sort we saw in Armenia or Europe during World War II.'

Joni has frequently declared that her goal is that of the apostle Paul, as recorded in Acts 20:24. To love God is to love life, and to love the gospel of His grace in Jesus Christ – no matter what.

SOME LESSONS

In another context, the Bible speaks of a great cloud of witnesses (Heb. 12:1). Here the New Testament is referring not to the angelic hosts, as is so often thought, but to the Old Testament saints recorded in Hebrews 11 who testified to the same God who finally revealed Himself in His eternal Son, Christ Jesus. After the New Testament period, down through the ages, there has also been a great cloud of witnesses who have borne that same testimony in all parts of the world.

Faith in Christ is, of course, faith in the Christ which the Scripture has made known. Charles Spurgeon was sure of this:

> It is proven by all observation that success in the Lord's service is very generally in proportion to faith. It is certainly not in proportion to ability, nor does it always run parallel to a display of zeal; but it is invariably according to the measure of faith, for this is the law of the kingdom without exception, 'According to your faith be it unto you.'

Faith is not a human decision so much as a God-given trust in God's Word.

Throughout history, those who trusted God's Word have been used to witness to the Lord. C.S. Lewis affirmed that:

> If you read history you will find that the Christians who did most for the present world were just those who thought most of the next. The Apostles themselves, who set on foot the conversion of the Roman Empire, the great men who built

up the Middle Ages, the English Evangelicals who abolished the Slave Trade, all left their mark on Earth, precisely because their minds were occupied with Heaven. It is since Christians have largely ceased to think of the other world that they have become so ineffective in this. Aim at Heaven and you will get Earth 'thrown in'; aim at Earth and you will get neither.

The men and women discussed above, albeit briefly for each one, illustrate the truth of Samuel Stone's hymn, 'The Church's One Foundation', with its lines:

Elect from every nation,
Yet one o'er all the earth

For all the differences in culture, time, language, gifts and status, there is a spiritual unity amongst all Christians, indwelt by the Spirit, resting on the Saviour and serving Christ as Lord. Dietrich Bonhoeffer wrote in his last work, *Ethics*: 'The form of Christ is one and the same at all times and in all places. And the Church of Christ also is one and the same throughout all generations.'

The purpose of this book is not for Christians to pick a hero or heroine, and follow the one of their choice. That kind of celebrity cult was precisely the problem in the Corinthian church in the first century. There were some who thought that they were following Paul, some Apollos, some Cephas (Peter) and some Christ (1 Cor. 1:12). Paul had to correct them by telling them that the truth was far more wonderful than they realized. By trying to follow one Christian hero, they were in fact short-changing themselves. The truth for Christians is that 'all things are yours, whether Paul or Apollos or Cephas ... all are yours. And you are Christ's, and Christ is God's' (1 Cor. 3:21-23). All true followers of the Lamb belong to each other, and are to learn from each other. All Christians have known what it is to have God's Word make an impact on their lives, for all know something of the truth of the psalmist's testimony: 'Your word is a lamp to my feet and a light to my path' (Ps. 119:105).

Christian Focus Publications

Our mission statement –

STAYING FAITHFUL

In dependence upon God we seek to impact the world through literature faithful to His infallible Word, the Bible. Our aim is to ensure that the Lord Jesus Christ is presented as the only hope to obtain forgiveness of sin, live a useful life and look forward to heaven with Him.

Our Books are published in four imprints:

CHRISTIAN FOCUS

popular works including biographies, commentaries, basic doctrine and Christian living.

CHRISTIAN HERITAGE

books representing some of the best material from the rich heritage of the church.

MENTOR

books written at a level suitable for Bible College and seminary students, pastors, and other serious readers. The imprint includes commentaries, doctrinal studies, examination of current issues and church history.

CF4•K

children's books for quality Bible teaching and for all age groups: Sunday school curriculum, puzzle and activity books; personal and family devotional titles, biographies and inspirational stories – Because you are never too young to know Jesus!

Christian Focus Publications Ltd,
Geanies House, Fearn, Ross-shire,
IV20 1TW, Scotland, United Kingdom.
www.christianfocus.com